6,000
SOUNDALIKES,
LOOK-ALIKES,
AND OTHER WORDS OFTEN CONFUSED

COMPILED BY MARY LOUISE GILMAN
WITH THE ASSISTANCE OF DOROTHY P. KENNEDY

How to Use This Book

Please read these paragraphs before dipping into this small volume. And note:

1. Although a great many words are cross-referenced, to keep the size of the book within reasonable limits I've omitted a cross-reference when its inclusion would come just a few lines below the word as defined. So glance back a bit before concluding the word you're looking for isn't there.

2. Because of space limitations, usually I've stuck to noun/noun or verb/verb usage in defining the two or more words (or phrases) discussed. Often the choice—noun vs. verb, say—depended on which usage normally involves the most confusion.

3. Lots of the words defined have so many meanings that it wouldn't be practical to try to list even a fourth of them. When you see (Etc.), in parentheses, that says the word has many other meanings and you'll have to consult a dictionary if the definition listed isn't the one you need. (This applies mostly to words in common use; less common terms rate longer definitions.)

4. In quite a few definitions you'll find, in brackets, an illustration of the word's usage. Often this will be a cliché—which is probably the form in which you'll have met the word in the first place!

5. Many word groupings consisting of three or more words may well appear to have quite disparate components. That's because Words A and B may sound or look somewhat alike, as do Words B and C—but not A and C. For that reason a cross-reference may appear a bit strange. (But trust me and do look up the word given in such cross-reference.)

There. Now go ahead and look up those problem words. By the way, though this book has been prepared basically for court reporters, I hope others will also find it useful.

—M.L.G.

Preface

"What could this word be? It sort of sounded like ...."

How often have you asked yourself, or a colleague, that question? It's my fervent hope that henceforth you'll be able to find a lot of answers in this book. Most of the more common soundalikes (*affect/effect*, *cite/sight/site*, and such) appeared in the two earlier editions, the first one that had 2,000 in its title, the more recent one with 3,000. But in addition to some common ones I'd managed to overlook, this book contains a great number of somewhat more sophisticated soundalikes*, look-alikes, and other problem words. It's obviously impossible to cover all technical vocabularies in our ever-expanding language, but you'll find quite a lot of medical and other technical material here.

In fact, most of us will never meet, in our work, reading, or listening, a great many of the words this book examines. But who can be sure just what words we *will* meet on the job or elsewhere? I did discard a number of words I found in going page by page through the new *Random House Dictionary of the English Language, Second Edition Unabridged.* An example: *paratoid*, which would have paired nicely with *parotid*. The longer word is defined as a gland near the ear of a toad, and I decided it probably would be of little interest (even to toad). Still, you never know.

*What, you may well ask, has happened to the hyphen in soundalike(s)? Well, my three newest dictionaries—Webster's Ninth New Collegiate, Random House Second Edition Unabridged, and Random House College—all now show the word written solid. (Previous editions didn't list it at all, and look-alike, which did appear before, still retains its hyphen.) We try to keep up with the times—despite inconsistencies in our language!

My sources for the 6,000 words chosen? Well, I've already mentioned *Random House.* I also used *Webster's Ninth New Collegiate Dictionary, Webster's Third New International Dictionary Unabridged* (now not so new), the *American Heritage Dictionary,* the *Oxford American Dictionary*—and in a few instances the *Oxford English Dictionary.* I even took some definitions from *The Official Scrabble Players Dictionary,* because they were so nice and short. Medical dictionaries: *Dorland's* and *Blakiston's*; legal: mostly *Black's.* Sometimes I ended up checking four or five dictionaries before I found a definition that seemed to cover the subject in not too many words.

And I'm most grateful to all the court reporters and others throughout the country who have sent me soundalike and other problem words in recent years. I'll mention only the three who furnished the most. Lynn Brooks, RPR, of Dallas sent me several typed pages of words, and retired reporter Virginia H. Rankin of Kansas City was a big help with medical terms. Another retired reporter, Dorothy P. Kennedy of Sacramento, suggested scores if not hundreds of words.

But that was only a small part of the tremendous help I received from Dorothy Kennedy. She gave me a typed critique on every batch of computer printout pages I mailed her. Not only did she catch a lot of stupid errors but in a great many instances suggested improved definitions—along with entries I'd overlooked. Also she helped proofread the final product. (We've never met, but I knew from previous correspondence that she was a fellow logophile. When I was trying to coax her into helping me proofread—I hadn't expected all the other services—I told her the book *needed* her. At the time I didn't realize how true that was, but I now know it's a much better book because of her.)

The book you're now looking at is a slightly revised version of the original *6,000 Soundalikes, Look-Alikes, And Other Words Often Confused* (copyright 1989). It contains a few corrections of errors in the previous edition, plus quite a few new entries. (We could, in fact, title this new edition *6,000-Plus*.) Some of the new words I myself stumbled on. Most of the rest came from Dorothy Kennedy, who assisted in the preparation of the original *6,000*; Lynn Brooks of Dallas and Marvin P. Birnbaum of New York contributed a number of them. (Mrs. Kennedy also helped with the proofreading of the revised pages.)

As I said in my preface to the *3,000* edition, words rank among man's most fascinating inventions. You might even find this small volume fun just to *read!*

Speaking of the preface to the *3,000*, here are some extracts from it, just for fun:

Soundalikes and sound-similars through the ages have formed the basis for most puns as well as other forms of humor.

Sometimes this humor involves phrases as well as single words. As [*New York Times*] columnist William Safire says, "The human ear hears words in its own way, not necessarily the way the human voice intends." The often humorous results he terms "mondegreens," from the line of an old ballad in which the words "laid him on the green" were distorted to "Lady Mondegreen."

You probably remember the story of the lawyer and the banker who were out fishing when their boat sank. As he struck out for the shore, the lawyer, a good swimmer, asked his friend, "Can you float alone?" The banker gasped, "I'm drowning, and you want to talk business!"

And here are two limericks, authors unknown, that illustrate the problems that soundalikes can create:

"I must leave here," said Lady de Vere,
"For these damp airs don't suit me, I fear."
　Said her friend, "Goodness me!
　If they do not agree
With your system, why eat pears, my dear?"

There was a young girl, a sweet lamb,
Who smiled as she entered a tram.
　After she had embarked
　The conductor remarked,
"Your fare." And she said, "Yes, I am."

Note that the second one involves two homophonic pairs: *your/you're* and *fare/fair*.

On the whole, look-alikes cause fewer problems—or at least they should. But they too account for a lot of spelling and other errors in writing. Here's a wonderful limerick involving a pair of look-alikes. A retired Yale University official, George D. Vaill, wrote it; and science-fiction author Isaac Asimov chose it as the best of 12,000 entries in a contest held several years ago.

The bustard's an exquisite fowl,
With minimal reason to growl;
　He escapes what would be
　Illegitimacy
By grace of a fortunate vowel.

Happy hunting for that right word that almost eluded you.

—MARY LOUISE GILMAN

A

Aaron	Masculine name.
Erin	Ireland; feminine name.
abdominal	Pert. to the part of the body between thorax and pelvis.
abominable	Detestable.
abduct	Kidnap; to move away from an axis.
adduct	To pull toward main axis.
abduction	Kidnapping; the action of turning outward.
adduction	The action of turning inward.
abductor	Kidnapper; a muscle that draws a part away from the axis of a body or an extremity.
adductor	A muscle that draws toward the median line of a body or toward the axis of an extremity.
aberration	Deviation.
abrasion	Wearing, grinding, or rubbing away by friction.
abient	Tending to move away from a stimulus or situation.
adient	Tending to move toward a stimulus.
ambient	Surrounding on all sides. [Ambient air.]
abjure	To renounce.
adjure	To command, as under oath.

ablation	Surgical removal of a part.
ablution	Washing of one's body or part of it.
abominable:	*See abdominal.*
abrade	To wear away.
braid	To interweave (hair, rope, etc.)
upbraid	To reproach.
abrasion	*See aberration.*
abridge	To reduce in scope.
bridge	To connect or link.
abrogate	To cancel or repeal.
arrogate	To appropriate for oneself presumptuously.
absence	State of being away.
absinthe	(also **absinth**) A green, aromatic liqueur.
absorb	To take in and make part of a whole; suck up.
adsorb	To gather on a surface in a condensed layer.
absorbent	Able to absorb moisture, etc.
adsorbent	Capable of adsorbing.
absorption	Act of absorbing.
adsorption	Act of adsorbing.
sorption	Act of taking up and holding by absorption or adsorption.
abstraction	Removing; an abstract idea.
obstruction	Something blocking or impeding.

abstruse	Hard to understand; profound.	**accident**	An unexpected or undesirable event; chance.
obtuse	Not sharp; stupid, slow at understanding.	**Occident**	The West as opposed to the Orient.
academe	The academic world.	**accidental**	Happening by accident.
academia	The milieu or interests of a university or college, etc.	**occidental**	Western. (Cap., n.) A native of the Western world.
academy	A secondary or high school, esp. a private one.	**acclaim**	Welcome with shouts of approval.
		exclaim	To cry out or speak in sudden emotion.
acaudal	Tailless.		
caudal	Of or at the tail.	**acclamation**	Loud expression of approval, praise, or assent.
acausal	Having no cause.	**acclimation**	Acclimatization, esp. under controlled conditions.
causal	Of or forming a cause.		
accede	To agree.	**exclamation**	Sharp or sudden utterance.
exceed	To surpass; to go beyond limits.		
		accrue	To accumulate.
accelerate	To speed up.	**ecru**	Light fawn color.
exhilarate	To enliven; excite.		
		accuse	To blame.
accept	To receive with consent.	**excuse**	To pardon.
except	To exclude; to object (take exception to).	**recuse**	To disqualify; to challenge as disqualified.
access	(v.) To be able to reach, approach, enter, etc.		
assess	To evaluate.	**acellular**	Being without cells.
axis	Straight line about which something revolves.	**cellular**	Of cells; composed of cells.
excess	Too much of something.	**acentric**	Not central; peripheral.
		centric	Central.
accessible	Capable of being reached.	**eccentric**	Unconventional in appearance or behavior.
assessable	Capable of being evaluated (or taxed).		
		acephalous	Headless.
accidence	Part of grammar dealing with inflections.	**cephalous**	Having a head.
accidents	Unforeseen events.		

acetal	Compound obtained by heating aldehydes or ketones with alcohols.	**acrophobia**	Abnormal dread of being at a great height.
acetyl	Acetic acid radical.	**agoraphobia**	Abnormal fear of open spaces.
acetic	Of vinegar.	**activate**	To make active.
aesthetic	Of or pert. to the sense of the beautiful.	**actuate**	To put into mechanical action or motion.
ascetic	Self-denying.	**acts**	Things done; deeds, etc.
acetin	A colorless liquid used chiefly in the manufacture of explosives.	**ax or axe**	Cutting tool.
		actual	Real.
		axial	Pertaining to an axis.
acetoin	A pleasant-smelling liquid used chiefly in the manufacture of flavors and essences.	**actuate**	*See activate.*
acetone	A volatile liquid used chiefly in paints and varnishes and as a solvent.	**adamantane**	A white crystalline hydrocarbon.
		adamantine	Utterly unyielding; adamant.
acetyl	*See acetal.*	**adapt**	To make fit, often by modification.
achromatic	Refracting light without dispersing it into its constituent colors.	**adept**	Skilled, proficient.
		adopt	To take by choice into a relationship; to take and use as one's own.
chromatic	Highly colored; pert. to the tones of a musical scale.	**addenda**	Additions.
		agenda	A list, outline, or plan.
acid	Sharp-tasting, sour.	**addict**	A person who is addicted to something, esp. drugs.
acrid	Having a bitter smell or taste.	**edict**	An order proclaimed by an authority.
aciform	Needle-shaped.	**addition**	Something added.
aciniform	Clustered like grapes.	**edition**	The form in which something is presented or published.
acme	Highest point.		
acne	Skin disorder.	**adduce**	To offer as an example, reason, or proof.
acolyte	Altar boy.	**educe**	To bring out or develop; to elicit. (*Also see deduce.*)
aconite	A plant belonging to the buttercup family.		
acrid	*See acid.*		

adduct	See *abduct*.	**adsorption**	See *absorption*.
adduction	See *abduction*.	**adulterer**	One who commits
adductor	See *abductor*.		adultery.
adept	See *adapt*.	**adulterator**	One who adulterates.
à deux	(F.) Being between two	**adulteress**	Female adulterer.
	persons in an intimate	**adulterous**	Relating to adultery.
	relationship.	**advantage**	Favorable condition or
adieu	Farewell.		circumstance.
ado	Fuss; to-do	**vantage**	Superior position or
adherence	The act of adhering.		opportunity.
adherents	Followers.		
		adventuress	Female adventurer.
adient	See *abient*.	**adventurous**	Disposed to seek
			adventure.
adit	An entranceway or		
	passage.	**adverse**	Opposed; hostile.
edit	To correct and prepare	**averse**	Unwilling; disinclined.
	for publication.	**obverse**	The front or principal
			surface of anything.
adjure	See *abjure*.		
		advert	To pay heed or
administer	To manage the		attention; to refer.
	business affairs of.	**avert**	To turn away; to avoid.
administrate	To act as administrator	**evert**	To turn outward or
	of. [A barbarism.]		inside out.
minister	To attend to people's	**invert**	To turn upside down.
	needs.		(*Also see covert, overt.*)
administration	Management of public	**advice**	(n.) Information,
	or business affairs.		counsel.
ministration	Attending to people's	**advise**	(v.) To offer advice.
	needs.		
		adz/adze	See *ads*.
ado	See *à deux*.		
adopt	See *adapt*.	**Aegean**	(n.) The Aegean Sea.
			(adj.) Pert. to the
adolescence	State or process of		Aegean Sea.
	growing up.	**Augean**	From Gk. mythology:
adolescents	Young people.		formidable, difficult
			task. [Augean stables.]
ads	Advertisements.		
adds	Increases; appends;	**aegis**	Protection;
	totals up.		sponsorship.
adz or adze	Cutting tool.		[Pronounced with a
			long *e*.]
adsorb	See *absorb*.	**ages**	Generations.
adsorbent	See *absorbent*.		

aerial	(adj.) Of or like air. (n.) Antenna.
Ariel	Shakespearean spirit; inner satellite of Uranus.
aerie	Bird nest on cliff or mountain.
airy	Of or rel. to air; light in weight or texture.
eerie	Weird.
Erie	Lake or city.
Aesop	Greek writer of fables.
ESOP	Employee stock ownership plan. (Same pronunciation: E-SOP.)
aesthetic	*See acetic.*
afebrile	Not marked by fever.
febrile	Feverish.
affect	(v.) To have an influence on. (n.) A feeling or emotion as distinguished from cognition, thought, or action (accent on first syl.: AF-fekt).
effect	(v.) To make; to bring about. (n.) Result; purport; intent.
affectation	Behavior put on for display, not natural or genuine.
affection	Love, liking.
affected	Influenced.
effected	Made; brought about.
affective	Arising from or influencing feelings or emotions.
effective	Producing a decisive or desired result.
afferent	Carrying toward.
efferent	Carrying away.
affinity	Close relationship; similarity; liking.
infinity	Endless or unlimited space, time, etc.
affluence	An abundant supply; wealth.
effluence	Something that flows out.
effluents	Materials that flow out.
affluent	Rich; abundant.
effluent	An outflowing; waste material.
afflux	Something flowing to or toward a point.
efflux	Outward flow, as of water.
affusion	Act of pouring a liquid on (as in baptism).
defusion	Separation of the life instinct from the death instinct.
diffusion	The act of diffusing (pouring out and spreading or dispersing).
effusion	Unrestrained expression of words or feeling; escape of gas or fluid.
infusion	Act of infusing; something introduced.
afterward	(also **afterwards**) At a later time.
afterword	Concluding section of a book, etc.
agenda	*See addenda.*
ages	*See aegis.*
aggravate	To heighten, increase, worsen.
aggregate	To combine and form a collection or mass.

aggression	Unprovoked attack; hostility.	**aisle**	Passageway or corridor.
		I'll	Contraction of *I will*.
egression	Going out; egress.	**isle**	Island (usu. poetic).
agoraphobia	*See acrophobia.*	**ait**	A little island.
		ate	Consumed.
ahold	(informal) A hold or grasp. [Better: He took hold (rather than ahold) of my arm.]	**eight**	Numeral.
		akinetic	Pert. to loss of motion.
		kinetic	Of or produced by motion.
a hold	A grasp; grip.		
		a la	(F.) In the manner of.
aides	Assistants.	**Allah**	Islamic Supreme Being.
aids	Helps.		
AIDS	Disease of the immune system.	**alarm**	Something that warns or alerts.
		alarum	Alarm (archaic), heard mostly now in the phrase *alarums and excursions*.
aigrette	A spray of feathers (or gems) worn in the hair.		
egret	Heron.		
		albumen	The white of an egg; albumin.
ail	To be unwell.	**albumin**	Any of a class of water-soluble proteins, including the main constituent of white of an egg.
ale	A malt beverage.		
ailment	Bodily disorder; slight illness.		
element	One of the parts making up a whole.		
		ale	*See ail.*
air	Atmosphere.	**align**	To bring into line.
e'er	Ever (poetic).	**A-line**	Having a flared bottom.
er	Interjec. showing hesitation, etc.		
ere	Before.	**alimentary**	Of or rel. to nourishment or nutrition.
err	To make a mistake. (Properly pronounced er, not air.)	**elementary**	Basic, fundamental.
heir	One who inherits.		
Ur	Ancient Babylonian city.		
aired	Ventilated.		
erred	Made a mistake—such as in mispronuncing the word!		
airy	*See aerie.*		

alkane	Any member of the alkane series (of saturated hydrocarbons).
alkene	Any member of the alkene series (of unsaturated hydrocarbons).
alkyne	(also **alkine**) Any member of the alkyne series (of unsaturated hydrocarbons).
all	The whole number, quantity, amount.
awl	Pointed instrument for piercing holes.
Allah	*See a la.*
allay	To alleviate.
alley	Narrow street.
ally	(n.) An associate. (v.) To join or enter into an alliance.
allegation	Something alleged.
allocation	Something apportioned.
allergenic	Pert. to an allergy.
allogeneic	Rel. to similarity and dissimilarity of cells or tissues.
allogenic	(Geol.) Formed elsewhere than in the rock in which it is found.
alleviate	To lessen, make less severe.
elevate	To raise.
alleys	Narrow streets.
allies	Countries in alliance with each other.
allision	The striking of one ship by another.
elision	Omission (as of an unstressed vowel.) *(Also see allusion, etc.)*
alliterate	To use alliteration (repetition of initial consonants or vowels).
illiterate	Unable to read and write.
allocation	*See allegation.*
allocator	A person who allocates.
allocatur	A kind of writ.
allocution	A formal speech; pronouncement delivered by the pope.
elocution	A person's manner of speaking or reading in public.
allot	To apportion.
a lot	Quite a bit. (*Never* correctly written as one word!)
allowed	Permitted.
aloud	With the speaking voice.
all ready	Set to go.
already	Previously.
all right	O.K.
alrite	A barbarism—don't use it.
all together	Together; in concert.
altogether	Wholly; thoroughly.
allude	To refer to.
elude	To evade.
elute	To remove by dissolving.

allusion	Reference. (*Also see allision and delusion.*)
elision	Omission (as of an unstressed vowel).
elusion	The act of eluding; evasion.
elution	Removal of an absorbed material by means of a solvent.
illusion	Misleading image presented to the vision.
allusive	Containing allusions.
elusive	Eluding; escaping.
illusive	Illusory; deceptive.
alluvial	Made of soil or sand left by rivers or floods.
eluvial	Pert. to eluvium: rock debris.
illuvial	Pert. to what washes or is washed in.
alluvion	The wash or flow of water against a shore.
alluvium	Detritus deposited by running water.
effluvium	Noxious vapor or odor.
eluvium	Rock debris produced by disintegration; fine soil or sand deposited by wind.
illuvium	Material accumulated from what has been leached out from another layer.
all ways	Total number of methods.
always	At all times; invariably.
ally	*See allay.*
a lot	*See allot.*
aloud	*See allowed.*
already	*See all ready.*
altar	(n.) A usu. raised platform for worship or sacrifice.
alter	(v.) To change.

alteration	Modification.
altercation	Noisy argument or controversy.
alternate	A deputy or substitute.
alternative	One of two or more possibilities.
altitude	Height.
attitude	Position, etc.; in aeronautics, the position of an aircraft relative to its axes and a reference point.
aluminium	(chiefly Brit. and Canadian) Aluminum.
aluminum	Silver-white metallic element.
alumna	Female graduate.
alumnae	Plural of *alumna*.
alumni	Plural of *alumnus*.
alumnus	Male graduate.
alveola	(pl. -*lae*) A small cavity, cell, or pit on the surface of an organ.
alveoli	(pl. of *alveolus*) The small air cells of the lungs.
always	*See all ways.*
ambient	*See abient.*
amend	To modify; change for the better.
emend	To edit or change; correct.
mend	To repair.
amenorrhea	Absence of the menses.
menorrhea	Menstrual flow.
amiable	Good-tempered.
amicable	Friendly.

aminase	An enzyme capable of promoting assimilation of ammonia.	**anabatic**	Moving upward (wind, etc.)
amylase	An enzyme that breaks down starch.	**anabiotic**	Coming back to life.
amylose	Any of various polysaccharides (as starch or cellulose).	**antibiotic**	Substance destroying or preventing bacterial growth.
among	Surrounded by.	**analyst**	One who analyzes.
amongst	Among.	**annalist**	A writer of annals; historian.
amoral	Being neither moral nor immoral. (*Also see moral.*)	**anaplastic**	(of cells) Having reverted to a more primitive form.
immoral	Not moral.	**antiplastic**	Unfavorable to the healing process.
ampule	A sealed glass tube containing medication.	**anchorite**	One who lives in seclusion, usu. for religious reasons.
ampulla	(pl. *ampullae*) A dilated portion of a canal or duct.	**ankerite**	A dolomitic iron-containing mineral.
amputation	The act of cutting or lopping off.	**androgenous**	Tending to produce male offspring.
imputation	The act of imputing; accusation.	**androgynous**	Having both male and female characteristics.
amulet	Talisman; charm to ward off evil.	**anecdotal**	Rel. to or containing anecdotes.
armlet	Ornamental band worn on the arm; small inlet or arm of the sea.	**antidotal**	Acting as an antidote.
omelet	(also **omelette**) Chef's special that starts with beaten eggs.	**anecdote**	Short narrative.
		antidote	Agent to counteract effects of poison.
amused	Found (something) humorous.	**anestrous**	Not showing estrus.
bemused	Confused; bewildered; lost in thought.	**anestrus**	(of a female mammal) An interval of sexual inactivity.
		estrus	Period of heat or rut.
amylase	*See aminase.*	**angel**	A spiritual being; backer of a play.
amylose	*See aminase.*	**angle**	A corner; method of achieving an objective.
an	Indefinite article.	**ankle**	Joint between foot and leg.
Ann/Anne	Feminine name.		

anhydride	A compound derived from another by removal of the elements of water.	**ante**	A stake put in by a poker player before seeing his hand.
anhydrite	A mineral.	**ante-**	(prefix) Before.
		anti	A person who is opposed to a certain practice, etc.
ankerite	*See anchorite.*	**anti-**	(prefix) Against.
anima	Soul, life.	**auntie**	Aunt.
animal	A living thing that can feel and move voluntarily.	**antecedence**	Priority; precedents.
		antecedents	Preceding things, circumstances, or people.
annalist	*See analyst.*		
annals	Yearly record of events.	**antibiotic**	*See anabatic.*
annuals	Plants, etc., lasting one season only.	**antic**	Caper; funny act.
annuls	Makes null and void.	**antique**	Something old.
annunciate	To announce.	**antidotal**	*See anecdotal.*
enunciate	To make a definite statement; to articulate or pronounce.	**antidote**	*See anecdote.*
		antimony	A chemical element.
annunciation	Announcement. (Cap.:) March 25, a church festival.	**antinomy**	Opposition between one law, principle, rule, etc., and another.
enunciation	Formulation; articulation.	**antiplastic**	*See anaplastic.*
		antonym	*See anonym.*
anonym	One who is anonymous; pseudonym.	**anuresis**	Retention of urine in the bladder.
antonym	A word of opposite meaning (*good* is the antonym of *bad*).	**enuresis**	Bedwetting; incontinence of urine.
ansiform	Loop-shaped.	**anus**	Opening at the end of the alimentary canal.
ensiform	Sword-shaped.	**heinous**	Very wicked; outrageous.
ant	Insect.	**anxious**	Worried.
aunt	Sister of one's mother or father.	**unctuous**	Oily; smugly earnest or virtuous.
		anyone	Anybody.
		any one	One of two or more. [Any one of you would help anyone in trouble.]

anyway	Nevertheless.	**apolitical**	Unconcerned with or detached from politics.
any way	No matter what means or method. [Any way you slice it, it's still baloney.]	**political**	Of or engaged in politics.
		apologue	Allegorical fable.
apatetic	(Zool.) Assuming colors and forms that effect deceptive camouflage.	**epilogue**	Concluding part added to a literary work.
apathetic	Showing little or no emotion.	**appalling**	Inspiring horror, dismay, disgust.
		appealing	Marked by earnest entreaty; pleasing.
apatite	Any of a group of calcium phosphate minerals.	**apperceive**	To have a conscious perception of; to comprehend.
appetite	Inherent craving for food, etc.	**perceive**	To become aware of.
aperiodic	Not periodic.	**apperception**	Conscious perception.
periodic	Occurring or appearing at intervals.	**perception**	Awareness; consciousness; understanding.
aphagia	Loss of ability to swallow.	**appertain**	Pertain.
aphakia	Absence of the crystalline lens.	**pertain**	To be relevant; to belong as part of.
aphasia	Loss or impairment of the power to use or comprehend words.	**appetite**	*See apatite.*
atasia	Inability to stand.	**appose**	To place in juxtaposition or proximity.
apiary	A place where bees are kept.	**oppose**	To resist, combat, withstand.
aviary	A place for confining birds.	**apposite**	Highly pertinent.
		opposite	Occupying opposing positions.
apical	Pert. to an apex.	**apposition**	Placing side by side.
epical	Heroic.	**opposition**	Resistance; disagreement.
epochal	Pert. to an epoch; momentous.		
a piece	A portion (of something).	**appraise**	To evaluate or estimate.
apiece	For each one; individually. [He gave us a piece of pie apiece.]	**apprise**	To give notice to; inform.
		apprize	To value; appreciate.

appropriate	To take possession of, annex.
expropriate	To deprive of possession or take away without approval.
approximate	Nearly correct or exact.
proximate	Imminent. [Proximate cause].
appurtenance	An incidental right; an adjunct.
pertinence	Relevance.
appurtenant	Auxiliary, accessory.
pertinent	Germane.
arachnid	Certain wingless insects.
arachnoid	Resembling a spider's web; of or belonging to the arachnids. (Med.) A thin membrane of the brain and spinal cord lying between the dura mater and pia mater.
arbiter	A person with power to decide a dispute; a judge.
arbitrator	A person chosen to settle differences; arbiter.
orbiter	One that orbits.
arc	Something arched or curved.
arch	Curved structure supporting a weight.
ark	Boat [Noah's]; something affording protection.
arcana	(pl. of *arcanum*) Secrets; knowledge known only to the initiated.
arcane	Known or understood only by a few; secret, esoteric.

area	Surface measure; scope.
aria	Operatic song for one voice.
areola	A ring of color, as around a human nipple. (*Also see aureole.*)
areole	An areola.
argentine	A silvery substance used in making artificial pearls. (Cap.:) Native of Argentina.
argentite	Silver sulfide.
arginine	An essential amino acid.
argol	Crude tartar deposited in wine casks during aging.
argyle	Diamond-shaped varicolored knitting pattern.
argot	Jargon or slang of a group or class, esp. criminals.
ergot	A fungus affecting rye and other cereal grains, dried for use in medicine.
aria	*See area.*
Ariel	*See aerial.*
ark	*See arc.*
armer	One that arms.
armoire	Tall cupboard or wardrobe.
armor	Defensive covering for the body, etc.
armlet	*See amulet.*
arouse	To awaken; incite.
rouse	Arouse.
roust	To rout, as from a place.

arraignment	Charge.	**artistic**	Of art or artists.
arrangement	Something arranged; preparation.	**autistic**	Having a form of mental illness that causes a person to withdraw into a private world of fantasy.
arrant	Extreme. [Arrant nonsense].		
errand	Mission; short trip.	**ascend**	To move upwards.
errant	Traveling; straying.	**ascent**	The act of rising or mounting upward.
arrhythmic	Lacking rhythm [*arrhythmia*: a disturbance in the rhythm of the heartbeat].	**assent**	Acquiescence.
		ascetic	*See acetic.*
eurhythmic	Having a pleasing rhythm.	**aseptic**	Free from bacteria that cause something to become septic.
rhythmic	Of, rel. to, or involving rhythm.	**septic**	Infected with harmful microorganisms that cause pus to form.
arrogate	*See abrogate.*		
arsenate	A salt or ester of an arsenic acid.	**asexual**	Having no sex or sexual organs.
arsenide	A binary compound of arsenic with a more positive element.	**sexual**	Of or pert. to sex.
		askew	Not straight or level.
arsenite	A salt or ester of arsenous acid.	**skew**	To turn or twist around.
arsine	Poisonous gas.	**asocial**	Not sociable.
arson	Malicious or fraudulent burning of a building.	**social**	Living in an organized community; not solitary.
arterial	Of, pert. to, or resembling the arteries.	**aspirate**	1. To start a word with an ''h'' sound. 2. To withdraw fluid from a body cavity.
arteriole	Very small branch of an artery.	**exasperate**	To annoy greatly.
arteriosclerosis	Thickening of the arterial walls.	**assay**	(n.) Examination and analysis. (v.) To analyze or test.
atherosclerosis	Arteriosclerosis with degenerative changes.	**essay**	(n.) Effort; attempt; a composition. (v.) To attempt.
artist	A person skilled in one of the fine arts.		
artiste	An artist, esp. a professional entertainer.	**assent**	*See ascent.*

assert	To state or declare positively.	astray	Off the right path.
assort	To classify; distribute into groups.	estray	A person or animal that has strayed.
assess	*See access.*	asymmetrical	(also **asymmetric**) Unsymmetrical.
assessable	*See accessible.*	symmetrical	Exhibiting symmetry; well-proportioned.
assimilate	To absorb.		
simulate	To copy, represent, or feign.	asymmetry	The quality or state of being asymmetric.
stimulate	To excite to activity or growth; arouse.	symmetry	Pleasing proportion between parts of a whole.
assistance	Help.		
assistants	Helpers.	asymptomatic	Showing no evidence of disease.
assort	*See assert.*	symptomatic	Serving as a symptom.
assorted	Mixed.	asynapsis	Failure of the pairing of homologous chromosomes.
sordid	Dirty; filthy.		
astatic	Unstable; unsteady.	synapse	The place where a nervous impulse is transmitted between neurons.
ecstatic	Intensely delighted.		
static	Not moving; stationary.		
aster	Flower.	synapsis	The pairing of homologous chromosomes.
Astor	Proper name.		
Esther	Feminine name.		
ester	A chemical compound.	asynchronism	Lack of synchronism.
		synchronism	Coincidence in time or rate.
asternal	Not reaching or connected with the sternum.		
sternal	Of or pert. to the sternum.	asynchronous	Not occurring at the same time.
		synchronous	Occurring at the same time.
astigmatism	A defect in an eye or lens preventing proper focusing.		
stigmatism	A condition of the refractive media of the eye in which rays of light are accurately brought to a focus on the retina.	asynergy	Defective coordination between parts, as muscles or limbs, that normally act in unison.
		synergy	Coordinated action or functioning.
astral	Relating to the stars.	atasia	*See aphagia.*
austral	Southern. (Cap.:) Australian.	ate	*See ait.*
		atherosclerosis	*See arteriosclerosis.*

atomic	Of, or rel. to, atoms, atomic energy, etc.	**Audubon**	Artist and ornithologist. [Audubon Society.]
atonic	Without accent or stress.	**autobahn**	German expressway.
atonal	(music) Not written in any particular key or scale system.	**Augean**	*See Aegean.*
tonal	Of a tone or tones.	**auger** **augur**	A tool for boring holes. To foretell from omens.
atonality	Absence of key or tonal center.	**aught**	Zero; cipher. *(Also see naught.)*
tonality	A particular scale or system of tones.	**ought**	Indicating obligation or duty.
atone **attain** **attorn**	To make amends. To reach or achieve. To agree to become tenant to a new owner or landlord.	**aunt** **auntie**	*See ant.* *See ante.*
atonic	*See atomic.*	**aura**	Atmosphere surrounding a person or thing.
atresia	Absence of an opening, passage, or cavity.	**aurora**	Dawn. (Cap.:) The Roman goddess of dawn.
atrichia	Congenital absence or loss of hair.	**aural**	Relating to the ear or sense of hearing.
attendance **attendants**	The act of attending. People who perform services for others; attendees.	**oral**	Spoken.
		aureole	Radiance; aura; corona. *(Also see areola.)*
attenuate	To make thin or slender.	**oriel** **oriole**	Bay window. Type of bird.
extenuate	To lessen the seriousness of; mitigate.	**auricle** **oracle**	An atrium of a heart. A wise person who states prophesies.
attitude **attorn**	*See altitude.* *See atone.*	**auspice**	Patronage; support. (Usu. plural.)
attrition	A reduction or decrease in numbers, size, or strength.	**hospice**	House or shelter for pilgrims or travelers.
detrition	The act of wearing away by rubbing.	**austral**	*See astral.*
atypical **typical**	Not typical. Regular; characteristic.	**autarchy** **autarky**	Absolute sovereignty. A national policy of economic independence.

autistic	*See artistic.*	**away**	From this or that place.
autobahn	*See Audubon.*	**aweigh**	Raised clear of the ground. [Anchors aweigh.]
automation	The use of automatic equipment to save labor.		
automaton	(pl. -*ta* or -*s*) Robot.	**awed**	Inspired with dread or reverence.
		odd	Strange; opp. of *even.*
avenge	To take vengeance for.		
revenge	To avenge; to take satisfaction by inflicting vengeance.	**awful**	Inspiring awe; terrible.
		offal	The viscera of slaughtered animals.
averse	*See adverse.*	**a while**	(n.) A certain length of time.
aversion	Dislike, repugnance.	**awhile**	(adv.) For a while. (Note that the *for* is built into this word.) [Stay for a while and rest awhile.]
eversion	Act of turning inside out.		
avert	*See advert.*		
aviary	*See apiary.*		
		awl	*See all.*
avocation	Minor occupation, hobby.	**ax/axe**	*See acts.*
evocation	Act of evoking, summoning (as a spirit).	**axel**	A jump in figure skating.
		axial	Pert. to or forming an axis. (*Also see actual.*)
vacation	Period for rest and relaxation.	**axil**	The angle between the upper side of a leaf and its supporting stem.
vocation	A person's trade or occupation.		
		axile	In or of an axis.
avoid	To shun.	**axle**	Shaft upon which a wheel revolves.
evade	To slip away; to elude.		
ovoid	Egg-shaped; oval.		
void	To make empty; to nullify.	**axes**	Plural of *ax/axe* or *axis.*
		axis	A straight line about which a body rotates. (*Also see access.*)
avulsion	Sudden cutting off or tearing away.		
evulsion	Act of plucking out.	**axiom**	Self-evident truth.
		axion	A hypothetical particle having no charge, zero spin, and small mass.
aw	(interjec.) Used to express sympathy, disgust, etc.	**axon**	The central process of a neuron.
awe	Respect combined with fear or wonder.		

16

ay	Aye.
aye	Yes.
eye	Organ of sight.
I	Personal pronoun. (Also note the construction term *I beam*: an iron or steel beam that is I- shaped in cross section.)

B

baa **bah**	The bleat of a sheep. (interjec.) Expression of contempt or disgust.
babble **Babel** **bobble**	To prattle; talk foolishly. Biblical tower. A repeated bobbing movement; fumble.
bauble **bubble**	Trinket. Small hollow globule filled with air or gas.
bach **bash** **batch**	To live as a bachelor. (Cap.:) German composer. A violent blow; a gala event. The quantity produced at one operation.
backside **backslide**	Buttocks. To relapse into bad habits.
bacon **beacon**	Smoked and cured side of pig. Light used as signal or warning. (*Also see beckon.*)
bad **bade**	Evil, etc. Past tense of *bid* (frequently mispronounced with long *a*).
baddie **batty**	(also baddy) Bad person or thing. Mentally unstable.

bail **bale**	(n.) Security given for appearance of a prisoner. (v.) To release under bail, etc.; to clear water from a boat. (n.) A large bundle of goods. (v.) To make up into a bale.
bailee **bailey**	The person to whom property is bailed. The outer wall of a castle. [Old Bailey: London court.]
bairn **barn**	(Scot.) Child. Farm building.
bait **bate**	To torment by jeering; to entice, as to bait a trap, etc. To reduce the force or intensity of. (Also consider *abate*.)
baited **bated**	Nagged or teased; set a trap. Restrained, reduced. [Bated breath.] (Also consider *abated*.)
baize **bays** **beys**	A coarse fabric. Inlets; parts of a building. Provincial governors in the Ottoman Empire.
bald **balled** **bawled**	Lacking natural or usual covering. Made into a ball; had intercourse with. Cried loudly; bellowed. [Bawled out: reprimanded severely.]
bale	*See bail.*
ball **bawl**	To make into a ball; have intercourse with. To cry out loudly.

balled	See *bald*.	**banister**	See *ballustrade*.
		bank	See *banc*.
ballet	Classical dance form.	**banned**	See *band*.
belly	Abdomen.	**banns/bans**	See *bands*.
ballustrade	A railing with supporting balusters.	**banquet**	Feast.
baluster	An upright often vase-shaped support for a rail.	**banquette**	A long upholstered bench.
banister	An upright supporting the handrail of a stair.	**barbed wire**	Wire with barbs to keep livestock in, etc.
		barbwire	Barbed wire (preferred).
balm	A fragrant resin; soothing influence.	**barberry**	A shrub.
bomb	An explosive device.	**Barbary**	Barbary Coast, Barbary States, etc.
bombe	A frozen dessert (one syllable).		
bombé	(of furniture) Curving or swelling outward (two syllables).	**bard**	A poet. [The Bard: Shakespeare.]
		barred	Having bars; excluded.
banc	(F.) In full court. [*En banc* (sometimes *in banc* or *in bank*): with all judges present.]	**bare**	To uncover or reveal.
		bear	To carry or support; endure, etc.
bank	Savings institution. (Etc.)	**baring**	Uncovering. (*Also see bearing.*)
band	A group of people joined for a common purpose. (Etc.)	**barring**	Fastening with a bar. (prep.) Excepting. [Barring unforeseen events....]
banned	Prohibited.		
banded	Having or marked with bands.	**bar mitzvah**	Religious ceremony for a Jewish boy of 13.
bandied	Tossed around.	**bat mitzvah**	Same ceremony for a girl.
bands	Groups of people playing music together. (Etc.)	**barn**	See *bairn*.
banns	Public announcement (esp. of a marriage).	**baron**	A nobleman.
bans	Prohibitions.	**barren**	Incapable of producing offspring (or vegetation); unproductive.
bang	Loud noise; resounding blow; fringe of hair over the forehead.	**baroness**	Wife of a baron.
bhang	(also bang) Hemp; cannabis.	**barrenness**	State of being barren; desolation.

baroque	Ornate style of architecture and art.	**bask**	To expose oneself to a pleasant warmth.
broke	Past tense of *break*.	**Basque**	A member of a people living in the western Pyrenees; their language.
barred	*See bard.*		
barrel	Large round container. (*Also see grouping under beryl.*)	**basque**	A tight-fitting bodice.
barrow	Wheelbarrow; prehistoric burial mound.	**bass**	*See base.*
		bastard	An illegitimate child; something of inferior quality.
barren	*See baron.*		
barrenness	*See baroness.*	**bustard**	Large ground-running bird.
barring	*See baring.*	**dastard**	Coward.
Barry	Masculine name.	**baste**	*See based.*
berry	Small fruit.		
bury	To inter; to conceal.	**bat**	A heavy stick; a flying mammal.
basal	Of or at the base.	**batt**	A sheet of cotton; batting.
Basel	Swiss city.		
basil	Sweet-smelling herb. (Cap.:) Masc. name.	**batch**	*See bach.*
		bate/bated	*See bait/bated.*
base	Foundation, etc.	**bathos**	Insincere or overdone pathos; triteness.
bass	(long *a*) A deep tone. (short *a*) A fish.		
		pathos	A quality arousing pity or sadness.
based	Made or formed to serve as a base.		
baste	To sew with loose stitches; to moisten (as meat) at intervals.	**bat mitzvah**	*See bar mitzvah.*
		baton	A stick of wood.
Basel	*See basal.*	**batten**	(n.) A thin strip of lumber. (v.) To furnish or fasten with battens. [Batten down the hatches.]
bases	Plural of *base* or *basis*.		
basis	Foundation.		
		batting	Cotton or wool in sheets.
bash	*See bach.*		
basic	Fundamental.	**batterie**	Ballet and tap-dancing term.
BASIC	A computer language.		
		battery	Device for generating electric current; the act of beating or battering. [The Battery: a park in Manhattan.]
basil	*See basal.*		

batty	*See baddie.*
bauble	*See babble.*
baud	A variable unit of data transmission speed.
bawd	A procuress.
bod	Body.
bawdy	Obscene; lewd.
bawdry	Coarse or obscene language.
body	Structure of bones, flesh, etc., of an animal. (Etc.)
bawl	*See ball.*
bawled	*See bald.*
bays	*See baize.*
bazaar	A market or fair.
bizarre	Strikingly odd.
be	To exist.
bee	Insect.
Bea	Short for *Beatrice.*
beach	(n.) Shore. (v.) To ground a boat.
beech	A tree.
beacon	Light used as signal or warning. (*Also see bacon.*)
beckon	To signal or summon by a gesture.
beadle	A minor parish official.
beagle	Small hound used for hunting.
Beatle	Member of the Beatles rock group.
beetle	(n.) Insect. (v.) To project or jut.
betel	East Indian pepper plant.

bean	Vegetable.
been	Form of verb *to be.* (Pronounced in U.S. like bin, in U.K. like bean.)
bin	Box, etc., for storage.
bear	*See bare.*
bearing	Carrying, supporting, enduring. (*Also see baring.*)
Bering	Sea/Strait.
bearish	Resembling a bear; rel. to falling prices on the stock market.
boorish	Crude; churlish.
beat	A single strike or blow.
beet	A vegetable.
beatification	The act of beatifying (defined below).
beautification	The act of beautifying.
beatify	To make supremely happy; to canonize.
beautify	To make beautiful.
Beatle	*See beadle.*
beau	(pl. *beaux* or *beaus.*) Suitor or sweetheart.
bow	A weapon; a curve; orna- mental knot.
beaut	Slang for *beauty.*
bute	(slang) Short for *phenylbutazone.*
butte	Knoll; isolated hill.
beautification	*See beatification.*
beautify	*See beatify.*
beckon	*See beacon.*
beech	*See beach.*
been	*See bean.*

beer	A malt beverage.		**benzene**	A colorless liquid mixture obtained from petroleum and coal tar, used as fuel and in the manufacture of plastics.
bier	A coffin or its stand.			
beet	*See beat.*		**benzine**	A colorless liquid mixture of hydrocarbons used as a solvent in dry cleaning.
beetle	*See beadle.*			
begat	Past tense of *beget.*		**benzoin**	An aromatic balsamic resin used in perfumery, etc.
beget	To procreate as the father.			
begot	Past tense of *beget.* (Past perfect: *begotten* or *begot.* Many people confuse the tenses, mixing up present and past.)		**bequest**	*See behest.*
			Bering	*See baring.*
			berg	Iceberg.
			burg	Town.
behest	A command; an earnest request.		**berm**	(also **berme**) A narrow path, shelf, or ledge typically at the top or bottom of a slope.
bequest	A legacy.			
bel	Ten decibels.		**birn**	Socket for mouthpiece in instruments of clarinet class.
bell	Metal instrument that makes a ringing sound when struck.			
belle	Popular, attractive woman.		**burn**	The act, process, or result of burning.
belay	To coil (a running rope) around a cleat, etc.		**berry**	*See Barry.*
belie	To show to be false.		**berth**	A place to sleep, esp. on a ship; allotted space.
bellows	(v.) Shouts in a deep voice. (n.) An apparatus for driving air through something.			
			birth	Emergence; beginning.
billows	Rises or rolls in waves or surges.		**beryl**	A mineral. (Cap.:) A feminine name. *(Also see barrel.)*
belly	*See ballet.*		**birl**	To cause a floating log to rotate by treading.
bemused	*See amused.*			
			burial	Interment.
			burl	A knot in wood, cloth, or wool.
			beseech	To implore.
			besiege	To surround with armed forces; to beset.

beside	At the side of.	**biddy**	A young chicken; an unpleasant woman.
besides	Over and above; other than, except.	**bitty**	Made up of or containing bits; small, tiny.
besmirch	To soil; to sully.		
smirch	To discolor or soil; tarnish or sully.	**bier**	*See beer.*
betel	*See beadle.*	**bight**	A loop, esp. in a rope.
		bite	A morsel; wound made by biting. (Etc.).
better	Of higher quality. (Etc.)	**byte**	A sequence of adjacent binary digits. (*Also see bit/bitt.*)
bettor	One who bets.		
bevel	A sloping edge or surface.	**bilious**	Relating to disordered liver function.
bezel	The sloped edge of a chisel; oblique face of a cut gem.	**bullous**	Marked by blisters.
level	An instrument for testing a horizontal line or plane.	**billed**	Past tense of *bill.*
		build	To construct.
beys	*See baize.*	**billion**	A thousand million. (*Also see bouillon.*)
bhang	*See bang.*	**billon**	An alloy used in coinage.
biannual	Happening twice a year.		
biennial	Happening every two years.	**billows**	*See bellows.*
		bin	*See bean.*
bias	Slant; prejudice.	**bind**	To tie or fasten.
bios	Biographies.	**bine**	A twining stem or flexible shoot.
bib	Cloth tied under the chin.		
bibb	Piece of timber bolted to a ship's mast.	**biogenetic**	Pert. to the production of living organisms from other living organisms.
Bibb	Variety of lettuce.	**biogenic**	Necessary for the life process.
bidder	One who bids.		
bitter	Sharp-tasting; unpleasant.	**bios**	*See bias.*
bidding	Making bids.	**biotite**	A common mineral of the mica group.
biding	Waiting.	**biotype**	A group of organisms having the same genotype.
biting	Cutting into with the teeth; causing a smarting pain.		

bird	A feathered friend.
burred	Having burrs.
Byrd	Proper name. [Admiral Byrd].
birn	*See berm.*
birr	Force, energy, vigor; a whirring sound.
bur	A rough prickly case around the seeds of certain plants; a dentist's rotary cutting tool.
burr	(also buhr) A rough or irregular protuberance; a small drill; a plant's seedcase or flower that clings to clothing, etc.
birth	*See berth.*
bisulcate	With two grooves; cloven- hoofed.
bisulfate	A salt of sulfuric acid.
bisulfide	A disulfide.
bisulfite	An acid sulfite.
bit	Small amount; cutting edge of a tool.
bitt	A post on ship's deck for securing lines.
bite	*See bight.*
biting	*See bidding.*
bitter	*See bidder.*
bitty	*See biddy.*
bizarre	*See bazaar.*
blanch	To bleach; to scald or parboil foods.
Blanche	Feminine name.
blench	To flinch; recoil.
blandish	To coax; to cajole.
brandish	To flourish or wave.

blat	To cry like a calf or sheep; bleat.
bleat	To utter the cry of a sheep or goat.
bleep	A short high-pitched sound; a censored word.
blip	A spot of light on a radar screen.
blench	*See blanch.*
bleu	(F.) Blue. [Bleu cheese].
blew	Past tense of *blow*.
blue	A color.
blip	*See bleep.*
bloc	A combination of persons, etc., with a common purpose.
block	A compact piece of material. (Etc.)
blond	Flaxen color; light-haired man.
blonde	Blond woman.
blotch	Imperfection; blemish.
botch	A piece of spoiled work; mess.
blue	*See bleu.*
boar	Male hog.
Boer	South African of Dutch descent.
boor	Rude or insensitive person.
bore	One who causes boredom.
board	A plank; daily meals; directors.
bored	Pierced with a rotary tool; weary with tedium.

boarder	One who is provided with regular meals.
border	Boundary or frontier; edge.
boarish	Of or like a boar; swinish.
boorish	Crude; insensitive.
bobble	*See babble.*
bod	*See baud.*
bode	To foretell or presage.
bowed	Shaped like a bow; past tense of bow (to bend forward).
body	*See bawdy.*
Boer	*See boar.*
bold	Fearless; impudent.
bowled	Past tense of *bowl.*
bolder	More bold.
boulder	Large stone.
bole	Tree trunk.
boll	The pod or capsule of a plant (cotton or flax, e.g.)
bowl	A concave vessel for holding liquids, etc.
bomb	*See balm.*
bombe	*See balm.*
bombé	*See balm.*
bomb bay	Compartment of a bomber containing bombs.
bombé	(F.) Curving or swelling outward (of furniture).
boor	*See boar.*
boorish	*See boarish.*
boos	Jeers.
booze	Intoxicating drink.

bootee	(also **bootie**) Baby's knitted or crocheted boot.
booty	Loot.
borane	A compound of boron and hydrogen, etc.
borate	A salt or ester of a boric acid.
boride	A binary compound of boron usu. with a more electropositive element or radical.
border	*See boarder.*
bore	*See boar.*
bored	*See board.*
born	Brought into existence.
borne	Past tense of *bear.*
bourn	(also **bourne**) Stream or brook.
borough	A division of government.
borrow	(v.) To take on loan. (n.) Material, as earth or gravel, used as a fill at another location (often pronounced burrow). [Ordinary borrow.]
bureau	Chest of drawers; office or department.
burro	Donkey.
burrow	Hole made by an animal.
botch	*See blotch.*
bother	Effort, work, or worry.
pother	Commotion; uproar.
bough	Branch of a tree.
bow	Forward part of a ship; bending of head or body in greeting.
bouillon	Broth.
bullion	Gold or silver in bulk.

boulder	*See bolder.*	**brake**	(n.) A device for arresting motion; a machine for forming sheet metal. (v.) To arrest the motion of a mechanism.
bounce	To spring back.		
jounce	To bump, bounce, or jolt.		
bourn	*See born.*	**break**	(n.) Breaking; an escape; a fair chance. (Etc.). (v.) To fracture. (Etc.)
bow	*See beau and bough.*		
bowed	*See bode.*		
bowl	*See bole.*		
bowled	*See bold.*	**braking**	Arresting the motion of a mechanism.
boy	Male child.	**breaking**	Fracturing.
buoy	A float.		
bracket	A support projecting from an upright surface.	**bran**	Ground inner husks of grain sifted out from flour.
brocket	Small red South American deer.	**brand**	Trademark; class of goods. (Etc.)
brae	A hillside (Scot.)	**brandish**	*See blandish.*
bray	To utter the loud harsh cry of a donkey; to spread thin, as printer's ink.	**brassie**	Golf club.
		brassy	Shamelessly bold; resembling brass.
braes	Hillsides (Scot.)	**brassiere**	Woman's undergarment.
braise	To cook slowly with very little moisture.	**brazier**	Pan for holding burning coals; one who works in brass.
brays	Utters the cry of a donkey; applies ink with a brayer.		
braze	To solder.	**brava**	Used in applauding a woman.
braid	Cord or ribbon having three or more component strands; plaited hair. (*Also see abrade.*)	**bravo**	Used in applauding a man.
		bray	*See brae.*
		brayed	*See braid.*
brayed	Uttered the cry of a donkey.	**brays**	*See braes.*
		braze	*See braes.*
		brazier	*See brassiere.*
brail	A line used to furl loose-footed sails.	**breach**	An infraction; a broken or ruptured condition.
Braille	A system of writing or printing for the blind.	**breech**	The hind end of the body, etc. [Breech birth; breech of a firearm.]
braise	*See braes.*		

bread	The staff of life.	**brighten**	To make brighter.
bred	Past tense of *breed*.	**Brighton**	Borough in southern England.
breadth	Distance from side to side; width.	**brilliance**	The quality of being brilliant.
breath	Air inhaled and exhaled.	**brilliants**	Gems with many facets.
breathe	To inhale and exhale.	**brim**	*See bream.*
break	*See brake.*	**brisk**	Lively.
breaking	*See braking.*	**brusque**	Blunt; harsh.
bream	A fish.	**Britain**	*See Breton.*
brim	Edge.	**Brittany**	*See Breton.*
breech	*See breach.*	**broach**	(v.) To open up (as a subject for discussion). (n.) A pointed, tapered tool.
bred	*See bread.*		
Breton	A native or inhabitant of Brittany.	**broche**	(one syllable, pronounced with a long *o*) A spindle.
Britain	A country (England).	**broché**	(F., two syllables) A pinstripe woven in the warp direction.
Brittany	Region in France.		
brewed	Steeped; boiled; fermented; fomented.	**brooch**	An ornament worn at the neck (preferably pronounced the same as *broach).*
brood	(n.) The young of an animal. (v.) To incubate; to meditate or worry.		
		brocket	*See bracket.*
		broke	*See baroque.*
brews	Brewed beverages.	**bromate**	A salt of bromic acid.
bruise	Contusion; abrasion.	**bromide**	A medicine; a commonplace or soothing remark.
briar	Tobacco pipe made from brier root.		
brier	A thorny plant. [Brier patch.]	**bromine**	A chemical element.
		bromize	To treat or combine with bromine or a bromide.
bridal	Pertaining to a bride.		
bridle	Headgear for a horse.	**brome**	Genus of grass.
bridge	*See abridge.*	**broom**	A shrub; brush for sweeping.
brier	*See briar.*	**brougham**	Type of carriage.
brigandine	Medieval body armor.		
brigantine	Masted square-rigged ship.		

broncs	Mustangs.	**buff**	Brownish-yellow color.
Bronx (the)	Borough of New York City.	**buffe**	Plate armor for the face and throat.
brooch	*See broach.*	**build**	*See billed.*
brood	*See brewed.*		
broom	*See brome.*	**bulbous**	Having or resembling a bulb.
brougham	*See brome.*	**bullous**	Resembling or characterized by bullae (large vesicles).
brows	Eyebrows; foreheads.		
browse	To graze; to look over casually.	**bullion**	*See bouillon.*
		buoy	*See boy.*
brucine	An alkaloid used chiefly in the denaturation of alcohol.	**bureau**	*See borough.*
		bur/burr	*See birr.*
brucite	A mineral used in magnesia refractories.	**burg**	*See berg.*
		burger	Hamburger.
bruise	*See brews.*	**burgher**	A middle-class townsman.
brusque	*See brisk.*	**burglar**	A person who breaks into a building with intent to steal.
bruit	To noise abroad; to report.		
bruit	(F., Med.) Abnormal sound heard on auscultation. (Pronounced broo-EE.)	**burial**	*See beryl.*
		burl	*See beryl.*
brut	Very dry (of champagne).	**burley**	A light type of tobacco.
brute	A beast; savage person.	**burly**	With a strong heavy physique; sturdy.
bubble	*See babble.*	**burn**	*See berm.*
		burred	*See bird.*
buccal	Pertaining to the cheek.	**burro**	*See borough.*
buckle	A fastener.	**burrow**	*See borough.*
bucchero	A black ceramic ware.	**bursa**	A sac or cavity containing a fluid to reduce friction, as at body joints.
buckaroo	A cowboy; broncobuster.		
buckra	(Southern U.S.) A white man (used disparagingly.)	**bursar**	Treasurer.
		purser	A ship's officer in charge of accounts, etc.
buckram	A stiff cotton fabric.		
buckle	*See buccal.*	**bury**	*See Barry.*

bus	1. Large motor-driven vehicle. 2. (Elec.) A conducting bar (bus bar) that carries heavy currents to supply several electric circuits.
buss	A kiss.
business	A task or duty; one's occupation.
busyness	State of being busy.
bussed	Carried by bus; kissed.
bust	Part of human anatomy; flop; police raid.
bustard	*See bastard.*
but	A conjunction.
butt	The end of something; a target. (Etc.)

butane	A colorless flammable gas.
butene	Butylene.
butylene	A gaseous isomeric hydrocarbon chiefly used in making synthetic rubber.
bute	*See beaut.*
butte	*See beaut.*
buy	To purchase.
by	(prep. and adv.) Near. (Etc.) [By-election; bylaw].
bye	A side issue; term used in bridge.
'bye	Good-bye.
by law	According to law.
bylaw	Local or corporate rule.
Byrd	*See bird.*
byte	*See bight.*

C

cabal	A small group of secret plotters.
cable	A wire or rope.
cabana	Shelter at a beach or swimming pool.
cabin	Small dwelling or shelter.
cacao	A tropical tree.
coco	The coconut palm or its fruit.
cocoa	A powder made from crushed cacao beans.
cache	A hiding place; something hidden.
cachet	A distinguishing mark; prestige. [Note: This two- syllable word should not conflict with the one- syllable *cache*, but the latter word is often mispronounced.]
cash	Ready money.
cad	Bounder; boor.
cat	Member of the feline family.
CAT	Computer-aided transcription; computerized axial tomography.
cadenza	(Music) A showy flourish or passage.
credenza	A sideboard.
cadge	To ask for a gift; beg.
catch	To capture. (Etc.)

Cain	First son of Adam and Eve. [To raise Cain: become angry or violent.]
cane	Walking stick; the hollow jointed stem of certain plants.
calcine	Product of calcination or roasting.
calcium	Chemical element present in bones and teeth.
calcite	A mineral consisting of calcium carbonate crystallized in hexagonal form.
calculous	Pert. to calculus or calculi.
calculus	1. A method of mathematical calculation. 2. A concretion of mineral substances, etc., found in ducts, cysts, etc.
calyculus	(also **caliculus**) A structure shaped like a cup.
calendar	A system for fixing divisions of a year.
calender	A machine with cylinders or rollers.
colander	A perforated pan.
calf	The young of a cow, whale, etc.; back of the leg.
calve	To give birth to a calf; to become detached (said of an ice mass).
caliber	Diameter of the inside of a tube or gun barrel; degree of excellence or importance.
caliper	(usu. *calipers*) An instrument for measuring diameters.

calix	(pl. *calices*) Cup.		**calm**	Quiet and still (pronounced by some as cam).
calyx	(pl. *calyxes* or *calyces*) Part of a flower; one of the cuplike divisions of the pelvis of the kidney.		**cam**	A rotating or sliding piece that imparts linear motion to other mechanical parts.
calk	A projection on a shoe sole or horseshoe to prevent slipping.		**caloric**	Rel. to heat; rel. to calories.
caulk	(also **calk**) To make watertight.		**choleric**	Hot-tempered.
cock	To turn up, tip, tilt; to position the hammer of a firearm for firing.		**Calvary**	Hill near Jerusalem.
cork	To stop up with a cork. [Note: witnesses in areas such as New England make little distinction in pronouncing some of these words.]		**cavalry**	Horsemen; mounted troops.
			calve	*See calf.*
			cam	*See calm.*
call	A shout or cry.		**calvous**	Lacking hair; bald.
caul	Sac in the womb in which the child lives during pregnancy.		**calvus**	Rel. to a cumulonimbus cloud.
cowl	A hood or hooded cloak; part of the front of an automobile body.		**calyculus**	*See calculous.*
			calyx	*See calix.*
caller	One that calls.		**camber**	A slightly arched surface; a setting of automobile wheels closer together at the bottom than the top.
choler	Irascibility.			
collar	A band of material around the neck.		**camper**	One that camps.
			camphor	Compound used as insect repellent, etc.
callosal	Pert. to the corpus callosum.			
colossal	Huge.		**can**	Container for liquid, etc.
			Cannes	Commune and port in SE France.
callous	Hardened; having calluses; feeling no emotion or sympathy for others.		**khan**	Title of rulers and officials in central Asia.
callus	A thickening, as of skin or a fractured bone.		**canal**	Channel; tubular passage in the body.
			cannel (coal)	A bituminous coal containing volatile matter that burns brightly.

canape	An appetizer.
canopy	Awning; marquee.
panoply	Ceremonial attire; magnificent or impressive display.
cancroid	A form of skin cancer.
chancroid	A painful lesion; venereal disease.
candid	Frank; honest.
candied	Encrusted or coated with sugar.
cane	*See Cain.*
cannel	*See canal.*
cannery	A canning factory.
channery	An accumulation of thin fragments of sandstone, etc.
cannon	An artillery piece.
canon	A regulation; rule; dogma.
canyon	Deep ravine.
canopy	*See canape.*
cant	Jargon; trite or pious phrases; tilted or sloping position.
can't	Contraction of *cannot.*
canter	Horse's gait.
cantor	Chief singer of the liturgy in a synagogue.
canvas	Firmly woven cloth; a sail.
canvass	Detailed examination; survey.
canyon	*See cannon.*

caparison	An ornamental covering for a horse; adornment.
comparison	The act or process of comparing.
capillary	A very small blood vessel; having a very small bore; pert. to surface tension.
papillary	Pert. to a small nipplelike eminence.
capital	Goods; an important city.
capitol	A building, usually found in a state or national *capital.*
caporal	Type of tobacco; overseer of a cattle ranch.
corporal	(n.) An Army noncom. (adj.) Of the body.
capstan	A vertical cylinder used for hoisting weights.
capstone	The top and last stone to be placed in a structure.
captain	Person in authority.
captan	A fungicide.
carat	(also **karat**) A unit of weight.
caret	A wedge-shaped mark.
carrot	Vegetable.
carbide	A carbon compound.
carbine	A light often semiautomatic rifle.
carbinol	Methyl alcohol.
carbonyl	A compound containing metal combined with carbon monoxide.

carbon dioxide	A heavy colorless gas that does not support combustion.	**carotene**	An orange or red substance that occurs in carrots, tomatoes, etc.—a good source of vitamin A.
carbon monoxide	A colorless odorless toxic gas that burns to carbon dioxide.	**keratin**	A strong protein forming the basis of nails, horns, claws, etc.
carbuncle	A large boil.	**keratome**	A knife used in eye surgery.
caruncle	A small, fleshy, red mark or nodule.		
carcass	Corpse; foundation structure (as of a tire).	**carotid**	One of two major arteries in the neck.
caucus	A meeting of a small group to decide policy.	**parotid**	A salivary gland at the base of each ear.
careen	To cause (a boat) to lean over on one side.	**carousal**	A drunken revel.
career	To go at top speed in a headlong manner. (Cars *career*, boats *careen*, but the distinction has become blurred so cars too now careen.)	**carousel**	(also **carrousel**) Merry-go- round; airport luggage conveyor.
		carpal	Rel. to the carpus (wrist).
		carpel	(Bot.) A simple pistil of a flower.
caressed	Stroked lovingly.	**corporal**	Physical; relating to the body or corpus. (*Also see caporal.*)
crest	Peak. (Etc.)		
caret	*See carat.*	**carpus**	Wrist; bones of the wrist.
caries	Tooth decay.	**corpus**	Main body or part.
carious	Affected with caries.		
carries	Transports.	**carrier**	One that carries.
		courier	Messenger.
carmen	Members of the crew of a streetcar, etc.	**currier**	One that curries (grooms horses, e.g.)
Carmen	Bizet opera; feminine name.	**Currier**	Famous U.S. lithographer. [Currier and Ives.]
carmine	A crimson or purplish-red color.		
		carries	*See caries.*
		carrot	*See carat.*
		cart	(n.) A conveyance. (v.) To carry or convey.
		carte	French word heard in phrases such as *carte blanche* and *carte de jour.*

carton	Cardboard box or container.
cartoon	Comic strip. (Etc.)
caruncle	*See carbuncle.*
cascara	A plant, its bark the source of a liquid drug.
mascara	A cosmetic for the eyelashes.
cash	*See cache.*
cashmere	A fine wool from the undercoat of the cashmere goat.
cassimere	A twill-weave, worsted suiting fabric.
Kashmir	Mountainous region of N India.
cask	A barrel.
casque	Medieval helmet.
cassock	A long garment worn esp. by certain members of the clergy.
hassock	A footstool.
cast	A mold; a rigid dressing; actors, etc.
caste	A division of society.
caster	A set of wheels.
castor	A plant (source of castor oil); an oily, odorous substance extracted from the groin of a beaver, used in perfume, etc.
casual	Informal.
causal	Expressing or indicating cause. [Causal connection.] *(Also see acausal.)*

casually	Informally; offhandedly.
casualty	One injured or killed in an accident or in battle.
cat/CAT	*See cad.*
cataclysm	Flood, deluge; disaster.
catechism	A summary of religious doctrine, often in the form of questions and answers.
catalectic	Lacking a syllable at the end of an incomplete foot.
cataleptic	Rel. to catalepsy (a type of seizure).
catalytic	Causing or rel. to catalysis (a change in chemical reaction). [Catalytic converter.]
catalepsy	A seizure in which a person becomes rigid and unconscious.
cataplexy	Sudden loss of muscle power following a strong emotional stimulus.
catarrh	Inflammation of a mucous membrane.
guitar	Stringed musical instrument.
catch	The act of catching or something caught. *(Also see cadge.)*
ketch	A small two-masted sailing boat.
kitsch	Something of tawdry design, appearance, or content, appealing to undiscriminating taste.

catch-up	The act of catching up or trying to catch up.	**cease**	To stop.
catsup	(also **catchup, ketchup**) A seasoned tomato puree.	**seas**	Bodies of water.
		sees	Observes.
		seize	To grab.
catechism	*See cataclysm.*	**cecal**	Pert. to the cecum (pouch in large intestine).
caucus	*See carcass.*	**fecal**	Pert. to feces.
caudad	Toward the tail or posterior end.	**cecum**	(also **caecum**) A cul-de-sac, esp. that in which the large intestine begins.
caudate	Having a tail or taillike appendage.		
caudal	Of, rel. to, or being a tail. *(Also see acaudal.)*	**sebum**	The fatty secretion of the sebaceous glands.
caudle	A warm drink for the sick.	**cedar**	Coniferous tree.
coddle	To pamper.	**ceder**	One that cedes.
cuddle	To hold closely and lovingly in one's arms.	**Seder**	A Jewish ceremonial dinner.
		seeder	One that sows.
caught	Past tense of *catch.*	**cede**	To yield or grant.
cot	Small bed.	**seed**	To sow.
caul	*See call.*	**ceil**	To furnish with a lining or ceiling.
caulk	*See calk.*	**seal**	To close securely.
causal	*See casual.*		
cause	Reason, motive. (Etc.)	**ceiling**	Overhead inside lining of a room.
caws	Cries of a crow.	**sealing**	Closing; fastening.
cautery	Cauterization.	**cel**	(also **cell**) A transparent celluloid sheet on which a character, etc., is drawn or painted and which constitutes a frame in the filming of an animated cartoon.
coterie	A select group of people.		
cavalry	*See Calvary.*		
cay	Low island or reef of coral (pronounced key or kay).		
key	Something providing access, control, or insight.	**cell**	Small compartment or unit.
quay	A wharf (pronounced key).	**sell**	To give up in return for something else.

celebrate	To observe (a day) or commemorate (an event).
cerebrate	To use the mind; think or think about.
celebration	Ceremony; festivities.
cerebration	Mental activity.
celery	Vegetable.
salary	Wages.
cellar	Basement.
seller	One who sells.
cellular	*See acellular.*
cellulase	An enzyme.
cellulate	Cellular.
cellulite	Lumpy fat deposits, esp. in thighs and buttocks.
cellulose	Organic substance found in all plant tissues.
cemetery	A burial ground for the dead.
symmetry	Pleasing proportion between parts as a whole.
censer	A covered incense burner.
censor	To inspect conduct, morals, etc.
censure	To criticize or reproach in a harsh manner.
senser	One that senses something.
sensor	A device that reacts to a certain stimulus.
census	Numbering.
senses	Faculties.
centimeter	(also **centimetre**) Metric measurement. [Note: Some doctors, et al., pronounce as sahn-ti-meter.]
sonometer	Instrument for determining the pitch of sounds.
centric	*See acentric.*
centrifugal	Moving or directed outward from the center.
centripetal	Directed toward the center.
cents	Monetary units; pennies.
scents	Odors.
sense	Meaning.
century	100 years.
sentry	Guard.
cephalus	*See acephalus.*
cere	A waxy protuberance at the base of a bird's bill.
sear	To burn, scorch, parch.
seer	One that sees; one that predicts the future.
sere	Dry; withered.
cereal	A grain; grain product.
serial	Work appearing in parts at intervals.
cerebellum	Portion of human brain that coordinates movement.
cerebrum	Portion of human brain that controls conscious thought.
cerebrate	*See celebrate.*
cerebration	*See celebration.*

cereus	A genus of cactus.	**chalcosis**	A deposit of copper particles in the tissues.
cerous	Containing trivalent cerium. *(Also see cirrous, etc.)*	**chalicosis**	An industrial lung disease.
serious	Grave, solemn; sober, thoughtful.	**chamber**	A room; legislative assembly. (Etc.)
serous	Of or resembling serum.	**chamfer**	Beveled edge on a piece of wood.
cervical	Rel. to the cervix.		
surgical	Rel. to surgery.	**champagne**	Sparkling wine. (Cap.:) Region in France.
cervices	Pl. of *cervix* (back of the neck; constricted part of an organ).	**champaign**	Level open country.
		Champaign	City in Illinois.
services	Pl. of *service*.	**chance**	Luck; opportunity. (Etc.)
cession	Ceding; yielding; concession.	**chants**	Songs; rhythmic monotonous utterances.
session	A meeting or series of meetings of court, etc.; a period spent continuously in an activity.	**chancellory**	A chancellor's position, department, or residence.
		chancery	A court of equity.
cetacean	Belonging to the Cetacea (marine mammals: whales, etc.)	**chancroid**	*See cancroid.*
		channery	*See cannery.*
cetaceum	Spermaceti (a solid obtained from the head of the sperm whale).	**chanter**	A person who chants; singer.
		chanteur	A male singer, esp. one who sings in nightclubs and cabarets. (Female form: *chanteuse.)*
cetaceous	Rel. to the Cetacea.		
setaceous	Bristlelike.		
chafe	To make sore by rubbing; to irritate.	**chantey**	(also **chanty**) Sailors' song.
chaff	To tease or joke.	**shanty**	A shack.
chairwoman	Feminine counterpart of *chairman*.	**chants**	*See chance.*
charwoman	Cleaning woman.	**char**	Type of trout; charred substance; charwoman.
chaise	(F.) A two-wheeled carriage (pronounced shaze). [Note also *chaise longue*, a long reclining chair.]	**chart**	Map; diagram. (Etc.)
chase	Pursuit.		
chez	(F.) At or in the home of (pronounced shay.)		

chard	Vegetable. [Swiss chard.]	**cheers**	Applause.
charred	Burned.	**jeers**	Boos.
shard	Fragment of a brittle substance.	**cheery**	*See chary.*
		cheetah	*See cheater.*
charwoman	*See chairwoman.*	**chef**	A professional cook.
		chief	A leader or ruler.
chary	Discreetly cautious.		
cheery	Cheerful.	**Chekov**	*See checkoff.*
cherry	Fruit.	**cherry**	*See chary.*
sherry	A wine.		
		chess	A game.
chase	*See chaise.*	**chest**	Container; part of the body.
chased	Pursued.	**chew**	To masticate.
chaste	Pure.	**eschew**	To avoid, shun.
chaser	Pursuer.	**chews**	Masticates.
chasseur	(F.) A hunter; a cavalry soldier; footman.	**choose**	To select.
		chez	*See chaise.*
cheap	Inexpensive; stingy.		
cheep	To chirp.	**chic**	Style; sophistication (pronounced sheek).
cheater	One that cheats.	**chick**	Chicken; girl (slang).
cheetah	Leopardlike animal of SW Asia and Africa.	**sheikh**	(also **sheik**) An Arab chief.
check	Sudden pause or break; verification; written order from a bank to pay out money (spelled *cheque* in U.K.)	**chief**	*See chef.*
		Chile	Country in South America.
Czech	Citizen of Czechoslovakia.	**chili**	(also **chile, chilli**) A hot pepper. [Chili con carne.]
checker	One that checks; a playing piece in checkers.	**chilly**	Cool.
exchequer	A national treasury.	**chinchy**	Stingy; cheap.
		chintzy	Decorated with chintz; cheap, inferior; stingy.
checkoff	Deduction from union dues, etc. (Two words as a verb.)		
Chekov	Russian dramatist and writer.		
cheep	*See cheap.*		

chirk	To cheer.
chirp	Short, sharp note made by a bird or insect, e.g. grasshopper.
chirr	Short vibrant sound of an insect.
chirrup	A series of chirps.
chitin	A substance that forms part of hard cover of insects and crustaceans.
chiton	A mollusk; an ancient Greek garment.
chloral	A pungent colorless oily aldehyde.
choral	Rel. to a chorus or choir.
chorale	A choral composition, using words of a hymn.
coral	A hard red, pink, or white substance built by tiny sea creatures.
corral	Pen or enclosure for animals.
kraal	A village of S African natives; an enclosure for animals.
chlorate	A salt of chloric acid.
chloride	A salt of hydrochloric acid.
chlorine	A greenish-yellow gas of suffocating odor.
chlorite	A green stone, resembling mica.
chloroethane	Ethyl chloride.
chloroethene	Vinyl chloride.
chlorophyll	The green coloring matter in plants.
chromophil	Staining readily with dyes.
choir	Group of singers or instruments.
quire	24 sheets of paper.

cholecystec-tomy	Surgical removal of the gallbladder.
cholecystos-tomy	Formation of an opening into the gallbladder.
cholecysto-tomy	Incision of the gallbladder.
choledo-chostomy	Formation of an opening into the common bile duct.
choledocho-tomy	Incision of the common bile duct.
choler	*See caller.*
choleric	*See caloric.*
choose	*See chews.*
choral	*See chloral.*
chorale	*See chloral.*
chord	Harmonious tones blended together.
cord	Rope, string, etc. [Vocal *cord*, not *chord*!]
cored	Removed the core of.
chorea	A nervous disorder.
Korea	Country in eastern Asia.
chose	1. Past tense of *choose*. 2. (L., pronounced like *shows*) A thing; an article of personal property. [Chose in action.]
shows	Performances. (Etc.)
chow	A type of dog; food (slang).
ciao	(It.) Greeting; hello or good-bye (pronounced chow).
chowder	A thick soup.
clowder	A group or cluster of cats.

chromate	A salt or ester of chromic acid.
chromite	An oxide of bivalent chromium.
chromatic	*See achromatic.*
chromatid	One of the paired complex constituent strands of a chromosome.
chromatin	The readily stainable substance of a cell nucleus.
chromic	Of, rel. to, or derived from chromium.
chronic	Marked by long duration or frequent recurrence.
clonic	Rel. to jerky muscle contractions or spasms.
colonic	Pert. to the colon.
chromophil	*See chlorophyll.*
chrysolite	(Mineral) Olivine.
chrysophyte	Any of a group of algae.
chucker	One that chucks.
chukar	A partridge.
chukker	A period of play in polo.
chute	An inclined plane or channel; slide; parachute.
shoot	New growth; firing of a missile.
ciao	*See chow.*
cinch	To make secure; to make sure of.
clinch	To fasten; to settle conclusively. *(Also see clench.)*

circlet	Small circle.
circuit	Line or route or distance around a place; district of a judge.
circumcise	To cut off the foreskin.
circumscribe	To draw a line around; restrict
cirrhosis	A disease of the liver.
sorosis	A fleshy fruit, composed of many flowers, seed vessels, etc.; pineapple, e.g.
cirrose	(Bot., Zool.) Having a cirrus or cirri.
cirrous	Resembling cirrus clouds.
cirrus	(Meteorol.) A wispy white cloud. (Bot.) A tendril. (Zool.) An appendage serving as a foot, tentacle, etc. (Pl. *cirri.*)
serous	Of, rel. to, or resembling serum. *(Also see series, serious.)*
cist	Burial chamber.
cyst	A sac enclosing a fluid.
schist	A rock with layers of different minerals that splits into thin irregular plates.
cistern	Tank or vessel for storing water.
cistron	A segment of DNA specifying a single functional unit.
cite	To quote by way of example.
sight	(n.) Something seen. (v.) To look at or through; to take aim.
site	(n.) Location. (v.) To locate.

citrine	Pale yellow; lemon-colored.	**clench**	To close (teeth or fingers) tightly.
citron	Fruit similar to a lemon.	**clinch**	To fasten; to settle decisively. (Also see cinch.)
clack	Chatter; a clapping noise.		
claque	A group hired to applaud.	**clew**	Clue.
		clue	Fact or idea that gives a solution to a problem.
clamber	To climb awkwardly.	**cue**	A long rod used in playing pool or billards; a signal or hint. [Note: These days people use clue in and cue in somewhat interchangeably to mean to inform or brief.]
clammer	One that digs clams.		
clamor	To make a din.		
clamp	A device for holding things tightly.		
cramp	Sudden painful involuntary tightening of a muscle.		
crimp	A bend or crease.	**queue**	A waiting line; a braid of hair.
clan	A group united by common interests.	**click**	See cleek.
Klan	Ku Klux Klan.	**clique**	See cleek.
classic	Traditional; enduring.	**climactic**	Of or rel. to a climax.
clastic	Made up of fragments of preexisting rocks.	**climatic**	Pert. to climate.
		climacteric	(n.) A major turning point or critical state. (adj.) Rel. to a critical period.
clause	Groups of words.		
claws	Curved nails of an animal.		
		climb	To go upward.
claustrum	A barrier, as a membrane partially closing an opening.	**clime**	Climate.
colostrum	The first milk secreted after giving birth.	**clinch**	See cinch and clench.
		clitic	Closely connected in pronunciation with a preceding or following word.
cleek	A large hook (as for a pot over a fire).		
click	A slight, sharp sound.	**critic**	A person who forms and expresses judgment.
clique	A narrow exclusive group of persons (preferred pronunciation klick).		
		clone	One or more organisms descended asexually from a single ancestor.
clef	A symbol on a stave in a musical score.	**cone**	Solid body that narrows to a point from a round flat base.
cleft	Split, partly divided. [Cleft chin.]		

clonic	See chromic.	coalition	Union; combination.
		collation	A light meal; act or
close	A conclusion; ending.		result of collating.
	2. A narrow lane or		
	alley (Brit.)	coaming	A raised frame around
clothes	Covering for the body.		the hatchway on a
cloze	Of, rel. to, or being a		ship's deck.
	test of reading	combing	Drawing a comb
	comprehension.		through.

closer	Nearer.
closure	An act of closing.
cloture	Closing or limitation of vote in a legislature.

coapt	To bring close together.
coopt	To take over an idea, etc., as one's own.

closet	To shut up in a private room.
cosset	To treat as a pet.

coarse	Unrefined.
course	Way or passage.

clot	A thickened mass formed from blood or other liquid.
clout	A blow; power of effective action.

coarser	More coarse; less refined.
courser	One that courses; hunting dog.

clothes	See close.
cloture	See closer.
clowder	See chowder.
cloze	See close.
clue	See clew.

coastal	Rel. to a coast.
costal	Resembling or pert. to a rib.

coat	Outer garment.
cote	Cottage.

clump	A cluster or mass.
lump	A protuberance or swelling.

coated	Covered.
coded	Put into a code.

coal	Kind of fuel.
col	A pass or depression in a mountain range or ridge.
cole	Cabbage (as in cole slaw).
kohl	A cosmetic to darken the eyelids.

coater	One that coats.
coder	One that uses or makes codes.

coax	To persuade; wheedle.
Cokes	Coca-Colas. (Also see coke.)

coaled	Fueled with coal.
cold	Chilly; frigid.

coca/cocoa	See cacao.

cocci	Pl. of coccus, a bacterium.
coccyx	Tailbone.

coalesce	To grow together; to unite.
convalesce	To grow strong or well.

coccid	A bug.
coccoid	Resembling a coccus; globular.

cochlea **trochlea**	Part of the inner ear. An anatomical structure resembling a pulley.	**coke** **Coke**	Residue of coal left after distillation; cocaine. Coca-Cola.
cock **coq**	Rooster. (Etc.) *(Also see calk.)* (F.) Cock. [Coq au vin].	**Cokes** **cola** **COLA**	*See coax.* Soft drink. An escalator clause esp. in union contracts (acronym for cost of living adjustment).
cocky **khaki**	Pert; arrogant. A kind of cloth; military uniform; a light yellowish brown.		
coda	Concluding musical section; conclusion of literary or dramatic work.	**colander** **cold**	*See calendar.* *See coaled.*
code	System of principles or rules. (Etc.)	**collaborate** **corroborate**	To work jointly with others. To get or give supporting evidence.
coddle **coded** **coder**	*See caudal.* *See coated.* *See coater.*	**collaboration** **corroboration**	Working jointly with another or others. Supporting evidence. *(Also see cooperation.)*
coequal **coeval**	A person who is the equal of another. Of the same period or age; contemporary.	**collage** **college**	An assembly of diverse fragments. A school.
cognition **recognition**	Act or process of knowing. Acknowledgment.	**collar**	*See caller.*
coffer **cougher**	Strongbox; treasury. One that coughs.	**collard** **collared**	Kale. [Collard greens.] Seized by the collar or neck.
coiffeur **coiffure**	Male hairdresser. Hairstyle.	**collation**	*See coalition.*
coign	Earlier spelling of *coin*, used now only in phrase *coign of vantage*: advantageous position.	**collie** **coolie** **coolly** **coulee**	Breed of dog. Unskilled laborer of Far East. In a cool manner. A deep ravine or gulch, usu. dry, that has been formed by running water.
coin **quoin**	Metal money. External angle of a building; cornerstone.		
coil **curl**	Series of loops; spiral. Ringlet.		

collision	Clash; impact.		**comfit**	Type of candy.
collusion	Secret agreement, usu.		**comfort**	Strengthening aid;
	for illegal purposes.			solace; ease; type of
				bed covering.
colonel	A commisioned officer.			
kernel	Central or essential		**comic**	Funny.
	part.		**conic**	Of or rel. to a cone.

colonic — *See chromic.*

comical — Funny.
conical — Resembling a cone, esp. in shape.

color — Shade; pigment; tint. *(Also see caller, collar.)*

comingle — Commingle.
commingle — To mix or mingle together; combine. (Prefer this word.)

culler — One that culls.
cruller — Twisted fried cake, cousin to a doughnut.

colossal — *See callosal.*

comity — *See comedy.*
comma — *See coma.*

colostomy — Formation of an artificial anus.
colotomy — Incision or opening of the colon.

command — To dominate; to order.
commend — To praise; to recommend.

colostrum — *See claustrom.*

commence — To begin.
comments — Remarks.

coma — Unconscious state.
comma — Punctuation mark.

committee — *See comedy.*

combine — To merge; unite; intermix.
confine — To restrict; to shut up.

comparable — Equivalent; similar.
comparative — Involving comparison; relative.

combing — *See coaming.*

compare — To represent as similar; liken; to contrast.
compeer — Companion; equal, peer.
compere — (Brit.) Master of ceremonies.

come — To arrive. (Etc.)
cum — (L.) With. [Dinner-cum-dancing, e.g.]

comedian — An actor who plays comic parts.
comedienne — Female comedian.

comparison — *See caparison.*

comedy — Humor.
comity — Courtesy; harmony.
committee — A group of people appointed to attend to a special function.

compartment — One of the spaces into which a structure is divided.
comportment — Behavior, manner of bearing.

compeer/ compere	*See compare.*
competence	The state of being competent.
competency	Competence (the preferable word).
complacence	Calm and secure satisfaction with oneself.
complaisance	Disposition to please or comply.
complacent	Self-satisfied.
complaisant	Willing to do what pleases others.
complected	(a barbarism) Complexioned.
complexioned	Pert. to color and appearance of skin. [Dark-complexioned.]
complement	Something that completes.
compliment	Expression of esteem; flattering remark.
complementary	Serving to fill out or complete; mutually supporting each other's lack.
complimentary	Expressing or containing a compliment; at no cost.
comportment	*See compartment.*
compose	To form, to make up.
comprise	To include, to consist of. [It's incorrect to say the board is *comprised* of six members.]
composer	One that composes.
composure	Calmness; self-possession.

comprehensible	Intelligible; understandable.
comprehensive	Inclusive; including much or all.
comprise	*See compose.*
comptroller	An official who audits accounts and certifies expenditures; controller.
controller	A person in charge of finances at an institution.
compulsive	Compelling; driven.
compulsory	Required.
concede	To accept as true, valid, or accurate.
conceive	To originate; to form a conception of.
concentrate	To bring or direct toward a common center or objective.
consecrate	To make or declare sacred.
concentration	A concentrated mass or thing; close attention.
consecration	The state of being consecrated.
conch	A large marine gastropod mollusk.
concha	A shell-like structure, esp. the outer ear; harness ornament.
conches	Plural of *conch*.
conscious	Awake; aware.
concord	Agreement.
conquered	Bested.
concordant	Agreeing.
concordat	An agreement or compact, esp. an official one.

concur	Agree; approve.	**conquer**	*See concur.*
conquer	Vanquish.	**conquered**	*See concord.*
condemn	To censure.	**conscience**	Consciousness of right or wrong.
contemn	To treat with contempt.	**conscious**	Awake; aware. *(Also see conches.)*
cone	*See clone.*		
confidant	One to whom secrets are entrusted (m.)	**conscien-tiousness**	Uprightness, honesty.
confidante	Same (f.)	**consciousness**	Awareness.
confident	Full of conviction or assurance.	**consecrate**	*See concentrate.*
		consecration	*See concentration.*
confidants	(Defined above.)	**consistent**	Conforming to a regular pattern or style.
confidantes	(Defined above.)	**constant**	Invariable or unchanging.
confidence	Full trust; assurance.		
confine	*See combine.*	**consonance**	Harmony; agreement.
		consonants	Letters of the alphabet other than vowels.
confirm	To give approval to; to ratify.	**constrict**	To tighten by making narrow; to squeeze.
conform	To bring into harmony or accord.	**construct**	(v.) To build. (n.) Something synthesized or constructed from simple elements, esp. a concept (accent on first syl.)
confirmation	Act or process of confirming.		
conformation	Producing conformity; adaptation.		
confuse	To throw into disorder; mix up; make unclear.		
contuse	To bruise.	**constriction**	A tightening or limiting.
		construction	Something constructed; an interpretation.
confusion	State of being confused.		
contusion	A bruise.	**consul**	An official, usu. in diplomatic service.
conga	Cuban dance.	**council**	An assembly, usu. an advisory group.
conge	(F.) Formal permission to leave.	**counsel**	Advice; an adviser or lawyer.
conger	Large marine eel.		
Congo	African republic (Zaire) and river.		
conic/conical	*See comic/comical.*	**contact**	Touching, coming together.
		contract	Formal agreement.
conjoined	Brought together so as to meet or overlap.		
conjoint	United; joint.		

contactor	(Elect.) A switch for an electric power circuit.	**coolie**	See collie.
contractor	One who contracts.	**coolly**	See collie.
contemn	See condemn.	**coop**	A pen.
		co-op	A cooperative. (Sometimes pronounced as one syllable; Harvard Coop, e.g.)
contemptible	Deserving to be scorned.		
contemptuous	Scornful, disdainful.		
contentious	Quarrelsome.	**coupe**	1. A closed two-door car shorter than a sedan of the same model (sometimes pronounced coo-pay). 2. A frozen dessert (pronounced coop).
contend	To struggle; to dispute.		
content	To satisfy.		
conterminus	Having a common boundary.	**coupé**	(F., two syllables) A ballet step; a closed carriage.
coterminus	Conterminous. (Prefer conterminous.)		
contest	Competition.	**coopt**	See coapt.
Kahn test	A test for syphilis.	**cooperation**	Working in a helpful way with another or others.
continence	Self-restraint.		
continents	The main land masses of the globe.	**corporation**	A group of people authorized to act as an individual, esp. in business.
countenance	Face; aspect; semblance.		
continual	Repeated regularly and frequently; recurring often.	**corroboration**	Supporting evidence. (Also see collaboration.)
continuous	Uninterrupted; unceasing.		
		cops	Police (slang).
contract	See contact.	**copse**	A wood of small trees and undergrowth.
contractor	See contactor.		
controller	See comptroller.	**corpse**	A dead body.
contuse	See confuse.		
contusion	See confusion.	**coq**	See cock.
convalesce	See coalesce.		
		coquette	A flirt.
convalescence	Gradual recovery of health.	**crochet**	Type of needlework (pronounced kro-SHAY).
convalescents	Those who are convalescing.		
		croquet	Lawn game (kro-KAY).
coo	A soft cry, as of a dove.	**croquette**	Small cake of minced food, deep-fried (kro-KET).
coup	A brilliant, sudden, and usually successful stroke.(Pronounced coo.)		
		crotchet	Peculiar trick or device; caprice (KROCH-it).

coracoid	Having the shape of a crow's beak. [Coracoid process of the scapula.]	**corolla**	Ring of petals forming the inner envelope of a flower.
coronoid	Shaped like a crown. [Coronoid process of the ulna, e.g.]	**corona**	A small circle or glow of light around something.
coral	*See choral.*	**corona**	(Defined above.)
cord/cored	*See chord.*	**karuna**	Czech unit of money.
		krona	Unit of money in Sweden (pl. *kronar*) and Iceland (pl. *kronur*).
core	Center.		
CORE	Congress of Racial Equality.	**krone**	Unit of money in Norway and Denmark (pl. *kroner*).
corps	Group of persons associated together (pronounced core).		
corpse	Dead body (a look-alike only).	**coroner**	*See corner.*
		coronoid	*See coracoid.*
corelate	(chiefly Brit.) Correlate.	**corporal**	Rel. to or affecting the body. (*Also see caporal.*)
correlate	To have a mutual or reciprocal relation.	**corporeal**	Physical; not spiritual or intangible.
corelation	(chiefly Brit.) Correlation.	**corporation**	*See cooperation.*
correlation	Mutual relation of two or more things or parts.	**corpus**	*See carpus.*
corespondents	Persons named as guilty of adultery with defendant in a divorce suit.	**corpuscular**	Rel. to corpuscles.
		crepuscular	Of, rel. to, or resembling twilight.
correspondence	Communication by letter, etc.	**corral**	*See choral.*
		correlation	*See corelation.*
correspondents	Those with whom one communicates.	**correlate**	*See corelate.*
		correspondence	*See corespondents.*
		correspondents	*See corespondents.*
cork	*See calk.*	**corrida**	(Sp.) Bullfight.
		corridor	Passageway; route.
corner	Angle or area where two sides (streets) meet.	**corroborate**	*See collaborate.*
coroner	Officer who holds an inquest.	**corroboration**	*See collaboration and cooperation.*
corn flour	Cornstarch.	**cosher**	1. To pamper. 2. To live at another's expense; sponge.
cornflower	Bachelor's button.	**kosher**	Conforming to Jewish dietary laws.

cosign	To sign jointly with another or others.	**coward** **cowered**	One that lacks courage. Shrank or crouched quivering with fear.
cosine	Ratio of angles (in trigonometry).		
		cowl	*See call.*
cosset	*See closet.*	**cozen**	*See cousin.*
costal	*See coastal.*		
		craft	Skill; a trade.
costume	Clothing.	**kraft**	Strong paper or board made from wood pulp.
custom	Usual practice.		
		cramp	*See clamp.*
cot	*See caught.*		
cote	*See coat.*	**crape**	Band of black paper or fabric used as a sign of mourning.
coterie	*See cautery.*		
coterminus	*See conterminus.*	**crepe**	(F.) Fabric with a wrinkled surface. [Crepe Suzette: a small sweet pancake served flambé.]
cougher	*See coffer.*		
coulee	*See collie.*		
council	*See consul.*		
councillor	(also **councilor**) Member of a council.	**crawfish** **crayfish**	Crayfish; spiny lobster. Crustacean resembling a lobster but much smaller.
counselor	(also **counsellor**) Adviser; lawyer.		
		creak	A grating or rasping noise.
counsel	*See consul.*		
countenance	*See continence.*	**creek**	A small stream (pronounced krik in many parts of the country).
counterpoise	Counterbalance.	**crick**	A painful spasmodic condition of muscles in back of neck.
counterpose	To place in opposition, contrast, or equilibrium.		
		cream	The butterfat part of milk.
coupe	*See coop.*		
courier	*See carrier.*	**crème**	(F., pronounced krem) Cream.
course	*See coarse.*		
courser	*See coarser.*		
		credenza	*See cadenza.*
courtesy	Courteous, polite behavior.		
curtesy	A husband's right to a deceased wife's estate.	**credible**	Plausible.
		creditable	Worthy of belief, esteem, or praise.
curtsy	A respectful bow.	**credulous**	Ready to believe, esp. on slight or uncertain evidence.
cousin	A child of one's uncle or aunt.		
cozen	To cheat, deceive, or trick.		
covert	Concealed; done secretly.		
overt	Open to view; manifest.		

creek	See *creak*.	**crews**	Groups of people working together.
cremate	To reduce (as a dead body) to ashes by burning.	**cruise**	A tour, usu. by ship.
		cruse	A small vessel for holding water or oil, etc.
crenate	(or **crenated**) Having the margin or surface cut into rounded scallops.		
		crick	See *creuk*.
		crimp	See *clamp*.
cremation	Burning.		
crenation	A crenate formation.	**cringle**	A loop or grommet at the corner of a sail to which a line is attached. (Note also *Kriss Kringle* : Santa Claus.)
creosol	Colorless liquid used as a disinfectant, etc.		
cresol	An isomeric compound also called methyl phenol.		
		crinkle	A wrinkle; crease.
creosote	Distillate of wood or coal tar, used in drugs, wood preservation, and ore-flotation processes.	**criteria**	Plural of *criterion*. [It's incorrect to say "One criteria is...."]
		criterion	A standard of judgment; rule.
crepe	See *crape*.		
crepuscular	See *corpuscular*.	**critic**	One who expresses judgment, etc. (*Also see clitic*.)
crest	See *caressed*.		
crevasse	A deep open crack, esp. in the ice of a glacier.	**critique**	Act of criticizing; a review.
crevice	A narrow opening or crack, esp. in a rock or wall.	**crochet**	See *coquette*.
		croquet	See *coquette*.
		croquette	See *coquette*.
crew	Group of persons working together.	**crossways**	Crosswise.
		crosswise	Across; transversely.
krewe	Social club in New Orleans sponsoring Mardi Gras balls, etc.		
		crotch	The part of the body or of a garment where the legs fork.
crewed	Served as a member of a crew.	**crutch**	Support for a lame person; any support.
crude	In a natural state, not refined; rough, rude.		
		crotchet	See *coquette*.
crewel	Yarn used for embroidery.	**crows**	Large black birds.
		croze	A tool used in barrelmaking.
cruel	Inhumane; mean.		
		crude	See *crewed*.

crudites	(French cookery) A raw- vegetable appetizer.	**crystalline**	Of or like crystal; transparent.
crudities	Crude actions or words.	**crystallite**	Any of minute crystalline bodies found in igneous rock.
cruel	*See crewel.*		
cruise	*See crews.*	**cube**	A solid body with six equal sides.
cruller	*See color.*	**tube**	A long hollow cylinder.
crumble	To break into small pieces.	**cuddle**	*See caudal.*
crumple	To collapse.	**cue**	*See clew.*
rumple	To wrinkle, tousle, muss up.	**culler**	*See color.*
		cum	*See come.*
crumbly	Apt to crumble; friable.	**curb**	(*kerb* in U.K.) Restraint; an edging of concrete, etc.
crumby	Full of crumbs.		
crummy	(also **crumby**) Dirty and run-down; shabby, seedy.	**curve**	A line of which no part is straight.
crunch	To crush noisily with the teeth; to walk or move with a sound of crushing.	**curd**	The thick casein-rich part of coagulated milk.
		Kurd	Member of a pastoral people of Kurdistan.
scrunch	To crunch, crush, or crumple; to contract or squeeze together.	**curt**	Terse; brusque.
		curios	Items considered novel, rare, or bizarre.
cruse	*See crews.*	**curiosa**	Curiosities; rarities.
		curious	Inquisitive; strange.
crustal	Of or pert. to a crust, as of the earth.	**curl**	*See coil.*
crystal	A quartz that is transparent or nearly so.	**currant**	A small seedless raisin.
		current	A flow, usu. marked by force or strength.
crutch	*See crotch.*	**currier/Currier**	*See carrier.*
cryogenics	The branch of physics dealing with very low temperatures and their effects.	**curser**	One who curses.
		cursor	(Computers) A movable symbol on the CRT.
cryonics	The practice of freezing a dead person in hopes of bringing him back to life later.	**curt**	*See curd.*
		curtsey	*See courtesy.*
		curtsy	*See courtesy.*
		custom	*See costume.*
crystal	*See crustal.*	**curve**	*See curb.*

cut-and-dried	Prepared or settled in advance.	**cynosure**	Center of attraction or attention.
cut-and-try	Marked by a procedure of trial and error.	**sinecure**	Office or position requiring little work.
cyanate	A salt or ester of cyanic acid.	**cyst**	*See cist.*
cyanide	(also **cyanid**) A very poisonous chemical substance.	**cystoscopy**	Examination with a cystoscope.
cyanine	A dye.	**cystostomy**	The formation of an artificial opening in the urinary bladder.
cyanite	A mineral (kyanite).		
cyclohexamide	An antibiotic substance.	**cystotomy**	Incision of the urinary bladder.
cyclohexyl-amine	A bad-smelling liquid used in the manufacture of rubber, etc.	**cytocrome**	A nerve cell with only a small amount of cytoplasm.
		cytosome	A cell body exclusive of the nucleus.
cycloid	Something having a curved or circular form.	**cytostome**	The oral aperture of a unicellar organism.
cytoid	Resembling a cell.		
cygnet	A young swan.	**cytoid**	*See cycloid.*
signet	A person's seal, used with or instead of a signature. [Signet ring.]	**cytology**	A branch of biology dealing with cells.
		psychology	The science of mind and behavior.
cymbal	A plate that produces a clashing musical tone.		
symbol	Token of identity; visible sign.	**Czech**	*See check.*

D

dado	Part of a pedestal or column; a groove or rectangular section for receiving the end of a board.
dido	An antic or prank.
dildo	An object serving as a penis substitute.
daemon	Var. of *demon*.
demon	A devil or evil spirit.
dairy	Milk enterprise.
diary	Daily log.
dale	Valley.
dell	Secluded hollow or small valley.
dam	To check the flow, esp. water.
damn	To condemn strongly; to curse.
damp	To diminish the activity or intensity of.
dancer	One that dances.
danseur	Male ballet dancer. (Fem.: *danseuse*.)
Dane	Citizen of Denmark.
deign	To condescend.
daring	Venturesome boldness.
derring-do	Daring action.
dastard	*See bastard.*
dauphin	Eldest son of a king of France. (His wife: dauphine.)
dolphin	Aquatic mammal.

dawn	Daybreak.
Don	(n., Sp.) Title of respect affixed to Christian name.
don	(v.) To put on, as clothes.
days	Plural of *day*.
daze	Stupefaction.
deaccelerate	To decelerate.
decelerate	To decrease the velocity.
deamidase	An enzyme that releases the amido group from a compound.
deaminase	An enzyme that releases the amino group from a compound.
deaminate	To remove the amino group from a compound.
dear	Beloved; expensive.
deer	Ruminant animal.
dearth	Scarcity.
dirt	Soil, etc.
deasil	Clockwise.
diesel	Type of engine.
debar	To bar from having or doing something; preclude.
disbar	To expel from the legal profession.
debauch	To seduce; to debase.
debouch	To march out (as from a defile) into open ground.
debility	Feebleness, weakness.
disability	Something that disables or disqualifies a person.

debride	To remove surgically lacerated, devitalized or contaminated tissue. (Second syllable pronounced breed.)
debris	Remains of something broken down or destroyed.
debouch	*See debauch.*
decadence	Deteriorating standards.
decadents	Those who become decadent.
decal	(shortened form of *decalcomania*) A picture transferred from paper to china, etc.
deckle	A frame around the edges of a mold used in making paper by hand. [Deckle edge.]
decane	A hydrocarbon of the methane series.
decay	Rot; deterioration.
decease	Death.
disease	Sickness; malady.
disseise	(also **disseize**) To dispossess.
deceased	Dead.
diseased	Unhealthy.
decedent	A deceased person.
descendant	A person or animal descended from a specific ancestor.
descendent	Descending; going or coming down.
dissident	One who differs or disagrees.
decelerate	*See deaccelerate.*

decent	Respectable; fit; modest.
descent	Act of coming down.
dissent	Disagreement.
decidedly	Without doubt.
decisively	Conclusively.
decimate	To destroy a great number or proportion of; (or, its original meaning) to select by lot and kill every tenth person of.
desiccate	To dry thoroughly; dehydrate. (*Also see exsiccate.*)
desquamate	To come off in scales
decision	Judgment.
discission	State of being torn apart; type of eye surgery.
decisively	*See decidedly.*
deckle	*See decal.*
decompose	To decay.
discompose	To disturb the composure of.
decry	To disparage.
descry	To catch sight of.
deduce	To draw a conclusion.
educe	To bring out or develop; to elicit. (*Also see adduce.*)
deduction	Conclusion reached by reasoning.
eduction	Something inferred or elicited.
induction	Formal installation, etc.
deductive	Of, rel. to, or provable by deduction.
inductive	Rel. to or employing mathematical or logical induction. [Inductive reasoning.]

deer	*See dear.*
defalcation	An act of embezzlement.
defecation	Emptying of the bowels.
defection	Abandonment of allegiance or duty.
defect	To desert one's country or abandon one's allegiance.
deflect	To turn or cause to turn aside.
defective	Flawed.
detective	One whose job is to investigate crimes.
defector	One who defects from a country, cause, etc.
detector	A person or thing (a smoke alarm, e.g.) that detects.
defer	To put off to a later time; to give way or yield.
differ	To disagree.
deference	Respect, esteem; yielding.
difference	Quality or state of being unlike.
diffidence	Shyness; hesitancy through lack of self-confidence.
deferential	Showing deference or esteem.
differential	Difference between comparable individuals or classes. (Etc.)
defervescence	The subsidence of a fever.
effervescence	Bubbles; high spirits.

defi	(F., pronounced day-fee) Challenge, defiance.
defy	To resist openly, refuse to obey.
definite	Clear, explicit.
definitive	Decisive, complete, final.
deflect	*See defect.*
deflection	Turning aside.
defluxion	Copious discharge of fluid matter, as in catarrh.
defuse	To remove the fuses of; to make less harmful or tense.
diffuse	Spread or scatter widely or thinly.
defusion	*See affusion.*
defy	*See defi.*
degas	To remove gas from.
degauss	To demagnetize.
deign	*See Dane.*
dejecta	Discarded bodily waste; excretion.
ejecta	Material cast out from the body or a volcano, e.g.; dejecta.
dell	*See dale.*
delimitate	To delimit (fix or mark limits).
delineate	To sketch or trace in outline.

delusion	A false belief or opinion. (*Also see allusion, illusion.*)	**depose**	To remove from a throne or other high position; to testify under oath.
disillusion	Disenchantment.		
dissolution	Act or process of dissolving (as a marriage).	**dispose**	To give a tendency to; to do away with.
demean	To degrade or debase.	**deposit**	To place, esp. for safekeeping.
demesne	Legal possession of land.	**posit**	To present or assume as fact.
domain	District or area under one's control.	**depositary**	A person to whom something is entrusted.
demon	*See daemon.*	**depository**	A place where something is deposited.
demonaic	Possessed or influenced by a demon.	**depravation**	Depravity.
demonic	Inspired as if by a demon.	**deprivation**	Loss.
demotic	Rel. to a simplified form of ancient Egyptian hieratic writing; popular, common.	**deprecate**	To belittle.
		depreciate	To lower in value.
		deprecatory	Apologetic; disapproving.
demur	To object.	**depreciatory**	Disparaging.
demure	Reserved; modest.		
demurrer	A pleading at law.	**deprivation**	*See depravation.*
dens	Plural of *den* (lair of wild animals).	**deputation**	The act of appointing a person or persons to represent or act for another.
dens	A tooth.		
dense	Thick; stupid.	**disputation**	The act of disputing or debating.
dents	Depressions or nicks.		
dent	Depression or nick.	**derange**	To disturb the operation or functions of.
dint	Force; power. [By dint of.]		
		disarrange	To disturb the arrangement or order of.
dependence	State of being influenced or supported by another.		
		deranged	Disturbed, esp. mentally.
dependents	Persons relying on another for support.	**disarranged**	Disturbed the arrangement of.
deploy	To spread out, to bring or come into action systematically.	**derring-do**	*See daring.*
		descendant	*See decedent.*
employ	To give work to; to use.		

descendent	See *decedent*.		**detent**	A mechanism that temporarily keeps one part in a certain position relative to another.
descry	See *decry*.			
descension	(Astrol.) The part of the zodiac in which the influence of a planet is the weakest.		**deténte**	(F.) A relaxing of tension, esp. between nations.
dissention	Disagreement that gives rise to strife.			
			determinant	A decisive factor.
descent	See *decent*.		**determinate**	Limited; of fixed and definite scope or nature.
deserts	(n., first syl. accented) Areas with insufficient natural water. (v., second syl. accented) Leaves, usu. without intent to return.		**deterrence**	The act of deterring.
			deterrents	Things that deter (e.g., nuclear weapons possessed by more than one country).
deserts	(n., second syl. accented) Deserved reward or punishment. [Just deserts.]		**detract**	To take away from or lower the value.
desserts	(n., second syl. accented) Last course of a meal or meals.		**distract**	To divert.
			detraction	Lessening of reputation or esteem; belittling.
deserve	To be entitled to.		**distraction**	Something that distracts attention; entertainment; mental upset or distress.
disserve	To serve badly.			
desiccate	See *decimate*.		**detrition**	See *attrition*.
desquamate	See *decimate*.			
			deuce	Playing card; tie in tennis; the devil.
desperate	Having lost hope.		**duce**	(It., pronounced doo-chay) Leader. [Mussolini: Il Duce.]
disparate	Markedly different.			
despite	In spite of.		**deviance**	Deviant quality or behavior.
respite	A delay or cessation for a time, esp. of something distressing or trying; reprieve (pronounced res- pit).		**deviants**	Those deviating from an accepted norm.
			device	Scheme, contrivance.
desserts	See *deserts*.		**devise**	To form in mind; invent. (Law:) To give real property by will; bequeath.
detective	See *defective*.			
detector	See *defector*.			

deviser	One who plans, contrives, etc.
devisor	One who bequeaths property in a will; testator.
divisor	A number by which another is to be divided.
devote	To give or use for a particular activity or purpose.
devotee	A person who is devoted to something; an enthusiast.
dew	Moisture, esp. in droplets.
do	To act.
due	Owing.
dexterous	(also **dextrous**) Adroit; clever; skillful.
dextrose	A form of glucose.
dextran	A viscous polysaccharide.
dextrin	(also **dextrine**) A gummy substance used as a thickening agent.
diabetic	Affected with diabetes.
diatetic	Of diet and nutrition.
diathetic	Having a predisposition toward a certain disease.
diuretic	Tending to increase the flow of urine.
diagram	A graphic drawing.
diaphragm	A wide muscle separating the abdominal and chest cavities of the body; a dividing membrane or thin partition.
diagrammatic	Shown by a diagram.
diaphragmatic	Rel. to the diaphragm.

diamide	A compound containing two amide groups.
diamine	A compound containing two amino groups.
diaphragm	See *diagram*.
diaphragmatic	See *diagrammatic*.
diary	See *dairy*.
diaschisis	A disturbance or loss of function in one part of the brain due to localized injury in another part.
diastasis	Separation of normally joined parts without fracture.
diathesis	Predisposition or tendency to a certain disease.
diatetic	See *diabetic*.
diathetic	See *diabetic*.
diatomic	Consisting of two atoms.
diatonic	(Music) Using the notes of the major or minor scale only.
dido	See *dado*.
die	(n.) An engraved device that stamps a design on metals [tool and die]; a marked cube used in games of chance (pl. *dice*).
dye	Coloring matter.
diesel	See *deasil*.
differ	See *defer*.
difference	See *deference*.
differential	See *deferential*.
diffidence	See *deference*.

diffraction	The separation of light into component parts.	**dioptic**	Pertaining to transmitted and refracted light.
refraction	The bending of a ray of light or heat or sound.	**diotic**	Pert. to both ears.
diffuse	*See defuse.*	**diplomat**	One employed or skilled in diplomacy.
diffusion	*See affusion.*	**diplomate**	One who holds a diploma, esp. a physician.
digitalin	A glucoside obtained from digitalis.		
digitalis	A plant (esp. the foxglove).	**dipstick**	A graduated rod for indicating depth.
dignify	To give dignity or importance to.	**lipstick**	Cosmetic for coloring the lips.
lignify	To change into wood or woodlike material.	**diptych**	Pair of pictures on two panels.
dilatation	Amplification, expansion, dilation. [Dilatation and curretage; i.e., D and C.]	**triptych**	Set of three panels bearing pictures, etc.
dilation	Making wider or larger (esp. neck of the womb).	**dire**	Dreadful, terrible, ominous.
		dyer	One that dyes.
dilution	A thinning down or weakening.	**dirt**	*See dearth.*
dilate	To make wider or larger.	**disability**	*See debility.*
dilute	To thin down or weaken.	**disapprove**	To have or express an unfavorable opinion.
		disprove	To refute.
dildo	*See dado.*	**disarrange**	*See derange.*
dine	To eat.	**disarranged**	*See deranged.*
dyne	A unit of force.	**disassemble**	To take apart.
dinar	Gold coin formerly used in Muslim countries.	**dissemble**	To assume a false appearance.
diner	One who dines; dining car; small restaurant.	**disassociate**	Dissociate.
dinner	A meal.	**dissociate**	To separate from association with.
dinghy	A small boat.	**disbar**	*See debar.*
dingy	Dirty; discolored.	**disburse**	To pay out.
dint	*See dent.*	**disperse**	To break up; to spread.

disc	A phonograph record; a coated plate for storing computer data; the working part of a disc harrow or plow.
disk	A thin circular object; any of various rounded or flattened anatomical structures (e.g., vertebral disk). [Note: *Disk* and *disc* are used somewhat interchangeably.]
discission	*See decision.*
discomfit	To frustrate, thwart, embarrass.
discomfort	State of being uncomfortable or uneasy.
discompose	*See decompose.*
discreet	Prudent; using good judgment.
discrete	Individually distinct; noncontinuous.
discus	A disk.
viscous	Sticky, adhesive.
viscus	Any internal organ, such as the stomach or intestines.
discussed	Talked about.
disgust	Repugnance.
disease	*See decease.*
diseased	*See deceased.*
disillusion	*See delusion.*
disinterested	Unbiased, impartial
uninterested	Not interested.
disk	*See disc.*
disparate	*See desperate.*
disperse	*See disburse.*

displace	To shift from its place; to take the place of.
displays	Shows; arranges.
disposal	Disposing of something.
Disposall	Trade-name of garbage disposal.
dispose	*See depose.*
disprove	*See disapprove.*
disputation	*See deputation.*
disseise	*See decease.*
dissemble	*See disassemble.*
disseminate	To scatter or spread widely.
dissimilate	To make dissimilar.
dissimulate	To dissemble (assume a false appearance).
dissent	*See decent.*
dissention	*See descension.*
disserve	*See deserve.*
dissidence	Dissent, disagreement.
dissidents	Those who differ or disagree. *(Also see decedent.)*
dissonance	Inharmonious or harsh sound; discord.
dissimilate	*See disseminate.*
dissimulate	*See disseminate.*
dissociate	*See disassociate.*
dissolution	*See delusion.*
distant	Separated in space; away.
distend	Swell; expand.
distract	*See detract.*
distraction	*See detraction.*
distrait	Absentminded; inattentive because of anxiety or apprehension.
distraught	Greatly upset.

disulfate	(also **disulphate**) A salt of pyrosulfuric acid.	**dogbane**	A plant.
disulfide	(also **disulphide**) A sulfide containing two atoms of sulfur.	**dogvane**	A small vane showing wind direction.
		doggy	Small dog.
diuretic	*See diabetic.*	**dogie**	A motherless calf.
diva	(pl. *divas* or *dive*) Prima donna.	**doily**	A small often decorative mat.
diver	One that dives.	**dolly**	A movable platform for a heavy object. (Etc.)
divers	Various.	**dolerite**	A coarse-grained variety of basalt.
diverse	Differing from one another.	**dolomite**	Calcium magnesium carbonite.
divisor	*See deviser.*	**dolphin**	*See dauphin.*
		domain	*See demean.*
djinni	(or **djinn** or **djin**) Var. of *jinni*.	**dominance**	Dominating position or influence.
jinni	(or **jinn**) A supernatural spirit that often takes human form.	**dominants**	Dominant genetic factors, organisms, etc.
do	*See dew.*	**don**	*See dawn.*
doc	Short for *doctor*.	**done**	Finished.
dock	Place for unloading freight cars, etc.	**dun**	(n.) Demand for payment. (adj.) Drab color.
docile	Easily led or managed.	**dossal**	*See docile.*
dossal	Ornamental cloth above an altar.	**dotty**	Mentally unbalanced.
		doughty	Valiant or stouthearted.
doe	Female deer.	**dowdy**	Not stylish.
dough	Flour mixture; money.	**dough**	*See doe.*
doer	One that takes an active part.	**doughy**	Of the consistency of dough.
dour	Stern; harsh; unyielding; sullen. (Preferably rhymes with *tour*, not *sour*.)	**doughty**	(Defined above.)
dower	A widow's share of her husband's estate.	**dour**	*See doer.*
does	(plural) Female deer.		
doze	Sleep.		

douse	To put into water; to extinguish.	**dram**	One-eighth of an ounce apothecaries' weight.
dowse	To search for underground water or minerals by use of a divining rod.	**gram**	One-thousandth part of a kilogram.
drowse	To be half asleep.	**dramatic**	Striking in looks or effect.
douser	One who douses.	**traumatic**	Pert. to physical or emotional injury.
dowser	Divining rod or person who uses it.	**draught**	*See draft.*
dowdy	*See dotty.*	**draw**	The act or process of drawing.
dowel	A pin fitting into a hole in an abutting piece to prevent motion or slipping.	**drawer**	A sliding box or receptacle. [Note: Many people, particularly in New England, say "dresser draw" and "desk draw."]
rowel	Small wheel at tip of a spur.		
towel	A piece of absorbent cloth or paper for drying.	**droop**	To bend or hang downward through tiredness or weakness.
dower	*See doer.*	**drop**	To fall by force; to allow to fall.
doyen	Senior member (in age, rank, etc.)	**drupe**	Fruit with juicy flesh around a stone with a kernel, as a peach.
doyenne	Fem. equivalent of doyen.		
doze	*See does.*	**drought**	*See draft.*
		drowse	*See douse.*
draft	The act of moving or pulling; a preliminary sketch; current of air. (Etc.)	**drowser**	*See douser.*
		dual	Twofold.
		duel	Combat between two persons.
draught	Something drawn—British var. of *draft* (and so pronounced).	**duce**	*See deuce.*
drought	Prolonged period of dryness.	**ducked**	Lowered (as the head); evaded.
		duct	Tube or pipe.
dragon	Mythical animal.	**ductal**	Of or pert. to a duct.
dragoon	(n.) A cavalryman. (v.) To coerce.	**ductile**	Capable of being drawn out or hammered thin.
		ductule	A small duct.

due	See dew.	**dutiable**	On which customs or other duties must be paid.
duly	In a correct or suitable way.	**dutiful**	Doing one's duty.
dully	Boringly; dimly.	**dye**	See die.
dunnage	Baggage or personal effects; packing material around cargo.	**dyeing**	Coloring.
tonnage	Capacity in tons.	**dying**	Expiring.
dun	See done.	**dyer**	See dire.
		dyne	See dine.
duplicative	Duplicating.	**dyscrasia**	An abnormal state of the body.
duplicitous	Marked by duplicity, i.e. deceit, double-dealing. (Sometimes misused to mean double or two-fold.)	**dysphagia**	Difficulty in swallowing.
		dysphasia	Difficulty in speaking or understanding language.
dusky	Somewhat dark; shadowy.	**dysplasia**	Abnormal development or growth.
dusty	Covered with dust.	**dyspraxia**	Inability to perform coordinated movements.

E

earn	To receive in return for effort.
erne	White-tailed sea eagle.
urn	Ornamental vase; a closed vessel usu. with a spigot for serving hot beverages.
earnest	Serious; grave.
Ernest	Masculine name.
earthly	Belonging to or characteristic of the earth.
earthy	Resembling or suggesting earth; crude. [Earthy humor.]
eau	(F.) Water. [Eau de cologne.]
O	Variant of *oh*. [O tempore! O mores!]
oh	Exclamation of surprise, etc.
owe	To be obligated.
eave	(usu. **eaves**) Overhanging lower edge of a roof.
eve	Evening (poetic).
Eve	First lady.
eccentric	*See acentric.*
ecdemic	Applied to diseases brought into a region from without.
endemic	Native; restricted to a locality.
epidemic	Widespread contagion.
pandemic	(of a disease) Occurring over a whole country or the whole world.

eclectic	Choosing or accepting from various sources.
ecliptic	The sun's path among stars.
electric	Of or producing electricity.
elliptic	Pert. to or having the form of an ellipse (defined below).
eclipse	The blocking of light from one heavenly body by another.
ellipse	A regular oval that can be divided into four identical quarters.
ellipsis	(pl. *ellipses*) Omission of words.
economic	Rel. to economics or the economy; profitable.
economical	Thrifty.
economics	A social science concerned with analysis of production, distribution, and consumption of goods and services.
ecru	*See accrue.*
ecstatic	*See astatic.*
ectogenous	Capable of growth outside the body of its host.
endogenous	Produced within; due to internal causes.
exogenous	Due to an external cause; not arising within the organism.
ectopic	In an abnormal position or place. (*Also see entoptic and entotic.*)
entopic	Occurring in the usual place.
edict	*See addict.*

edifice	A large building.	**el**	An elevated railroad in a city.
Oedipus	(Gk. legend) A king who unwittingly killed his father and married his mother. [Oedipus complex.]	**ell**	A wing of a building at right angles to the main part.

edit	*See adit.*	**elastic**	Resilient; flexible.
edition	*See addition.*	**elastin**	A protein similar to collagen.
educe	*See adduce and deduce.*		
eduction	*See deduction.*	**elective**	Optional.
e'er	*See air.*	**selective**	Selecting or tending to select.
eerie	*See aerie.*		
effect	*See affect.*		
effected	*See affected.*	**electric**	*See eclectic.*
effective	*See affective.*		
efferent	*See afferent.*	**elegy**	Sorrowful or serious poem.
effervescence	*See defervescence.*	**eulogy**	Speech or piece of writing in praise of a person or thing.
effluence	*See affluence.*		
effluent	*See affluent.*		
effluents	*See affluence.*		
effluvium	*See alluvion.*	**element**	*See ailment.*
efflux	*See afflux.*	**elementary**	*See alimentary.*
effusion	*See affusion.*	**elevate**	*See alleviate.*

egg	Ovum.	**elicit**	To draw forth or bring out.
yegg	A safecracker; thug.	**illicit**	Unlawful.
		licit	Lawful.

egoist	A self-centered person.	**eligible**	Qualified to be chosen.
egotist	A selfish person; egoist.	**illegible**	Indecipherable.
		legible	Capable of being read.

egression	*See aggression.*	**eliminate**	To get rid of something.
egret	*See aigrette.*	**illuminate**	To light up; to shed light on something.
eight	*See ait.*		

either	Which of two.	**elision**	Omission of an unstressed vowel, etc. *(Also see allusion, illusion, etc.)*
ether	The clear sky; liquid used as an anesthetic and as a solvent.		
		Elysian	Of or relating to Elysium. [Elysian field.]
ejaculate	To eject (as semen); to utter suddenly and vehemently.	**Elysium**	(Gk. mythology) The abode of the blessed dead.
jaculate	To throw or hurl (dart, javelin, etc.)		

ejecta	*See dejecta.*	**ell**	*See el.*

ellipse	*See eclipse.*	emigrate	To leave for residence elsewhere.
ellipsis	*See eclipse.*	immigrate	To enter a country for permanent residence.
elliptic	*See eclectic.*		
elocution	*See allocution.*		
		eminent	*See emanant.*
elude	To avoid or escape. (*Also see allude/delude.*)		
		emit	To throw out or give off.
elute	(Chem.) To remove by dissolving.	omit	To leave out.
elusion	*See allusion.*	emission	An act of emitting; emanation.
elusive	*See allusive.*		
elution	*See allusion.*	omission	An act of omitting.
eluvial	*See alluvial.*	remission	State or period of relief.
eluvium	*See alluvion.*		
Elysian	*See elision.*	empathize	To experience empathy.
Elysium	*See elision.*	emphasize	To place emphasis on.
em	The width of a piece of type about as wide as it is tall.	empathy	The ability to identify oneself mentally with a person or thing.
en	Half an em.	sympathy	A feeling of pity or tenderness for another's grief or troubles.
emanant	Issuing from or as if from a source.		
eminent	Prominent; famous.	emphysema	A lung disease.
immanent	Inherent.	empyema	The presence of pus in a body cavity.
imminent	Ready to take place; threatening.		
		employ	*See deploy.*
emend	*See amend.*		
		empress	Female ruler; wife or widow of an emperor.
emerged	Came into view.		
emersed	(Bot.) Risen or standing out of water, leaves, etc.	impress	To apply with pressure so as to imprint; to influence.
immersed	Plunged into something; engrossed, absorbed.		
		empyema	*See emphysema.*
emersion	The emergence of a heavenly body from an eclipse.	emulate	To strive to equal; to imitate.
		immolate	To offer in sacrifice.
immersion	State of being immersed.		
		emulation	Ambition to equal or excel.
emigrant	One who leaves one's country.	immolation	Act or state of immolating.
immigrant	One who comes to a country to take up residence.		

en	*See em.*	entoptic	Pert. to the internal eye.
endemic	*See ecdemic.*	entotic	Pert. to the internal ear. *(Also see ectopic and ectotic.)*
endocrine	Secreting internally.		
exocrine	Rel. to a secretion released outside its source.	entrance	Means or place of entry; entering.
		entrants	Those who enter, esp. in competition.
endogenous	Growing or originating from within. *(Also see ectogenous.)*		
		entree	(F.) Main dish of a meal; entrance (pronounced ahn-tray).
indigenous	Native.	entry	Act, right, or privilege of entering.
endure	To suffer, bear; to last.		
inure	To accustom, esp. to something unpleasant. *(Also see immure.)*	entrepreneur	One who organizes, manages, and assumes the risk of a business enterprise.
enervate	To lessen vitality or strength of.	intrapreneur	An employee of a large corporation given freedom and financial support to create new products, etc.
innervate	To supply with nerves.		
innovate	To introduce a new process or way of doing things.		
		enumerable	Countable.
en gros	(F.) In gross.	innumerable	Countless.
engross	To occupy the whole of; to prepare the text of an official document.	enunciate	*See annunciate.*
		enunciation	*See annunciation.*
in gross	A large quantity or shipment.	enuresis	*See anuresis.*
		envelop	To enclose or enfold.
ensiform	*See ansiform.*	envelope	A flat usu. paper container, as for a letter.
ensure	To make certain; to insure. [Note: some publications, or at least the *New Yorker* and *New York Times*, always use *insure*, never *ensure*.]	epic	A long narrative poem.
		epoch	A point or period of time. [Note: The British pronounce this word with a long *e*, so there would be no soundalike!]
insure	To give, take, or procure insurance on; to take necessary measures.		
enthralled	Held spellbound.	epical	*See apical.*
in thrall	In bondage.	epidemic	*See ecdemic.*
entomology	Science rel. to insects.		
etymology	History of words.		

epigram	Witty saying.
epigraph	A quotation suggesting a theme.
epilogue	*See apologue.*
epitaph	Inscription on a tomb.
epithet	Descriptive term, usu. abusive.
epoch	*See epic.*
epochal	*See apical.*
equable	Uniform; even, unvarying, even-tempered.
equitable	Fair and just.
equivalence	Equality.
equivalents	Things that are equivalent.
[equivocably]	No such word!
equivocally	Tending to mislead or confuse.
erasable	Capable of being erased.
irascible	Hot-tempered.
er	*See air.*
ere	*See air.*
ergot	*See argot.*
Erie	*See aerie.*
Erin	*See Aaron.*
erne	*See earn.*
Ernest	*See earnest.*
erotic	Of sexual love; arousing sexual desire. *(Also see erratic.)*
esoteric	Intended for people with special knowledge or interests.
exotic	Introduced from abroad, not native; unusual.
err	*See air.*
errand	*See arrant.*
errant	*See arrant.*
erratic	Irregular and uneven in motion, habits, etc.
erotic	Of sexual love or desire.
erred	*See aired.*
estray	*See astray.*
erupt	To burst forth.
irrupt	To rush in forcibly. [Note: The words have very similar meaning, but *irrupt* conveys more force and violence.]
eruption	Act or process of erupting; to break out (in a rash, etc.)
irruption	A forcible or violent rushing in; intrusion.
eruptive	Erupting or tending to erupt.
irruptive	Irrupting or tending to irrupt.
escalade	To mount, pass, or enter by means of ladders.
escalate	To increase or cause to increase in intensity or extent.
eschatological	Pert. to eschatology (defined below).
scatological	Obscene. (See below.)
eschatology	Branch of theology concerned with death, afterlife, etc.
scatology	Obscenity, esp. words or humor relating to excrement.
eschew	*See chew.*
ESOP	*See Aesop.*
esoteric	*See erotic.*

especial	Special, outstanding; belonging chiefly to one person or thing.	**ethanal**	Acetaldehyde.
		ethanol	Alcohol.
special	Of a particular kind, not general; exceptional in amount, quality, or intensity.	**ethynyl**	A univalent chemical radical.

especial	Special, outstanding; belonging chiefly to one person or thing.
special	Of a particular kind, not general; exceptional in amount, quality, or intensity.
especially	Specifically; particularly.
specially	Uniquely; distinguishably. *(Also see specialty.)*
Esquire	An unofficial title of respect, sometimes placed, esp. in abbreviated form, after a name: in the U.S., usu. applied to lawyers, women as well as men.
squire	A country gentleman in England; a woman's escort.
essay	*See assay.*
ester	*See aster.*
Esther	*See aster.*
estimate	Evaluation, calculation.
guesstimate	An estimate made without adequate information.
estrange	To alienate.
strange	Odd; peculiar.
estrous	Being in heat. *(Also see anestrous.)*
estrus	(Zool.) The period of heat or rut.
etch	To engrave with acid.
itch	To have an itchy sensation or a restless desire.

ethanal	Acetaldehyde.
ethanol	Alcohol.
ethynyl	A univalent chemical radical.
ether	*See either.*
ethics	Moral principles or values.
ethnics	Members of a minority group.
ethnology	A branch of anthropology that analyzes cultures.
ethology	The study of animal behavior.
ethyl	A univalent hydrocarbon radical; an antiknock fluid.
methyl	A chemical unit present in methane, etc.
methylal	A volatile liquid used as a solvent, in perfumery, etc.
etiology	Cause or origin (esp. of a disease).
ideology	A systematic body of concepts, esp. about human life or culture.
etymology	*See entomology.*
eulogy	*See elegy.*
eurythmic	*See arrhythmic.*
evade	*See avoid.*
evaluation	Act or process of valuing.
valuation	Estimation of a thing's value; appraisal.
evaporate	To turn or be turned into vapor.
evaporite	Sedimentary rock formed by evaporation of seawater.
eve/Eve	*See eave.*

eversion	*See aversion.*
evert	*See advert.*
everyday	(adj.) Ordinary; routine.
every day	Each day. [We wear our everyday clothes every day but Sunday.]
evocation	A calling forth.
invocation	Calling upon God in prayer.
revocation	Act of revoking.
evoke	To call forth.
invoke	To call for help or protection.
revoke	To withdraw or cancel.
evulsion	*See avulsion.*
ewe	Female sheep.
yew	Evergreen tree or shrub.
you	Personal pronoun.
ewer	Vase-shaped pitcher or jug.
your	Personal pronoun.
you're	Contraction of *you are.*
ewes	Plural of *ewe.*
use	To utilize.
yews	Plural of *yew.*
exacerbate	To worsen.
exaggerate	To make a thing seem larger, better, smaller, or worse than it really is.
exasperate	To annoy greatly.(*Also see aspirate.*)
exalt	To raise high; to glorify.
exult	To rejoice.
exaltation	Elation; spiritual delight.
exultation	Rejoicing.
exasperate	*See exacerbate.*

exceed	*See accede.*
except	*See accept.*
exceptionable	Objectionable.
exceptional	Rare; better than average.
excess	*See access.*
exchequer	*See checker.*
exclaim	*See acclaim.*
exclamation	*See acclamation.*
exclusion	Shutting out.
extrusion	Forcing, pressing, or pushing out.
excursion	A short journey.
incursion	A raid or brief invasion into someone else's territory.
excuse	*See accuse.*
exercise	To use; to exert oneself physically or mentally.
exorcise	To expel, as an evil spirit.
exhausted	Used up completely; tired out.
exhausting	Using up; tiring.
exhaustive	Thorough, trying all possibilities.
exhilarate	*See accelerate.*
exhort	To urge, advise, or caution earnestly.
extort	To obtain by force or threats.
ex mora	(L.) From or in consequence of delay.
ex more	(L.) According to custom.
exocrine	*See endocrine.*
exogenous	*See ectogenous.*
exorcise	*See exercise.*

exotic	*See erotic.*	**expiration**	Breathing out (air); the end of life, etc.
expand	To increase; to enlarge.	**extirpation**	Complete removal of a part; eradication.
expend	To spend; to consume.	**extrication**	Removal; disentanglement.
expound	To set forth or explain; to defend. [Note: Lawyers often use *expand upon* and *expound upon* somewhat interchangeably.]	**explanation**	Statement explaining something.
		explication	Detailed explanation.
expandable	Capable of being expanded.	**explicit**	Free from ambiguity.
expansible	Capable of being expanded. (The *Random House Dictionary* gives as an illustration, "Most metals are expansible.")	**implicit**	Implied.
		explode	To burst (out) violently.
		implode	To burst inward.
		expound	*See expand.*
		expropriate	*See appropriate.*
expansive	Able or tending to expand; (of a person) genial, outgoing.	**exsiccate**	To dry or remove moisture from. (*Also see decimate.*)
expensive	Costly.	**extricate**	To release or free from entanglement.
expatiate	To enlarge in discourse or writing.	**extant**	In existence.
expatriate	To banish; to withdraw (oneself) from one's native country and live abroad.	**extent**	Range; limit.
		extemporary	Unrehearsed; offhand.
		extempore	On the spur of the moment.
expedience	Expediency.	**extenuate**	*See attenuate.*
expediency	Suitability; fitness.		
expedients	Temporary means to an end.	**extern**	A nonresident doctor or medical student.
expend	*See expand.*	**intern**	(also **interne**) An advanced student or graduate gaining supervised practical experience.
expensive	*See expansive.*		
expertise	Expert knowledge or skill.		
expertize	To give a professional opinion on, usu. after careful study.	**extirpate**	To root out and destroy completely.
		extricate	To dissentangle or release from entanglement. (*Also see exsiccate.*)

extirpation	*See expiration.*
extort	*See exhort.*
extrados	The exterior curve of an arch.
intrados	The interior curve of an arch.
extramural	Existing or functioning outside (beyond the walls).
intramural	Within the limits (walls) of an association, etc.
extraordinaire	(F.) Markedly exceptional; extraordinary. [Reporter extraordinaire.]
extraordinary	Going beyond what is usual, regular, or customary.
extricate	*See exsiccate and extirpate.*
extrication	*See expiration.*
extrinsic	Originating from outside; external.
intrinsic	Belonging to the basic nature of a person or thing.
extrude	To force, press, or push out.
exude	To ooze out.
extrusion	*See exclusion.*
exult	*See exalt.*
exultation	*See exaltation.*
eye	*See ay.*
eyed	Looked at.
I'd	Contr. of *I would* or *I had.*
eyelet	A small hole; grommet.
islet	Island (poetic).

F

facet	A small plane surface; phase.
faucet	A device for controlling flow of liquid from a pipe.
facetious	Jocular.
factious	Promoting dissension.
factitious	Artificial.
fictitious	Imaginary; false.
fractious	Irritable, peevish; unruly.
facial	Pert. to the face.
fascial	Pert. to fascia: a type of connective tissue; a distinct band of color. (Etc.)
facility	Quality of being easy; an aid, equipment, structure, etc., that makes it easy to do something.
faculty	Any of the powers of body or mind; a school's teaching/ administrative staff.
facilitate	To make easier.
felicitate	To make happy.
faction	A small united group within a larger one, esp. in politics.
fiction	Stories, books; figment of the imagination.
fraction	A small part.
friction	The rubbing of one body against another; disagreement.
factious	*See facetious.*

factitious	*See facetious.*
facts	Things known with certainty.
fax	Facsimile.
faculty	*See facility.*
faddish	Inclined to take up fads.
fattish	Somewhat plump.
fetish	An object believed to have magical power.
faerie	(also **faery**) Fairyland.
fairy	Elf; imaginary being.
ferry	A type of boat.
faggot	(slang, offensive) A male homosexual.
fagot	A bundle of sticks or twigs.
faille	Shiny dressgoods.
file	A device for keeping papers in order; a steel tool used for cutting or smoothing, esp. metal.
phial	Vial.
phyle	The largest political subdivision of an ancient Greek city-state.
fain	Gladly; willingly. [I would fain....]
fane	Temple; church.
feign	To pretend.
faint	To lose consciousness.
feint	To make a deceptive movement.
fair	An exhibition for sale of goods.
fare	Price charged for transportation.
fairy	*See faerie.*

faker	One that fakes.	**fate**	Destiny.
fakir	A Hindu ascetic.	**fete**	Festival. (Note also *fait accompli,* F., an accomplished fact.)
fallow	(of land) Plowed but left unplanted in order to restore its fertility.		
fellow	Comrade; associate; man.	**fated**	Destined.
		feted	Honored or commemorated with a fete.
false	Untrue.	**fetid**	Having an offensive smell.
faults	Weaknesses.		
familial	Pert. to a family.	**fattish**	*See faddish.*
familiar	Well known; often seen or experienced.	**faucet**	*See facet.*
		faults	*See false.*
fane	*See fain.*	**faun**	Figure from Roman mythology.
far away	A long way off.	**fawn**	(n.) A young deer. (v.) To court favor by a cringing or flattering manner.
faraway	(adj.) Remote; dreamy, abstracted.		
fare	*See fair.*	**fay**	A fairy; elf.
faro	A gambling game.	**fey**	Crazed; touched.
farrow	(n.) A litter of pigs. (v.) To give birth to a litter of pigs.	**fax**	*See facts.*
Pharaoh	A ruler of ancient Egypt.	**fays**	Fairies.
		faze	To disconcert.
farther	At or to a greater distance or more advanced point.	**phase**	To adjust so as to synchronize.
further	In addition, moreover. [These words are often used interchangeably, but purists prefer the distinction: Let me further say that it lay five feet farther down.]	**feat**	Notable act or achievement.
		feet	Plural of *foot.*
		febrile	*See afebrile.*
fascial	*See facial.*	**fecal**	Of or rel. to feces.
		fetal	Rel. to a fetus. (*Also see fatal.*)
fatal	Causing death.		
fetal	Relating to a fetus.	**feet**	*See feat.*
		feign	*See fain.*
		feint	*See faint.*
		felicitate	*See facilitate.*
		fellow	*See fallow.*

74

ferment	To undergo fermentation.	**fibula**	Bone on the outer side of lower part of the leg.
foment	To incite.	**tibia**	The shinbone.
		[tibula]	No such word!
ferrate	A salt compound containing iron and oxygen.	**fiche**	Microfiche, a piece of microfilm that can be filed like an index card.
ferrite	A compound formed when ferric oxide is combined with a more basic metallic oxide.	**fish**	Cold-blooded animal living in water.
serrate	Notched on the edge like a saw.	**fiction**	*See faction.*
		fictitious	*See facetious.*
ferrule	Metal ring or cap.	**figment**	Something made up or contrived. [Figment of the imagination.]
ferule	A rod for punishing children.		
		pigment	Coloring matter.
ferry	*See faerie.*		
		file	*See faille.*
fervent	Glowing; impassioned.		
fervid	Burning; marked by extreme fervor.	**filet**	A lace net with a pattern of squares.
		fillet	A ribbon; a strip of material; a slice of boneless meat or fish. [But it's *filet mignon*.]
fervor	Warmth and intensity of feeling; zeal.		
fever	An abnormally high body temperature; nervous excitement.		
		Filipino	Native of the Philippines.
fetal	*See fatal and fecal.*	**Philippine**	Of or rel. to the Philippine Islands.
fete/feted	*See fate/fated.*		
fetid	*See fated.*	**fillip**	A quick smart blow or stroke given with a fingertip; something that tends to arouse or excite.
fetish	*See faddish.*		
feudal	Pert. to medieval laws, etc.		
futile	Useless.	**flip**	Act of flipping; a somersault.
		Philip	(also **Phillip**) Masc. name.
fever	*See fervor.*		
fey	*See fay.*		
		filter	A device for removing suspended material.
fiancé	Man engaged to be married.	**philter**	(also **philtre**) A potion credited with magical power.
fiancée	Woman engaged to be married.		

fin	A thin flat projection, as from the body of a fish, etc.; a five-dollar bill.	**fjord**	(also **fiord**) A narrow inlet of the sea between steep cliffs.
Finn	Native of Finland.	**ford**	A shallow place where a river may be crossed by wading or riding through.
final	At the end, coming last.		
finale	The final selection of a musical composition, etc.		
		flack	Press agent.
		flak	Antiaircraft guns; dissension.
finally	At last.		
finely	Precisely; minutely.	**flacks**	Press agents.
		flax	An annual herb, source of linen.
find	To come upon accidentally.		
fined	Given a penalty.	**flagrant**	Glaring; conspicuously bad.
finish	End.	**fragrant**	Having a pleasant odor.
Finnish	Pert. to Finland or Finns.	**flail**	To wave or swing about wildly.
fire	Combustion producing light and heat.	**flay**	To criticize harshly; excoriate.
pyre	A pile of wood, etc., for burning a corpse in a funeral rite.	**flair**	A natural aptitude. (Cap.:) A make of pen.
		flare	An unsteady, glaring light.
firs	Evergreen trees.		
furs	Pelts; coats.		
furze	A European shrub.	**flak**	*See flack.*
fiscal	Financial.	**flambé**	(of food) Covered with liquor and ignited before serving.
physical	Having material existence.		
		flambeau	A flaming torch.
fish	*See fiche.*		
		flamenco	A dance (Gypsy).
fisher	One that fishes. (Cap.:) A proper name.	**flamingo**	Aquatic bird.
fissure	A separation; crack.	**flammable**	Able to be set on fire.
		inflammable	Able to be set on fire; flammable.
fizz	A hissing sound; carbonation.	**nonflammable**	Unable to be set on fire.
phiz	A face or facial expression.	**flanges**	Ribs or rims for strength.
		phalanges	Fingers or toes. (Sing.: *phalanx.*)

flare	*See flair.*
flash	A sudden burst of flame or light. (Etc.)
flesh	Tissue of animal bodies. (Etc.)
flaunt	To display in a gaudy manner.
flout	To scorn, to mock. [He flouts convention.]
flax	*See flacks.*
flay	*See flail.*
flea	An insect.
flee	To run away.
flecks	Tiny spots or streaks.
flex	To bend.
flesh	*See flash.*
fleshly	Of or like flesh; not spiritual.
fleshy	Plump.
flew	Past tense of *fly.*
flu	Virus disease (influenza).
flue	An enclosed passageway for directing a current.
flex	*See flecks.*
flic	(slang) A police officer.
flick	A sudden light blow or tap; (slang) a motion picture.
flip	*See fillip.*
floc	A flocculent mass resembling tufts of wool.
flock	Group of birds or animals.
flocks	Plural of *flock.*
phlox	A flower.
floe	Large mass of floating ice.
flow	Uninterrupted movement.
floral	Of or rel. to flowers.
florid	Excessively flowery; ruddy.
flounder	To move clumsily and with difficulty.
founder	To collapse; to become disabled. [Boats and overfed horses founder.]
flour	Finely ground grain.
flower	A blossom.
flout	*See flaunt.*
flow	*See floe.*
flu/flue	*See flew.*
flume	A ravine with a stream; an artificial channel conveying water.
plume	A large feather; plumage; a column of smoke, etc.
fluoride	A compound of fluorine and one other element.
fluorine	The most reactive nonmetallic element.
fluorite	A common mineral, the principal source of fluorine.
foaled	Gave birth to a colt.
fold	To lay one part over another.
foggy	Filled with fog.
fogy	(also **fogey**) A person with old-fashioned ideas.

foment	*See ferment.*
fondling	Caressing, petting.
foundling	An abandoned child.
font	A basin or vessel holding water for baptism; a set of printing type.
fount	A fountain; a source.
for	Directed or sent to.
fore	The front part of something.
four	A number.
foramen	An opening, orifice, or small passage.
foremen	Persons in charge.
foray	A quick raid.
fray	Fight, battle, or skirmish.
forbear	To abstain; to forgo.
forebear	An ancestor.
forceful	Powerful, vigorous, effective.
forcible	Done by force; forceful.
ford	*See fjord.*
fore	*See for.*
forego	To precede. [A foregone conclusion.]
forgo	To give up or go without.
foreword	Preface.
forward	Situated in advance.
froward	Habitually disposed to disobedience.
form	Shape; structure.
forum	A place or meeting where a public discussion is held.

formal	Conforming to accepted rules or customs.
formyl	The radical HCO of formic acid.
formally	Ceremoniously; conventionally.
formerly	Previously.
fort	A strong or fortified place.
forte	1. One's strong point (one syl.) 2. A direction in music (two syl.: for-tay).
forth	Onward; forward.
fourth	No. 4 in a series.
fortuitous	Happening by chance; accidental. (Now also used to mean felicitous or fortunate, but not by careful writers and speakers.)
fortunate	Lucky.
forum	*See form.*
forward	*See foreword.*
fought	Past tense of *fight.*
fraught (with)	Full of; accompanied by. [Fraught with danger.]
wrought	Worked (esp. in shaping or hammering metals).
foul	Offensive.
fowl	A bird, esp. domestic cock or hen.
founder	*See flounder.*
foundling	*See fondling.*
fount	*See font.*
four	*See for.*
fourth	*See forth.*
fraction	*See faction.*
fractious	*See facetious.*

fragrant	*See flagrant.*	**fro**	Back, away. [To and fro.]
franc	French monetary unit.	**frow**	(Also **froe**) A cleaving tool.
frank	Forthright; honest; (cap.:) Masc. name.		
frantic	Emotionally out of control.	**froward**	*See foreword.*
frenetic	Frenzied; frantic.	**fryable**	*See friable.*
		fryer	*See friar.*
frater	A brother (in a religious order); comrade.	**fundus**	(pl. *fundi*) The inner basal surface of a bodily organ.
freighter	A ship carrying mainly freight.	**fungous**	Of, pert. to, or caused by fungi.
fraught	*See fought.*	**fungus**	(pl. *fungi*) Any of a major group of lower plants (incl. mushrooms, toadstools, etc.)
fray	*See foray.*		
frays	Brawls; fights.	**funeral**	Burial ceremony.
phrase	A group of grammatically related words.	**funereal**	Rel. to a funeral; solemn.
frees	Turns loose; extricates.	**furlong**	One-eighth of a mile.
freeze	To congeal into ice.	**furlough**	Leave of absence, esp. for a soldier.
frieze	A coarse woolen fabric; an architectural term.		
		furry	Covered with fur.
freighter	*See frater.*	**fury**	Violent anger.
frenetic	*See frantic.*		
		furs/furze	*See firs.*
friable	Easily crumbled.	**further**	*See farther.*
fryable	Suitable for frying.		
viable	Able to exist.	**fuse**	(also **fuze**) A short length of wire designed to melt and thus break the circuit if current exceeds a safe level; a mechanical or electrical detonating device (usu. spelled *fuze*).
friar	A member of a mendicant order.		
fryer	(also **frier**) A young chicken suitable for frying.		
		fusee	(also **fuzee**) A large-headed friction match; a red signal flare used esp. for protecting stalled vehicles.
friction	*See faction.*		
frieze	*See frees.*		
frigid	Intensely cold.		
rigid	Stiff; inflexible.	**futile**	*See feudal.*

G

Gael	Celtic.
gale	A very strong wind.
gaff	A sharp hook for spearing fish.
gaffe	A social blunder.
gage	A token of defiance; glove thrown to the ground.
gauge	A measurement.
gait	A manner of walking.
gate	An opening in a wall or fence.
gaiter	A covering of cloth or leather for the ankle and lower leg.
gator	(also **gater, 'gator**) Alligator.
gale	*See Gael.*
galleon	A large Spanish sailing ship, 15th-17th centuries.
gallon	Four quarts.
gallop	A horse's fastest pace.
Gallup	Proper name. [Gallup poll.]
galosh	A high overshoe.
goulash	A kind of stew, Hungarian specialty.

gambit	A chess move; stratagem.
gamut	A whole series, such as of musical notes. [It ran the gamut from *a* to *z*.] (*Also see gantlet/ gauntlet.*)
gamble	To wager.
gambol	To skip about in play.
gambrel	A roof with two slopes on each side.
gamin	Urchin.
gammon	Backgammon. 2. (Brit.) Ham or bacon. 3. Leg or thigh (U.S. slang).
gamut	*See gambit.*
gantlet	1. A stretch of railroad track where two lines of track overlap. 2. A former kind of military punishment. [He ran the gantlet.] 3. Var. of *gauntlet.*
gauntlet	Glove worn with medieval armor to protect the hand; a challenge to combat. [He threw down the gauntlet.] (*Also see gambit/gamut.*)
garble	To alter so as to create a wrong impression or change the meaning.
gargle	(n.) Something gargled; mouthwash.
gargoyle	A grotesque carved face or figure, esp. one used as a rainspout carrying water clear of a wall.
googol	A number equal to 1 followed by 100 zeros.

gastroscopy	Examination with a gastroscope.
gastrostomy	Establishing an artificial opening into the stomach.
gastrotomy	Incision into the stomach.
gate	*See gait.*
gate array	(electonics) A geometric pattern of basic gates contained in one chip.
Gatorade	(TM) A refreshing drink.
gator	*See gaiter.*
gauge	*See gage.*
gauntlet	*See gantlet.*
gays	Homosexuals.
gaze	A long steady look.
geek	(slang) A carnival performer who performs morbid or disgusting acts; any strange or eccentric person.
gook	l. (slang, disparaging and offensive) A native of SE Asia or the S Pacific. 2. (slang) Thick makeup. *(Also see guck, etc.)*
gel	Gelatin.
jell	To set as jelly; to take definite form.
geld	To castrate.
gelt	(Ger. and Yid.) Money.
gild	To overlay with gold.

geminal	Rel. to or characterized by two usu. similar substituents on the same atom.
germinal	In the earliest stages of development; creative.
geminate	To become double or paired.
germinate	To begin to grow; to sprout.
gemination	Doubling or pairing.
germination	Beginning to grow; sprouting.
generic	Of a whole genus or group; (of a drug) not protected by trademark.
genetic	Of or rel. to genetics; inherited.
genes	Genetic units.
jeans	Levi's; blue jeans.
genius	One with exceptional gifts or intelligence.
genus	Kind, sort, or class.
genteel	Elegant; affectedly polite and refined.
Gentile	One of non-Jewish faith.
gentle	Soft; not harsh.
geodesic	Pert. to the geometry of curved surfaces.
geodetic	Of, rel. to, or determined by geodesy (a branch of mathematics dealing with the Earth's shape and area).
geranium	A flower.
germanium	A scarce metallic element used chiefly in transistors.
German	Native of Germany.
germane	Relevant.

germinal	*See geminal.*	**gild**	To overlay with gold.
germinate	*See geminate.*		*(Also see geld, etc.)*
germination	*See gemination.*	**guild**	An association of craftsmen, etc.
gestation	The process of carrying or being carried in the womb.	**gilder**	One who gilds.
gustation	The act or sensation of tasting.	**guilder**	Dutch monetary unit; gulden.
gesture	An expressive movement of any part of the body.	**gill**	Four fluid ounces; the organ with which a fish breathes in water.
jester	A person who makes jokes.	**jill**	Girl; sweetheart. (Cap.:) Fem. name.
ghastly	Shockingly frightful; dreadful.	**gilt**	1. Gold or something resembling it. *(Also see geld.)* 2. Young female
ghostly	Of or like a ghost; spectral.		pig.
ghillie	(also **gillie**) A low-cut tongueless shoe.	**guilt**	The fact of having committed an offense.
gilly	A truck or wagon, esp. to transport circus equipment.	**gist**	The point of the matter.
		jest	Joke.
gib	A plate of metal, etc., to hold other parts in place.	**glacier**	A huge mass of ice.
		glazier	One that glazes.
glib	Offhand; superficial.	**glance**	A quick intermittent flash or gleam.
jib	A triangular sail stretching forward from the mast. [The cut of one's jib.]	**glimpse**	A fleeting view.
		glands	Organs that secrete bodily substances.
gibe	To utter taunting words.	**glans**	The tip of the penis or clitoris.
jibe	To be in accord; (naut.) to shift suddenly.	**glazier**	*See glacier.*
		glib	*See gib.*
jive	To talk jive (the jargon assoc. with swing music and early jazz), esp. if trying to deceive; to perform or dance to jive music.	**glimpse**	*See glance.*
		globule	A small rounded drop.
		lobule	A small lobe.
		glucoside	A compound yielding glucose upon hydrolysis.
gig	An engagement to play jazz, etc.	**glycoside**	A compound yielding sugar and aglycon upon hydrolysis.
jig	A lively dance.		

82

gluey	Sticky; like glue.	**gorilla**	An ape.
gooey	Messy, sticky, viscid.	**guerrilla**	One who engages in irregular warfare.
gluten	A tough elastic protein substance.	**goulash**	*See galosh.*
glutton	A person who eats to excess.	**gourmand**	A lover of food, a glutton.
glutinous	Viscid; gluelike.	**gourmet**	A connoisseur of good food and drink. [Pronounced goor-may.]
gluttonous	Voracious.		
glyceryl	A trivalent radical.	**graciously**	Done in a gracious manner. [Note: It's not very modest to say, "I graciously accept this plaque"!]
glycol	An alcohol containing two hydroxyl groups.		
glycyl	A univalent radical.		
glycoside	*See glucoside.*	**gratefully**	Expressing gratitude.
gneiss	A coarse-grained rock of quartz, etc.	**grade**	A stage in a process. (Etc.)
nice	Pleasant, satisfactory; fastidious.	**grayed**	(also **greyed**) Grew gray.
gnu	A large antelope (habitat Africa and crossword puzzles).	**graded**	Assigned a grade to.
knew	Realized. (Etc.)	**grated**	Reduced to small particles; caused irritation.
new	Fresh, unused. (Etc.)		
godly	Sincerely religious.	**graffiti**	Plural of *graffito*.
goodly	Rather large or great.	**graffito**	Word or drawing scratched or scribbled on a wall.
gofer	A person who runs errands for another.		
gopher	A short-tailed burrowing rodent.	**graft**	Something grafted (as living tissue); illegal gain.
gooey	*See gluey.*	**graph**	A diagram or chart.
googol	*See garble.*	**graphed**	Plotted on a graph.
gook	*See geek.*		
		grain	Unit of weight (.065 gram).
Gordian (knot)	An intricate problem.	**gram**	Unit of weight (15.43 grains). *(Also see dram.)*
guardian	One who guards or protects.		
gorgeous	Beautiful.	**Granada**	Spanish city.
gorges	(n.) Narrow steep-sided valleys. (v.) Overeats.	**Grenada**	One of the Windward Islands.

grate	A frame of parallel bars or lattice; fireplace.	**grisly**	Inspiring horror or fear.
great	Large; distinguished.	**gristly**	Consisting of or containing gristle.
grated	*See graded.*	**grizzly**	(adj.) Somewhat gray, grizzled. [A grizzly bear.] (n.) A device for screening ore, consisting of a row of iron or steel bars.
gratefully	*See graciously.*		
grayed	*See grade.*		
grays/greys	Turns gray (grey).		
graze	To feed on growing herbage; to abrade or scratch.		
		groan	A moan.
		grown	Mature.
grease	Rendered animal fat.	**grocer**	One who sells groceries.
Greece	A country.	**grosser**	More repulsive; less refined.
great	*See grate.*		
Grenada	*See Granada.*	**groin**	The fold where each thigh joins the trunk.
grievance	A cause of distress.	**loin**	The side and back of the body between the ribs and the hipbone.
grievants	Those who submit a grievance for arbitration.		
		grown	*See groan.*
		guardian	*See Gordian.*
griffin	(Gk. mythology) A creature with eagle's head and wings on a lion's body.	**guarantee**	An assurance of the fulfillment of a condition.
griffon	A breed of dog.	**guaranty**	Warranty; guarantee. *(Also see warranty.)*
grill	Food broiled on a grill; an informal restaurant.	**guck**	Slime or oozy dirt.
grille	A grating forming a barrier or screen. [Note: If a restaurant misspells its own name and calls itself the Greasy Spoon Grille, you'd better spell it that way.]	**gunk**	Filthy, sticky, or greasy material.
		junk	Trash.
		guerrilla	*See gorilla.*
		guessed	Estimated.
		guest	One receiving hospitality.
grip	A strong or tenacious grasp; a suitcase.	**guesstimate**	*See estimate.*
gripe	A complaint.	**guide**	To lead or direct.
grippe	Flu.	**guyed**	Steadied or reinforced with a guy (rope or chain).

guide wires	*See next entry.*
guy wires	Ropes or cables to keep something steady or secured (*not* guide wires).
guild	*See gild.*
guilder	*See gilder.*
guilt	*See gilt.*
guise	A form or style of dress; semblance.
guys	Fellows; rope, chain, etc., to brace or guide. (See entry under *guide wires*.)
guitar	*See catarrh.*
gummite	A mixture of hydrous oxides of uranium, thorium, etc.
Gunite	A mixture of cement, sand, etc., used in concrete construction.

gunk	*See guck.*
gunnel	1. An eellike fish. 2. Gunwale.
gunwale	[Naut.] The upper edge of a ship's side. (Usu. pronounced gunnel.)
gustation	*See gestation.*
gutta	An ornament in Doric architecture. [Gutta-percha: Rubberlike gum produced by a SE Asian tree.]
gutter	A trough along the eaves to carry off rainwater.
guyed	*See guide.*
guys	*See guise.*

H

hail	Pellets of frozen rain; a greeting or signal for attention.
hale	Healthy.
hair	A threadlike growth.
hare	A rabbit. [Not only hares are *harebrained*!]
Herr	The title of a German man.
hairbreadth	Extremely close..
hairsbreadth	Hairbreadth.
hairy	Hirsute.
harry	To harass or annoy. (Cap.:) A masc. name.
hale	*See hail.*
Halcion	(TM) A sleep remedy.
halcyon	Calm; peaceful.
halide	A chemical compound.
halite	Rock salt.
hall	A large room for assembly.
haul	Act or instance of hauling.
halve	To divide in half.
have	To be in possession of.
hammock	A hanging bed of canvas or rope mesh.
hummock	A hump in the ground.
handcraft	Handicraft.
handicraft	Work that needs both skill with the hands and artistic design.

Handel	Famous composer.
handle	To touch with the hands.
handiwork	Work done by the hands.
handwork	Handiwork.
handmaid	A personal maid or female servant.
handmade	Made by hand.
handsome	Beautiful; sizable.
hansom	Type of carriage. [Hansom cab.]
hangar	Shelter for an airplane.
hanger	One that hangs; loop or device for hanging.
happi (coat)	Japanese lounging jacket.
happy	Contented.
harass	To bother persistently.
Harris	Proper name.
hardwood	Hard compact wood of various trees (oak, etc.)
heartwood	The dense inner part of a tree trunk.
hardy	Capable of enduring cold, etc.
hearty	Showing warmth of feeling; vigorous, strong.
hare	*See hair.*
Harold	Masculine name.
herald	Announcer; forerunner.
Harriet	Feminine name.
heriot	Feudal tribute or payment
harry/Harry	*See hairy.*

hart	Male deer.	hear	To perceive by the ear.
heart	Organ of the body; core.	here	In or at this place.
			Note: Indication of approval of a speaker's statement is "Hear, hear," not "Here, here."
hassock	*See cassock.*		
haul	*See hall.*	heard	Past tense of *hear*.
		herd	(n.) A drove. (v.) To drive in a group, esp. animals. (*Also see erred* under *aired* grouping.)
haunch	The fleshy part of the buttock and thigh; the leg and loin of deer etc. as food.		
paunch	A protruding abdomen.	hearsay	Something heard from another.
		heresy	Opinion or doctrine contrary to accepted beliefs.
have	*See halve.*		
		heart	*See hart.*
haws	(n.) Hawthorn berries. (v.) Equivocates. [Hems and haws.]	heartwood	*See hardwood.*
		hearty	*See hardy.*
hawse	Part of a ship's bow.	hectare	A unit of surface measure.
hay	Dried grass.	hector	To intimidate by bullying. (Cap.:) A masc. name.
heigh	An exclamation used to call attention, etc. (Pronounced either as hay or hi.)		
		heel/he'll	*See heal.*
hey	Expression of surprise, etc.	heeled	*See healed.*
		heigh	*See hay and hi.*
hayrack	A frame used in hauling hay.	heinous	*See anus.*
		heir	*See air.*
hayrick	A haystack.		
		heist	A robbery or holdup.
hays	Cuts, cures, and stores hay.	hoist	To raise or haul up.
haze	Thin mist; mental confusion.	helpmate	Companion, helper, esp. wife.
		helpmeet	Helpmate.
heal	To cure.		
heel	Part of the foot.		
he'll	Contraction of *he will*.		
healed	Cured.		
heeled	Supplied with a heel; (of a dog) followed at one's heels.		

hence	From this time; for this reason.
thence	From that place or source.
whence	From where, from what place or source, from which. [It's incorrect to say *from whence* because the *from* is built in.]
herald	*See Harold.*
herd	*See heard.*
here	*See hear.*
heresy	*See hearsay.*
heriot	*See Harriet.*
heroin	Narcotic drug.
heroine	Principal female character; brave girl or woman.
Herr	*See hair.*
hertz	Unit of frequency of electromagnetic waves.
hurts	Injuries or sorenesses.
heterogamous	Having unlike gametes (reproductive cells).
heterogeneous	Different in kind; incongruous.
heterogenous	Originating outside the body.
heterogonous	Characterized by the alternation of sexual and asexual generations.
heterogymous	Having females of two different kinds, one sexual and the other infertile (as ants).

heteromerous	Having unequal or different parts within the same structure.
heteronomus	Subject to external or foreign laws or domination.
heteronymous	Having different names; (optics) relating to crossed images of an object seen double.
hew	To cut with an ax, etc.
hue	Color; shade.
Hugh	Masculine name.
hewed	Cut.
hued	Colored.
hey	*See hay.*
hi	Hello.
hie	To hasten.
high	Tall. (Note also *heigh*, defined under the *hay* group, which is pronounced either hi or hay. In *heigh-ho* it usually has the long *i*.)
hide	To conceal.
hied	Hastened.
higher	Loftier.
hire	To employ; to rent, as a cab.
him	Personal pronoun.
hymn	A song of praise to God.
hippie	A nonconformist, usu. young.
hippy	Having big hips.
Hippocratic (oath)	An oath taken by doctors about to enter the practice of medicine.
hypercritic	Excessively critical person.

hire	*See higher.*
his	Personal pronoun.
hiss	To make a sharp sibilant sound.
hissed	Past tense of *hiss.*
hist	Interjec. used to attract attention.
historic	Famous or important in history; momentous.
historical	Belonging to or dealing with history or past events.
hysterical	Wildly emotional or uncontrolled.
hither	To or toward this place.
thither	To or toward that place; there.
whither	To which place.
ho	Interjec. expressing surprise.
hoe	Implement for cultivating.
hoar	Frost.
hoer	One that hoes.
whore	Prostitute.
hoard	(n.) A hidden supply or fund stored up. (v.) To gather and store away.
horde	A multitude.
whored	Acted as a whore.
hoarse	Rough or harsh in sound.
horse	Equine quadruped.
hoax	A plot to trick or deceive.
hokes	Treats in a falsely contrived way.

hockey	(ice or field) A team game.
hooky	(Playing) truant. [Schoolkids have been known to play both of these simultaneously!]
hoer	*See hoar.*
hoes	Implements for cultivating.
hose	A flexible tube; stockings.
hoist	*See heist.*
hokes	*See hoax.*
hold	To maintain possession.
holed	Made a hole. [Cf. *holed up* and *hold up.*]
hole	An opening.
whole	Complete; entire.
holey	Containing holes.
holly	Evergreen shrub with red berries.
holy	Sacred.
wholly	Completely; entirely.
home	To go home; to proceed toward an objective.
hone	To sharpen. [You home in on your goal as you hone your skills.]
homely	Plain.
homey	Homelike.
homily	A sermon.
homeotype	A biological specimen that has been carefully compared with and identified with an original or primary type.
homotype	A part or organ of the same fundamental structure as another.

hominid	A primate of the family Hominidae, which includes modern man.
hominoid	Resembling or relating to man.
homogeneous	Of the same or a similar kind or nature.
homogenous	Rel. to mating like with like.
hone	*See home.*
hooch	(slang) 1. Liquor. 2. A thatched hut of SE Asia.
hutch	A cabinet; a pen for rabbits.
hooky	*See hockey.*
hoop	A ring; a circular strip.
whoop	A loud yell.
horde	*See hoard.*
horse	*See hoarse.*
hose	*See hoes.*
hospice	*See auspice.*
hostel	Inn; lodging for travelers.
hostile	Antagonistic; unfriendly.
hours	60-minute periods.
ours	Yours and mine. (No apostrophe!)
hue/hued	*See hew/hewed.*
Hugh	*See hew.*
hulk	Body of an old ship; clumsy-looking person or thing.
hull	Outer covering of a fruit or vegetable, etc.; basic frame of a ship or aircraft.

human	Of or relating to a person.
humane	Marked by compassion.
humerus	Long bone of the upper arm.
humorous	Funny.
hummock	*See hammock.*
humpback	A hunchback; type of whale.
hunchback	A person with a hump on his back.
hurdle	To leap over.
hurtle	To move or hurl rapidly.
hurts	*See hertz.*
hutch	*See hooch.*
hyaloid	Glassy; transparent. [The hyaloid membrane encloses the vitreous humor of the eye.]
hyoid	A bone between the root of the tongue and the larynx.
hydronic	Of, rel. to, or being a system of heating and cooling that involves heat transfer.
hydroponic	Pert. to the art of growing plants without soil.
hymn	*See him.*
hyper-	(prefix) Above or beyond.
hypo-	(prefix) Less than or below normal.

NOTE: A number of word groupings follow that have *hyper-* and *hypo-* as prefixes. Rather than cross-index all the *hypo-* words, I refer you to the *hyper-* soundalikes.

hyperacidity	Excessive acidity.
hypoacidity	Acidity in a lesser degree than usual or normal.
hyper-alimentation	Overfeeding.
hypo-alimentation	Insufficient nourishment.
hyperbaric	Having a specific gravity greater than that of cerebrospinal fluid.
hypobaric	Having a specific gravity lower than that of cerebrospinal fluid.
hypercalcemia	An abnormally large amount of calcium in the blood.
hypocalcemia	An abnormally small amount of calcium in the blood.
hyper-cholesterolemia	Excessive amount of cholesterol in the blood.
hypo-cholesteremia	An abnormally low amount of chlolesterol in the blood.
hypercritic	*See Hippocratic.*
hypercritical	Censorially critical.
hypocritical	Characterized by hypocrisy.
hyperesthesia	An abnormally acute sense of pain, heat, cold, or touch.
hypesthesia	(also **hypoesthesia**) Impairment of sensation.
hyperglycemia	An abnormally high level of glucose in the blood.
hypoglycemia	An abnormally low level of glucose in the blood.

hyperhidrosis	Excessive sweating.
hypohidrosis	Abnormally diminished sweating.
hyperkalemia	Abnormally high concentration of potassium in the blood.
hypokalemia	Abnormally low concentration of potassium in the blood.
hyperkinesia	Excessive movement.
hypokinesia	Abnormally diminished muscular function or mobility.
hypermotility	Excessive motility of the stomach or intestine.
hypomotility	Abnormally slow motility.
hyperphagia	Bulimia.
hyperplasia	Abnormal multiplication of cells.
hypoplasia	Abnormal deficiency of cells.
hyperpnea	Increase in depth of inspiration.
hypopnea	Shallow breathing.
hyper-potassemia	Hyperkalemia (defined above).
hypo-potassemia	Hypokalemia (defined above).
hypersecretion	An excessive secretion.
hyposecretion	Diminished secretion.
hypertension	Abnormally high arterial blood pressure.
hypotension	Low blood pressure.
hypertensive	Characteristic of or causing high blood pressure.
hypotensive	Characterised by or causing low blood pressure.

hyperthermia	(also **hyperthermy**) Abnormally high fever.
hypothermia	Subnormal body temperature.
hyperthyroidism	Overactivity of the thyroid gland.
hypothyroidism	Deficient activity of the thyroid gland.

hypertonic	Having extreme muscular or arterial tension.
hypotonic	Having less than normal tone or tension.
hysterical	*See historic.*

I

I	See ay.
idealogy	See etiology.
I'd	See eyed.

idle	Not occupied; unemployed.
idol	Symbol of worship; false god.
idyll	(also idyl) Narrative poem; romantic interlude.

ileac	Pert. to ileus (intestinal obstruction).
iliac	Pert. to or situated near the ilium.

ileum	Part of the small intestine.
ilium	A bone of the pelvis.

I'll	See aisle.
illegible	See eligible.
illicit	See elicit.
illiterate	See alliterate.

illuminance	Illumination.
illuminants	Illuminating agents.

illuminate	See eliminate.
illusion	See allusion.
illusive	See allusive.
illuvial	See alluvial.
illuvium	See alluvium.
immanent	See emanant.
immersed	See emerged.
immersion	See emersion.
immigrant	See emigrant.
immigrate	See emigrate.
imminent	See emanant.
immolate	See emulate.
immolation	See emulation.

immoral	Not moral. (Also see amoral.)
immortal	Exempt from death or oblivion.

immunity	The state of being protected from a disease, etc.
impunity	Exemption or freedom from punishment or harm.

immure	To imprison; to shut in.
inure	To accustom, esp. to something unpleasant.

impassable	Incapable of being passed or traveled.
impassible	Incapable of suffering pain; impassive.
impossible	Incapable of occurring.

impatience	Lack of patience.
impatiens	Type of flower.
inpatients	Persons remaining in a hospital for treatment.

impediment	Something that impedes; obstacle.
pediment	A triangular gable crowning the front of a building; a gently sloping rock surface at the foot of a steep slope.

impersonal	Not influenced by personal emotion.
interpersonal	Of the relations between persons.

impersonate	To pretend to be another person for entertainment or in fraud.
personate	To act or play a part; to pass oneself off as someone else.

93

impervious	Not able to be penetrated; not influenced by.	**in**	To or toward; at.
		inn	A public lodging house.
pervious	Admitting of passage or entrance; permeable; accessible.	**inane**	Silly, lacking sense.
		insane	Not sane; mad.
impinge	To make an impact; to encroach.	**inapt**	Not suitable.
infringe	To violate; to encroach.	**inept**	Lacking in fitness or aptitude; incompetent.
implicit	*See explicit.*	**unapt**	Not likely; inappropriate.
implode	*See explode.*	**inbred**	Produced by inbreeding; inborn.
imply	To suggest; to hint.	**interbred**	Crossbred.
infer	To reach an opinion from facts or reasoning.	**Incas**	Members of an American people in Peru before the Spanish conquest.
impostor	(also **imposter**) One who assumes a fraudulent identity.	**incus**	Bone in the middle ear.
imposture	A fraudulent deception.	**uncus**	A hooked anatomical part.
impotent	Powerless to take action.	**incidence**	Rate of occurrence or influence.
impudent	Cocky, insolent.	**incidents**	Occurrences; happenings. [Note: *Incidences* (pl. of *incidence*) is rarely used. But the plural of *incident* is frequently mispronounced with the extra syllable.]
impotence	The condition or quality of being impotent; weakness.		
impotents	Impotent persons.		
impracticable	While both words mean not practical, the longer one suggests difficulty of accomplishment; something impractical is unwise or imprudent.	**instance**	An illustration; example.
impractical		**incite**	To move to action; urge on.
		in sight	In view.
		insight	Intuitive discernment.
impress	*See empress.*	**incompetent**	Not legally qualified; incapable.
impudent	*See impotent.*	**inconsonant**	Not in accord.
impugn	To assail or oppose.	**incontinent**	Unable to control bodily functions; lacking in self-control.
impute	To attribute; to lay blame.		
impunity	*See immunity.*		
imputation	*See amputation.*		

incredible	Hard to believe; unbelievable.	**indiscreet**	Imprudent.
incredulous	Skeptical; unbelieving, showing disbelief.	**indiscrete**	Not divided into distinct parts.
		indite	*See indict.*
incredibility	Unbelievability.		
incredulity	Disbelief.	**induce**	To persuade; to produce or cause.
incubation	Hatching.	**induct**	To install as an officer or member of a group.
intubation	Introduction of a tube into a hollow organ.		
		induction	*See deduction.*
incubous	(of leaves) Overlapping, with the upper part of each leaf covering the base of the leaf above it.	**inductive**	*See deductive.*
		industrial	Of or engaged in industries.
incubus	A nightmare; an evil spirit.	**industrious**	Hardworking.
		ineffective	Not effective.
incursion	*See excursion.*	**ineffectual**	Not producing the intended effect.
incus	*See Incas.*		
		inept	*See inapt.*
independence	Freedom.		
independents	People not subjected to control by others.	**inequity**	Injustice; unfairness.
		iniquity	Wickedness.
independent	Not dependent on or controlled by another.	**infarction**	An infarct (an area of dead or damaged tissue) or formation of one.
interdependent	Dependent on each other.		
		infraction	Violation.
indeterminable	Impossible to discover or decide.	**infect**	To contaminate.
indeterminate	Not fixed in extent or character; vague.	**infest**	To overrun in large numbers.
indict	To charge with an offense.	**infer**	*See imply.*
indite	To write down; to proclaim.	**infinity**	*See affinity.*
		infirm	Physically weak.
indigence	Poverty.	**inform**	To give information.
indigents	Poor people.		
		inflammable	*See flammable.*
indigenous	*See endogenous.*		
indigent	Poor.		
indignant	Angry.		

inflect	To change the pitch of the voice in speaking.	**innocence**	Freedom from sin or guilt.
inflict	To cause (a blow or penalty, etc.) to be suffered.	**innocents**	Those who are innocent.
		innovate	*See enervate.*
inflection	Modulation of voice, change of pitch or tone.	**innumerable**	*See enumerable.*
		inpatients	*See impatience.*
infliction	The act of inflicting.	**insane**	*See inane.*
influence	The power to produce an effect.	**insanitary**	Unsanitary.
		unsanitary	Unclean.
influents	Tributaries; fluids or other material flowing in.	**insensate**	Without physical sensation; unfeeling.
inform	*See infirm.*	**insensible**	Unconscious; without feeling; unaware.
infraction	*See infarction.*		
infringe	*See impinge.*	**insensitive**	Not sensitive.
infusion	*See affusion.*		
		insert	To put (a thing) in or between or among.
ingenious	Clever, resourceful.	**inset**	To set or place in.
ingenuous	Showing innocent or childlike simplicity.		
		insidious	Seductive; spreading or developing or acting inconspicuously but with harmful effect.
ingest	To take in as food.		
inject	To introduce a new element into.	**invidious**	Likely to cause resentment because of real or imagined injustice.
in gross	*See en gros.*		
inhuman	Lacking pity; savage.	**insight**	*See incite.*
unhuman	Inhuman.	**in sight**	*See incite.*
inhumane	Cruel.	**insigne**	Badge of authority; emblem.
unhumane	Inhumane.	**insignia**	Plural of *insigne*, but used as a singular itself.
iniquity	*See inequity.*		
inject	*See ingest.*	**installation**	Act of installing or state of being installed.
injure	To harm.	**instillation**	Injection; imparting gradually.
in jure	(L.) According to law.		
inn	*See in.*	**instance**	An illustration; example. (*Also see incidence.*)
innervate	*See enervate.*		
		instants	Small spaces of time.

insure	*See ensure.*
intense	Existing in an extreme degree.
intents	Purposes; meanings.
intension	Intensification; intensity.
intention	Determination to act in a certain way.
inter	To bury.
intern	To confine or impound, esp. during a war; to serve an internship. (*Also see extern.*)
interbred	*See inbred.*
inter-	(prefix) Between.
intra-	(prefix) Within.
intro-	(prefix) 1. In, into. 2. Inward, within.

NOTE: A number of the word groupings that follow have *inter-*, *intra-*, and *intro-* as prefixes. Rather than cross-index all the *intra-intro* words, I refer you to the *inter-* soundalikes.

intercellular	Situated between or among cells.
intracellular	Within a cell or cells.
intercoastal	Existing or done between seacoasts.
intercostal	Situated or extending between the ribs.
interdependent	*See independent.*
interfering	Dealing with other people's affairs without right or invitation.
interferon	A protein substance that prevents development of a virus in living cells.

intergallactic	Of, existing, or occurring in the space between galaxies.
intragallactic	Existing or occurring within a single galaxy.
interject	To throw in between or among other things; to interpolate.
introject	To incorporate (attitudes or ideas) into one's personality unconsciously.
interjection	Something interjected, as a remark.
introjection	Process of introjecting.
interlobar	Between two lobes.
intralobar	Within a lobe.
intermission	An interval; a pause in work or action.
intromission	An insertion.
interment	The act or ceremony of interring (burying).
internment	Imprisonment.
intermittent	Coming and going at intervals; not continuous.
intromittent	Being inserted.
intermural	Of, pert. to, or taking place between two buildings, etc.
intramural	Involving only students of the same school, etc. (*Also see extramural.*)
interocular	Being, or situated, between the eyes.
intraocular	Located in or occurring or administered within the eye.

interpellate	To question (a foreign minister) formally to explain an act or policy.	**iodide**	A compound of iodine with another element.
interpolate	To interject.	**iodine**	A chemical element, used in solution as an antiseptic.
interpellation	A procedure of asking a government official to explain an action.	**irascible**	*See erasable.*
interpolation	Something interpolated, as a passage introduced into a text.	**irregardless**	Regardless. [Nonstandard. Don't use it.]
interpersonal	*See impersonal.*	**regardless**	Despite everything.
interspecies	Existing or occurring between species.	**irrelevant**	Not responsive or germane.
intraspecies	Existing or occurring within a species.	**irreverent**	Lacking in proper respect.
interstate	Between states.	**irrigate**	To supply with water by artificial means.
intestate	Not having made a will.	**irritate**	To annoy.
intrastate	Within a state.		
		irrupt	*See erupt.*
in thrall	*See enthrall.*	**irruption**	*See eruption.*
		irruptive	*See eruptive.*
intimate	To make known, esp. by hinting.	**isle**	*See aisle.*
intimidate	To subdue or influence by threats or force.	**islet**	*See eyelet.*
		isogonic	Having or pert. to equal angles.
intrados	*See extrados.*	**isonomic**	Pert. to equality of political rights.
intrapreneur	*See entrepreneur.*	**isotonic**	Having the same osmotic pressure.
intrinsic	*See extrinsic.*		
intubation	*See incubation.*	**isotopic**	Pert. to isotopes.
inure	*See endure and immure.*	**isotropic**	Identical in all directions.
invade	To encroach upon; infringe.		
inveighed	Attacked in words; assailed.	**itch**	*See etch.*
		its	Possessive pronoun. (It *never* takes an apostrophe!)
invert	*See advert.*	**it's**	Contraction of *it is.*
invidious	*See insidious.*		
invocation	*See evocation.*		
invoke	*See evoke.*		

J

jack	A portable device for raising heavy weights. (Etc.) (Cap.:) Masc. name.
jock	(slang) An athlete.
jackal	Wolflike animal.
Jekyll	(and Hyde) Protagonist in a novel by R. L. Stevenson, now used to describe a split personality.
jaculate	See ejaculate.
jam	A crush; difficult spot; jelly.
jamb	Side of a door or window.
jammies	Pajamas (baby talk).
jimmies	(v.) Forces open a door, etc., with a jimmy. (n.) A topping for cupcakes, etc.
Japanese	Native of Japan; of or pert. to Japan.
Javanese	Native of Java; of or pert. to Java.
jealous	Envious.
zealous	Ardent.
jeans	See genes.
jeers	See cheers.

jejuno-jejunostomy	Surgical formation of an anastomosis between two parts of the jejunum.
jejunostomy	Making of an artificial opening through the abdominal wall into the jejunum.
Jekyll	See jackal.
jell	See gel.
jest	See gist.
jester	See gesture.
jetsam	Goods thrown overboard from a ship in distress to lighten it. [Flotsam and jetsam.]
jettison	To throw (goods) overboard; to discard.
jewelry	Personal adornment.
Jewry	The Jewish people.
jury	A group of persons sworn to render a verdict.
jib	See gib.
jibe	See gibe.
jig	See gig.
jiggle	To rock or jerk lightly.
joggle	To shake slightly; to move by light jerks.
juggle	To toss and catch a number of objects skillfully.
jill/Jill	See gill.
jimmies	See jammies.
jinni/jinn	See djinni.
jive	See gibe.
jock	See jack.
joiner	One that joins.
jointer	A tool for joining.
jointure	Act of joining; wife's estate.

joist	A timber or metal beam supporting a floor or ceiling.
joust	A combat on horseback between two knights; personal combat.
jounce	*See bounce.*
judicial	Pert. to courts of law.
judicious	Wise; discreet.
juridical	Of or rel. to the administration of justice.
juggle	*See jiggle.*
juggler	One who juggles.
jugular	Large vein in the neck.
julep	A drink. [Mint julep.]
tulip	A flower.
junction	The act of joining.
juncture	A point of time, a critical convergence of events.
Juneau	City and port in Alaska.
Juno	Jupiter's wife.
junk	*See guck/gunk.*
junta	A group of people who combine to rule a country.
junto	A group of persons joined for a common cause.
jury	*See jewelry.*

K

Kahn test	*See contest.*
karat	*See carat.*
karuna	*See corona.*
Kashmir	*See cashmere.*
kay	*See cay.*
kayak	An Eskimo canoe.
kyack	A packsack swung on either side of a packsaddle.
keratin	*See carotene.*
keratode	The horny substance forming the skeleton of some sponges.
keratoid	Resembling horn.
keratome	*See carotene.*
kernel	*See colonel.*
ketch	*See catch.*
ketchup	*See catch-up.*
ketene	A colorless toxic gas.
ketone	An organic compound with a carbonyl group attached to two carbon atoms.
key	A means of gaining entrance; clue. *(Also see cay.)*
quay	A wharf (pronounced key).
khaki	*See cocky.*
khan	*See can.*
kibbutz	A communal settlement in Israel.
kibitz	To watch and comment on a game of cards.

kill	An instance of killing.
kiln	A special type of oven.
kind	A class of similar things; type.
kine	Cattle.
kinesic	Pert. to kinesics (study of body movements).
kinesthetic	Pert. to kinesthesia (muscle sense).
kinetic	Of or produced by movement. (*Also see akinetic.*)
kitsch	*See catch.*
kiwi	1. Flightless bird of New Zealand. 2. A fruit (also called Chinese gooseberry).
kiyi	A small whitefish.
Klan	*See clan.*
knave	Rogue.
nave	Main part of church interior.
knead	To press with the hands (as dough); to mold.
kneed	Struck with the knee.
need	To want; to lack.
knew	*See gnu.*
knickers	Short pants.
nickers	Neighs, whinnies.

knight	Medieval gentleman-soldier.
night	Opposite of day.
knightly	Of or belonging to a knight; noble, courageous.
nightly	Happening every night.
knit	To link or cause to grow together.
nit	A louse or its eggs.
knob	A rounded protuberance.
nob	(slang) The head; one in a superior position in life.
knot	A tying; lump or knob.
not	Negative. (*Also see naught-nought.*)
knotty	Full of knots; complex. [Knotty pine.]
naughty	Disobedient.
know	To be aware of. (Etc.)
no	Not any; negative.
knows	Is aware of.
noes	Plural of *no.*
nose	Organ of smell.
kohl	*See coal.*
Korea	*See chorea.*
kraal	*See choral.*
kraft	*See craft.*
krewe	*See crew.*
krona/krone	*See corona.*
Kurd	*See curd.*
kyack	*See kayak.*

L

label	Identifying slip, description, etc.
labial	Of the lips.
labile	Unstable.
laboratory	Place equipped for scientific experiment.
lavatory	Washbasin; washroom.
lacerate	To injure flesh by tearing; to wound.
macerate	To soften by steeping in a liquid.
laches	Undue delay in asserting a legal right.
latches	Bars, etc., fastening a door or gate.
lacs	Resinous substances.
lacks	Deficiencies.
lax	Not strict or stringent.
lactase	An enzyme.
lactose	A sugar present in milk.
lade	To load.
laid	Past tense of *lay*. [He laid it down.]
[layed]	No such word!
lager	A light beer.
lagger	Laggard.
logger	One that logs.
lain	Past perfect of *lie*. [She had lain there.]
lane	Narrow road.
lair	Shelter for a wild animal.
layer	Stratum.
lam	Sudden flight. [Take it on the lam.]
lamb	A young sheep.
lama	A Lamaist monk.
llama	South American animal.
lame	Crippled.
lamé	A fabric in which gold or silver thread is interwoven.
lane	*See lain.*
Lapps	Natives of Lapland.
laps	Numbers of turns around a racetrack, etc.
lapse	A slight error; decline. [Also consider *elapse*. Lawyers often use *lapsed time* and *elapsed time* interchangeably.]
largess	(also **largesse**) Money or gifts generously given.
large S	Capital S.
laryngeal	Of, pert. to, or located in the larynx.
pharyngeal	Of, pert. to, or situated near the pharynx.
laryngitis	Inflammation of the larynx.
pharyngitis	Inflammation of the mucus membrane of the pharynx; sore throat.
larynx	The part of the throat containing the vocal cords.
pharynx	Cavity at the back of nose and throat.

laser	A device that amplifies light waves.	**lea**	Grassland.
maser	A device for amplifying electrical impulses.	**lee**	The side protected from the wind. (Cap.:) Masc. name or surname.
latches	See *laches*.	**leach**	To subject to the action of percolating liquid. [Leaching field.]
latent	Present but not visible; dormant.	**leech**	A blood-sucking worm.
patent	(adj.) Obvious; unconcealed (pronounced with a long *a* in this usage).	**lead**	(n.) A metal. (v.) To guide or conduct. (Etc.)
later	Tardier; at a future time.	**led**	Past tense of *lead*.
latter	Being the second mentioned of two.	**leader**	One that leads or guides.
lath	A thin narrow strip of wood.	**lieder**	A German song.
lathe	A type of machine.	**liter**	(also **litre**) Metric measurement.
Latin	Classical language.	**leaf**	Part of a plant; page of a book.
latten	A brasslike alloy.	**Leif**	Masculine name.
lattice	A structure consisting of interlaced strips of material.	**lief**	Willing; glad. [I'd as lief go as not.]
lettuce	Leafy vegetable.	**leak**	A crack or hole that lets something escape.
laudable	Praiseworthy.	**leek**	A vegetable.
laudatory	Containing or expressing praise.	**lean**	To deviate from a vertical position.
lavatory	See *laboratory*.	**lien**	A legal right to a debtor's property.
lay	Something that lies or is laid.	**leaps and bounds**	(*by*) With very rapid progress.
lei	Garland of flowers, etc.	**metes and bounds**	The boundaries or limits of a piece of land.
layed	See *lade*.	**Leary**	Proper name.
layer	See *lair*.	**leery**	Suspicious.
lays	Deposits, as an egg.	**leased**	Rented.
laze	To act or lie lazily.	**least**	Smallest.
lax	See *lacs*.	**lest**	For fear that. [Worried lest she be late.]

lectern	A stand to hold a speaker's notes, etc.	**leopard**	Spotted Asian or African carnivore.
podium	A platform for a lecturer, conductor, et al.	**leotard**	Skintight one-piece garment worn by acrobats, et al.
led	*See lead.*	**lesion**	*See legion.*
lee	*See lea.*		
leech	*See leach.*	**less**	Not so much of.
leek	*See leak.*	**loess**	A loamy deposit formed by the wind (pronounced les, LOW-es, or lus).
leery	*See Leary.*		
legible	*See eligible.*		
legion	A large military force; a very large number.	**lessen**	To shrink or decrease.
lesion	A change in tissue structure caused by injury or disease.	**lesson**	Something learned or studied.
		lesser	Of less size, quality, or significance.
legislator	One that makes laws.	**lessor**	One that conveys property by lease.
legislature	Body of persons having power to make laws.		
lei	*See lay.*	**lest**	*See leased.*
Leif	*See leaf.*		
		lets	Allows; rents.
lends	Makes a loan.	**let's**	Contraction of *let us*.
lens	(pl. *lenses*) Optical glass; part of eye.	**lettuce**	Leafy vegetable. *(Also see lattice.)*
lengths	Measured distances or dimensions.	**let us**	Allow us.
links	Connecting structures, as in a chain.	**levee**	An embankment.
lynx	Wild animal.	**levy**	An assessment. (Cap.:) Proper name.
lenticel	A mass of cells on a plant stem.	**level**	An instrument for testing a horizontal line or plane. *(Also see bevel.)*
lenticle	A window in a clock case showing the pendulum bob.	**lever**	A rigid body used to lift weights.
lenticule	A tiny lens on the base side of film used in stereoscopic or color photography.	**lewd**	Indecent; lustful.
		lude	(slang) Short for *Quaalude* (TM), a brand of methaqualone.
lentil	A kind of bean plant.		
lintil	A horizontal supporting beam.		

lexicography	The writing of dictionaries.
lexicology	The study of the formation, meaning, and use of words.
liable	Held responsible by law. (Don't confuse with *likely*: "He is liable to get mad" is colloquial.)
libel	To defame, usu. in writing.
liar	Prevaricator.
lier	A person or thing that lies, as in wait or ambush.
lyre	Ancient musical instrument.
licensor	One that grants a license.
licensure	The granting of a license.
lichen	Type of fungus-like plant.
liken	To compare.
licit	*See elicit.*
licker	One that licks.
liqueur	A sweetened alcholic beverage.
liquor	A beverage, esp. alcoholic.
lie	A falsehood.
lye	A caustic substance.
lieder	*See leader.*
lief	*See leaf.*
lien	*See lean.*
lier	*See liar.*

lieu	Place; stead. [In lieu of.]
loo	A card game; (Brit.) a toilet.
Lou	(or **Lew**) Given name or nickname.
lifelong	Continuing for a lifetime.
livelong	(pronounced LIV-long) Entire; whole. [The livelong day.]
lightening	Reducing in weight, quantity, or color.
lighting	Illumination.
lightning	Atmospheric electrical discharge.
lignify	*See dignify.*
liken	*See lichen.*
limb	An appendage (leg, arm, branch).
limn	To delineate.
lime	1. A white substance (calcium oxide) used in making cement, etc. 2. A fruit.
Lyme (disease)	An acute inflammatory disease caused by a tick- borne virus.
limey	(slang) An Englishman.
limy	Smeared with or consisting of lime.
limpet	A marine gastropod mollusk.
limpid	Transparent; clear and simple in style. (*Also see lipid.*)
linage	Number of lines of printed or written matter.
lineage	Descent in line from a common progenitor.

lineal	Composed of or arranged in lines; hereditary.
linear	Of, rel. to, or resembling a line; straight.
lineament	An outline, feature, contour of body.
liniment	A salve.
links	*See lengths.*
lintel	*See lentil.*
lipid	Fats and fatlike substances normally present in the body. (*Also see limpid.*)
lipoid	Fatty; resembling fat.
lipstick	*See dipstick.*
liqueur	*See licker.*
liquor	*See licker.*
liter	*See leader.*
literal	Actual; obvious, not figurative.
littoral	Of, rel. to, or growing on or near a shore.
literature	A writing in prose or verse.
litterateur	A literary person; professional writer.
llama	*See lama.*
lo	An expression of wonder or surprise. [Lo and behold!]
low	(adj.) Opposite of *high*. (n.) Depth; a cow's moo.
load	A burden.
lode	An ore deposit.
lowed	Mooed.
loan	Something borrowed.
lone	Sole; solitary.

loaner	Something lent.
loner	Solitary person or thing.
loath	Unwilling; reluctant.
loathe	To detest.
lobule	*See globule.*
local	A train or bus that makes all stops.
locale	A locality.
lochs	Lakes (Scot.)
locks	Devices for fastening.
lox	Smoked salmon.
locus	A place; locality.
locust	A type of grasshopper.
lode	*See load.*
loess	*See less.*
logger	*See lager.*
lone/loner	*See loan/loaner.*
loo	*See lieu.*
loon	A diving waterfowl.
lune	A crescent-shaped figure.
loop	More or less circular figure formed by cord, etc., folded back across itself.
loupe	Small magnifier used by jewelers.
loose	To untie; to free from constraint.
lose	To fail to keep or use.
looser	Less tight.
loser	One that loses.
loot	Goods taken as spoils of war; something appropriated illegally.
lute	Guitar-like instrument.

lore	Knowledge.
lower	Less high in place or position.
Lou	*See lieu.*
louver	(also **louvre**) One of a set of overlapping slats admitting air but excluding light or rain.
Louvre	A national museum in Paris.
low	*See lo.*
lowed	*See load.*
lox	*See lochs.*
lubricious	Lustful; lecherous.
lubricous	Having an oily smoothness; slippery.
lucid	Clearness of order or arrangement.
pellucid	Admitting the maximum passage of light; clear as crystal.

lude	*See lewd.*
lumbar	Of or in the lower back.
lumber	(n.) Timber sawed into planks. (v.) To move in a heavy, clumsy way.
lump	*See clump.*
lune	*See loon.*
lupous	Pert. to lupus.
lupus	A skin disease.
lute	*See loot.*
luxuriant	Lush; profuse.
luxuriate	To indulge oneself luxuriously.
luxurious	Opulent; sumptuous.
lye	*See lie.*
Lyme	*See lime.*
lynx	*See lengths.*
lyre	*See liar.*

M

ma	Short for *mama*.
maw	Mouth, throat, gullet, jaws.
macerate	*See lacerate.*
mackintosh	A raincoat.
McIntosh	Type of apple; surname.
macr-, macro-	(prefix) Long; large.
micr-, micro-	(prefix) Small; minute.
macro	(adj.) Large, thick, or prominent.
micro	(adj.) Very small.

NOTE: The *macro-/micro-* words listed below will not be cross-indexed. (They are only a partial listing—consult your dictionary for others.)

macrocephalic	Having a skull with a large cranial capacity.
microcephalic	Having an abnormally small head.
macrocosm	The great world, the universe.
microcosm	A world in miniature.
macrocyte	An abnormally large red blood cell.
microcyte	An abnormally small red blood cell.
macrodontia	Abnormally large teeth.
microdontia	Abnormally small teeth.

macroorganism	An organism that can be seen with the naked eye.
microorganism	An organism too small to be seen with the naked eye.
macrophage	A large white blood cell.
microphage	A small cell in blood or lymph.
macroscopic	Visible to the naked eye.
microscopic	Visible only through a microscope.
madam	A word used in speaking politely to a woman. (But it might not be polite to refer to her as *a* madam!)
Madame	(F.; abbrev. *Mme*) The title of a French-speaking woman, esp. a married woman.
maddening	Enraging.
madding	Frenzied. [Far from the madding crowd.]
madder	A plant yielding vegetable dye.
matter	Substance. (Etc.)
natter	To chatter.
made	Manufactured; produced.
maid	Young girl; servant.
maggot	A grub, worm.
magnate	Person of power or influence.
magnet	Something that attracts.
magisterial	Having or showing authority; imperious.
magistral	Prescribed or prepared for a particular occasion, as a remedy.

magma	Molten rock material within the earth.		**malfeasance**	An unlawful act.
magna	(L., great) A college degree (magna cum laude) or a person receiving such a degree.		**misfeasance**	A transgression, esp. the wrongful exercise of lawful authority.
			nonfeasance	Failure to do what ought to be done.
magnate	*See maggot.*		**mall**	Area set aside as for shopping.
magnet	*See maggot.*		**maul**	To beat; to handle roughly.
magnificent	Grand; sumptuous.		**moll**	A gangster's female companion.
munificent	Lavish; liberal.			
maid	*See made.*		**malleolus**	Rounded process on either side of ankle joint.
mail	Postal matter.		**malleus**	One of the small bones of the internal ear.
male	Masculine.			
mailer	One who mails; an advertising brochure, etc.		**mallow**	A flowering plant.
malar	Of or pert. to the cheek or zygomatic bone.		**mellow**	Sweet and rich in flavor; genial, jovial.
main	Principal.		**maltase**	An enzyme that hydrolyzes maltose to glucose.
Maine	New England state.		**Maltese**	Native of Malta, or its language; a breed of cat.
mane	Long hair growing around the neck.		**maltose**	A sugar produced by the hydrolysis of starch.
maize	Corn.			
maze	Confusing, intricate network of passages; labyrinth.		**mammary**	Of or pert. to the milk-secreting glands of mammals.
malady	Ailment.		**memory**	Remembering; a thing remembered.
melody	Tune.			
malar	*See mailer.*		**manage**	To have under effective control.
male	*See mail.*		**ménage**	A household. [Ménage à trois.]
Malay	Peninsula; of or pert. to its people, culture, etc.		**manakin**	A small songless bird.
melee	Confusion; turmoil; jumble.		**manikin**	(also **mannikin**) A little man; dwarf; pygmy.
			mannequin	A dummy for displaying clothes.

mandatary	A person or nation holding a mandate.	**marital**	Of or rel. to marriage.
mandatory	Authoritatively ordered; obligatory; compulsory.	**martial**	Warlike.
		marshal	Officer in charge of prisoners.
		Marshall	Common surname.
mandrel	Metal bar, axle, spindle.	**markup**	Amount added to cost of an article to give selling price.
mandrill	Large fierce baboon.		
mane	*See main.*	**mock-up**	An experimental model, built to scale, for display, etc.
maniac	Lunatic; madman.		
manic	Afflicted with or pert. to a mania.	**marlin**	Saltwater game fish.
manioc	A plant grown in the tropics for its edible rootstock; cassava; tapioca.	**merlin**	A small falcon. (Cap., Arthurian Romance:) A magician.
manifold	Numerous and varied.	**marquee**	A permanent canopy.
manyfold	By many times; by multiples.	**marquis**	A European nobleman.
		marquise	Wife or widow of a marquis; a gem cut, yielding many facets.
manikin	*See manakin.*		
mannequin	*See manakin.*	**marrow**	Soft fatty substance in the cavities of the bones.
manner	A way of acting. [To the manner born.]	**narrow**	Of small width.
manor	A mansion.	**marry**	To wed.
		Mary	Feminine name.
mantel	A shelf above a fireplace.	**merry**	Full of gaiety or high spirits.
mantle	A cloak.		
manyfold	*See manifold.*	**marshal**	*See marital.*
		Marshall	*See marital.*
mare	A female horse.	**marten**	Small animal.
mayor	A city's chief executive.	**martin**	European sparrow.
margarita	Tequila-based cocktail of Mexican origin.	**martial**	*See marital.*
margarite	A mineral, related to mica.	**Mary**	*See marry.*
		mascara	*See cascara.*
marguerite	A large daisy-like flower. (Cap.:) A feminine name.	**maser**	*See laser.*
		mask	Anything that disguises or conceals, esp. worn on the face.
		masque	A masquerade; type of entertainment.

mass	Aggregate; a religious service.
mess	A confused jumble; a meal.
massage	Rubbing and kneading of the body to lessen pain or stiffness.
message	A spoken or written communication.
massed	Gathered or assembled into a mass.
mast	1. A long pole on a ship that supports the sails and rigging. 2. The fruit of beech, oak, chestnut trees used as food for pigs.
massif	Mountain heights forming a compact group.
massive	Large and heavy or solid.
mastic	An aromatic resin.
nastic	Pert. to an automatic response of plants.
mat	Rug for wiping shoes, etc.
matte	(adj.) Having a dull or lusterless surface.
material	Matter, goods.
matériel	Equipment and supplies used by an organization.
matter	*See madder.*
maul	*See mall.*
maunder	To talk in a rambling way.
meander	To ramble; wander aimlessly.
maw	*See ma.*

may be	Could be.
maybe	Possibly; perhaps.
mayor	*See mare.*
maxim	A general truth; adage.
maximum	Greatest possible amount.
maze	*See maize.*
mean	(n.) A middle point between extremes.
mesne	(Law) Intermediate; intervening (pronounced like mean).
mien	Bearing; demeanor.
meander	*See maunder.*
meat	Food; flesh; substance.
meet	(n.) A gathering. (adj.) Proper.
mete	Measure, boundary. [Metes and bounds.]
medal	A piece of metal, usu. with a stamped design, given as an award.
meddle	To interfere.
metal	Any of various fusible, ductile, lustrous substances.
mettle	Courage and fortitude; disposition or temperament.
nettle	A wild plant covered with stinging hairs.
medial	Being or occurring in the middle.
median	In the middle or in an intermediate position.
medium	Intermediate in amount, quantity, position, or degree.
mesial	Middle; esp. dividing an animal into right and left halves.

111

mediate	To reconcile differences.	**menorrhea**	*See amenorrhea.*
meditate	To ponder.	**menu**	A list of dishes served or available to be served at a restaurant, etc.
Medicaid	A government health program.		
Medicare	Government program of hospitalization, etc.	**venue**	(Law) The locale of an event; the proper place or places for the trial of a lawsuit.
medicate	To treat with medicine.		
medium	*See medial.*		
meet	*See meat.*	**merci**	(F.) Thank you.
		mercy	Compassion.
meiosis	(Biol.) A process of division of cell nuclei whereby the number of chromosomes is halved. (Rhet.) Understatement.	**merengue**	A ballroom dance of Dominican and Haitian origin.
miosis	(also **myosis**) Excessive constriction of the pupil of the eye.	**meringue**	A mixture of beaten eggs and sugar, baked crisp.
mitosis	The usual method of cell division.	**meretricious**	Showily attractive but false or insincere.
meld	1. To declare for a score in some card games. 2. To merge, blend.	**meritorious**	Deserving of honor or award.
melt	To become liquid by heat.	**meticulous**	Extremely careful about details.
melee	*See Malay.*	**merlin**	*See marlin.*
		merry	*See marry.*
		mesial	*See medial.*
melliferous	Yielding or producing honey.	**mesalliance**	(F.) Marriage with a person of inferior social position.
mellifluous	Sweet-sounding.		
mellow	*See mallow.*	**misalliance**	An unsuitable alliance, esp. an unsuitable marriage.
melody	*See malady.*		
melt	*See meld.*		
memento	A souvenir; a reminder.	**mesne**	*See mean.*
momento	From misuse, now accepted by most dictionaries as a variant of *memento*. Avoid.	**mess**	*See mass.*
		message	*See massage.*
		metacarpal	Of or pert. to the metacarpus; a bone in the metacarpus.
memory	*See mammary.*	**metatarsal**	Of or pert. to the metatarsus; a bone in the metatarsus.
ménage	*See manage.*		
mend	*See amend.*		

metacarpus	The bones forming the palm of the hand.
metatarsus	The bones forming the middle part of the foot.
metal	*See meddle.*
metastasis	Spread of a disease such as cancer within the body.
metathesis	The transposition of sounds or letters in a word; chemical interchange of atoms.
metastasize	(of malignant cells, etc.) To spread to other parts of the body by way of blood, etc.
metathesize	To undergo or cause to undergo metathesis (defined above).
mete	*See meat.*
meteor	A small celestial body that enters the earth's atmosphere.
meter	1. (also **metre**) Unit of length in metric system. 2. A mechanical measuring device.
métier	A person's trade, profession, or department of activity; one's forte or specialty.
meteorite	A fallen meteor.
meteoroid	A meteor revolving around the sun.
metes and bounds	*See leaps and bounds.*
methyl	*See ethyl.*
methylal	*See ethyl.*
meticulous	*See meretricious.*
mettle	*See medal.*

mewl	To cry, as a baby or young child; whimper.
mule	Domestic animal; a backless slipper.
mews	(n.) A back street; alley; stables with living quarters. (v.) Makes the high-pitched sound characteristic of a kitten or cat.
muse	Source of inspiration. (Cap.:) Any of nine sister goddesses in Greek mythology presiding over song, poetry, arts, sciences.
microcopy	A photographic copy in which graphic material is reduced in size.
microscopy	The use of or investigation with the microscope.

NOTE: For *microcosm* and other words with prefix *micro-*, see under *macrocosm*, etc., earlier in this book—or consult your dictionary.

midst	The middle.
missed	Past tense of *miss*.
mist	Water vapor near the ground.
mien	*See mean.*
might	Power; energy; strength.
mite	Tiny arachnid; very little bit; small coin. [The widow's mite.]
mil	One-thousandth of an inch.
mill	One-tenth of a cent; machinery for grinding grain, etc.

mileage	Distance measured in miles.	**mind**	Brain.
millage	Tax rate expressed in mills.	**mined**	Dug (as ore) from the earth.
milestone	A stone functioning as a milepost.	**mine**	*See mime.*
millstone	One of a pair of circular stones between which grain is ground; a heavy mental or emotional burden. [Millstone around one's neck.]	**miner**	One who works in a mine.
		minor	A person under legal age.
		minim	The smallest unit of liquid measure; the least quantity of anything.
militate	(usu. with *against*) To have weight or effect.	**minimal**	Very small; least possible.
mitigate	To make less harsh or painful; extenuate.	**minimum**	(n., adj.) The least quantity possible or allowable.
milk toast	Buttered toast served in hot milk.	**minister**	*See administer.*
milquetoast	A timid, spineless person. [Caspar Milquetoast: a character in a cartoon strip by H. T. Webster (1885-1952).]	**ministration**	*See administration.*
		minks	Certain fur-bearing animals; furs.
		minx	A pert girl.
mill	*See mil.*	**minor**	*See miner.*
millage	*See mileage.*	**mints**	*See mince.*
		miosis	*See meiosis.*
millenary	Pert. to a thousand, esp. 1000 years.	**misalliance**	*See mesalliance.*
millinery	Women's hats.	**miscible**	Capable of being mixed.
		mixible	Miscible.
millstone	*See milestone.*	**misfeasance**	*See malfeasance.*
milquetoast	*See milktoast.*		
		misogamist	One who hates marriage.
mime	Acting with gestures and without words; a performer who does this.	**misogynist**	One who hates, dislikes, or distrusts women.
mine	Possessive pronoun. (Etc.)	**misogamy**	Hatred of marriage.
		misogyny	Hatred, dislike, or mistrust of women.
mince	Small chopped bits (specif. mincemeat).		
mints	Confections flavored with mint.		

missal	A prayer book.	**mobility**	The quality of being mobile. (Sociol.) The movement of people in a population, as from job to job, etc.
missile	An object or weapon that is thrown or projected.		
missive	A written communication.	**motility**	(Biol.) The capability of moving spontaneously.
mistral	A cold dry wind common in southern France.	**mock-up**	*See markup.*

missed   *See midst.*

misses   Young ladies.

missus   (also **missis**) Wife. [I'll have to ask the missus.]

Mrs.   Title of respect for a married woman.

Mses.   Pl. of *Ms.*, title of respect for women. (Source: *Random House Dictionary*.)

missile   *See missal.*
missive   *See missal.*
mist   *See midst.*
mistral   *See missal.*
mite   *See might.*
mitigate   *See militate.*
mitosis   *See meiosis.*
mixible   *See miscible.*

moan   Low sound of pain; a lament.

mown   Past tense of *mow*.

moat   A trench or large ditch.
mote   A small particle; speck.

mobile   Capable of moving or being moved readily.

motile   (Biol.) Moving or capable of moving spontaneously.

modal   1. Of or pert. to mode, manner, or form. 2. (Music) Pert. to mode, as distinguished from key; based on a scale other than major or minor.

model   A standard or example for imitation or comparison. (Etc.)

mode   Current fashion. (Etc.)
mowed   Cut (grass, etc.)
node   A swelling.

modeled   Shaped after a pattern.
mottled   Marked with spots or blotches.

modern   Up to date; contemporary.
moderne   Pretentiously modern.

moiré   A fabric that looks like watered silk.
moray   A tropical eel.

mole   A small burrowing animal. (Etc.)
vole   Any of several small animals resembling mice or rats.

moll   *See mall.*
momento   *See memento.*

monogamy	Marriage with only one person at a time.	**moral**	(n.) The significance or lesson to be drawn from a story. (adj.) Virtuous; honorable. (*Also see amoral.*)
monotony	Wearisome uniformity or lack of variety. [No comparison intended here.]		
		morale	An individual's mental and emotional condition.
Monseigneur	A French title of honor given to princes, bishops, et al.	**morel**	An edible mushroom.
		mortal	(n.) A human being. (adj.) Having caused or about to cause death; subject to death.
Monsignor	The title of certain Roman Catholic priests and officials.		
		morality	Moral conduct; a doctrine or system of morals.
mood	One's emotional state.		
mooed	Lowed (cattle).	**mortality**	The quality or state of being mortal. [Mortality table: actuarial table.]
moors	Expanses of open grassland.		
Moors	Members of a Muslim people living in NW Africa.		
		moray	*See moiré.*
mores	Moral attitudes; customs.	**mordant**	Sharply caustic or sarcastic.
mowers	Those that mow (grass, etc.)	**mordent**	(Music) A melodic ornament in which a principal note is rapidly ornamented with a note a half or whole step below.
moot	Open to question; debatable, undecided. [Moot court.]		
mute	Characterized by absence of speech or sound.		
		morel	*See moral.*
moose	A ruminant animal.	**mores**	*See moors.*
mouse	Small rodent.		
mousse	A chilled dessert; a foamy hair-styling preparation.	**morn**	(Poetic) Morning.
		mourn	To feel or express sorrow or grief.
moraine	Glacial deposit.	**morning**	Forenoon.
murrain	An infectious disease in cattle.	**mourning**	The act of grieving.
		morpheme	The smallest meaningful grammatical unit of a language.
		morphine	A drug made from opium, used for relieving pain.

morsal	Pert. to a tooth's grinding surface.		**multiparous**	Producing more than one at a birth.
morsel	Small bite of food, etc.		**nulliparous**	Describing a woman who has never borne a child.

morsal Pert. to a tooth's grinding surface.
morsel Small bite of food, etc.

mortal *See moral.*
mortality *See morality.*
mote *See moat.*

motif A dominant idea or theme (as in a work of art).
motive Something that causes a person to act in a certain way; incentive.

motile *See mobile.*
motility *See mobility.*
mottled *See modeled.*
mourn *See morn.*
mourning *See morning.*
mouse *See moose.*
mousse *See moose.*
mowed *See mode.*
mowers *See moors.*
mown *See moan.*

moxa A flammable substance obtained from the leaves of certain Chinese and Japanese plants.
moxie (slang) Vigor, verve, pep. (Cap.:) Trademark of a soft drink.

Mrs. *See misses.*
Mses. *See misses.*

mucous (adj.) Secreting or containing mucus.
mucus A viscous bodily secretion.

mule *See mewl.*

mull To study; to think about carefully.
null Having no legal effect.

multiparous Producing more than one at a birth.
nulliparous Describing a woman who has never borne a child.

munificient *See magnificent.*
murrain *See moraine.*

muscat Variety of grape.
musket A heavy large-caliber shoulder firearm.

muscle A body tissue consisting of long cells that contract when stimulated and produce motion.
mussel A marine bivalve mollusk.
muzzle 1. The projecting nose and jaws of dogs, etc. 2. The open end of a firearm. 3. A strap or wire, etc., put over an animal's head to prevent it from biting or feeding.

muse *See mews.*

musical Of, pert. to, or producing music.
musicale A social entertainment featuring music.

musket *See muscat.*

Muslim (also **Moslem**) An adherent of Islam.
muslin A sheer to coarse cotton fabric.

mussed	Untidy; rumpled.	**mutual**	Having the same feelings one for the other.
must	Auxiliary verb used to express necessity or obligation.	**mutuel**	(short for *pari-mutuel*) A betting pool.
musth	(also **must**) Violent, destructive frenzy occurring with the rutting season in male elephants.	**muzzle**	*See muscle.*
		myatonia	Deficient muscle tone.
mussel	*See muscle.*	**myotonia**	Muscle spasm or muscle rigidity.
mustard	A condiment.	**myelogram**	X-ray photograph of the spinal cord.
mustered	Formally assembled or enrolled.	**myogram**	Tracing of muscular contraction.
mute	*See moot.*		
mutter	To speak or utter in a low unclear tone; to utter subdued grumbles.	**mystic**	Of hidden or symbolic meaning, esp. in religion.
utter	To make (a sound or word) with the mouth; to put (as currency) into circulation.	**mystique**	An aura of mystery or mystical power.

N

Nader (Ralph) Political reformer and consumer advocate.
nadir The lowest point.

naif A naive or inexperienced person.
naive Artless, ingenuous; deficient in worldly judgment.

nap 1. A short snooze. 2. Short raised fibers on the surface of cloth or leather.
nape Back part of the neck.
nappe A type of rock formation.

naphthol (also **naphtol**) A chemical compound.
naphthyl Containing a certain chemical group.

narcotic A drug that dulls the senses.
necrotic Pert. to the death of living tissue.

narrow *See marrow.*
nastic *See mastic.*

natal Of or pert. to a person's birth.
Natal S African province (pronounced Na-TAHL).

natter *See madder.*

naught Nothing; zero.
nought A var. of *naught*, but lawyer-language expert Morton S. Freeman says in his "Word Watcher" column, "Use *nought* for zero in a strictly numerical sense ('Nought from four is four'). In other contexts use *naught*."
nowt (Brit. dialect) Nothing.

naughty *See knotty.*

nauseated Affected with nausea.
nauseous Causing nausea.

naval Of or rel. to a navy.
navel Depression in center of abdomen. [Navel oranges.]

nave *See knave.*

nay A negative reply or vote.
né Born with the name of (m.)
née Born with the name of (f.)
neigh The cry of a horse.

necrotic *See narcotic.*
need *See knead.*

neither Not either.
nether Situated down or below.

nettle *See medal.*

neuter (Grammar, of a noun) Neither masculine nor feminine.
neutral Not aligned with either side.

new	*See gnu.*	node	*See mode.*
nice	*See gneiss.*	noes	*See knows.*
nickers	*See knickers.*	nose	*See knows.*

Nice City and port in SE France on the Mediterranean (pronounced like niece.)

niece Daughter of one's brother or sister.

nicks Small cuts or notches.

nix (slang) Nothing. ["Macht nix," often heard from American soldiers in Germany (corruption of "Es macht nichts"): it doesn't matter.]

night *See knight.*
nightly *See knightly.*
nit *See knit.*

nitrate A salt or ester of nitric acid.

nitride A binary compound of nitrogen with a more electropositive element.

nitrite A salt or ester of nitrous acid.

nix *See nicks.*
no *See know.*
nob *See knob.*

nocturn A religious (Roman Cath.) service.

nocturne A dreamy piece of music.

noisome Offensive or disgusting, as an odor.

noisy Making loud sounds.

none Not any; nothing.

nun Woman with a religious order.

nonfeasance *See malfeasance.*
nonflammable *See flammable.*
not *See knot.*
nought *See naught.*
nowt *See naught.*

noxious Physically harmful; distasteful. [Noxious fumes.]

obnoxious Very unpleasant; objectionable.

nuclei Plural of *nucleus.*

nuclide A species of atom defined by the composition of its nucleus.

null *See mull.*
nulliparous *See multiparous.*

numerous Many; consisting of many items.

numinous Supernatural; mysterious; holy.

nun *See none.*

O

O	*See eau.*
oar	Long shaft for propelling a boat.
o'er	Over (poetic).
or	A conjunction suggesting an alternative.
ore	A mineral containing valuable metal.
obdurate	Stubborn; unyielding.
obturate	To close a hole or cavity so as to prevent a flow of gas through it.
object	Something solid that can be seen or touched.
objet	(or **objet d'art**, F., pronounced ob zhe DAR) An object of artistic worth or curiosity.
obligate	To bind or oblige morally or legally.
obviate	To anticipate and prevent or eliminate (difficulties, etc.)
obligee	One to whom another is obligated.
obliger	One who obliges.
obligor	One who places himself under legal obligation.
obnoxious	*See noxious.*
obsequies	Funeral rites; a funeral.
obsequious	Excessively or sickeningly respectful.

obsolescent	Becoming obsolete.
obsolete	No longer in general use.
obstruction	*See abstraction.*
obturate	*See obdurate.*
obtuse	*See abstruse.*
obverse	*See adverse.*
obviate	*See obligate.*
Occident	*See accident.*
Occidental	*See accidental.*
odd	*See awed.*
odder	More peculiar; stranger.
otter	An aquatic furbearing weasellike mammal.
ode	A lyric poem.
owed	Obligated to.
odor	Smell.
order	Command. (Etc.)
ordure	Excrement.
odious	Hateful, detestable.
odorous	Smelly.
Oedipus	*See edifice.*
offal	*See awful.*
o'er	*See oar.*
official	Of an office or position of authority; authenticated; authorized.
officious	Objectionably aggressive in offering one's unrequested and unwanted services.
oh	*See eau.*
oleo	Short for *oleomargarine.*
olio	A mixture; hodgepodge.
omelet	*See amulet.*
omission	*See emission.*
omit	*See emit.*

121

omnificent	Creating all things; having unlimited powers of creation.	**oracle**	See auricle.
		oral	See aural.
		orbiter	See arbiter.
omnipotent	Almighty or infinite in power, as God.	**order**	See odor.
omniscient	Knowing everything.	**ordinance**	Authoritative decree or direction.
once	One time and no more; formerly.	**ordnance**	Military supplies, weapons, ammunition, etc.
wants	Desires; needs.		
one	The first in a series.	**ordure**	See odor.
won	Past tense of *win*.	**ore**	See oar.
onside	(Sports) Illegally in advance of the ball or puck.	**organism**	A living being, an individual animal or plant.
on-site	Carried out or located at the place of a particular activity.	**orgasm**	Sexual climax.
oozy	Exuding moisture.	**oriel**	See aureole.
Uzi	A submachine gun.	**orient**	(v.) To locate a place in relation to the points of the compass. (n., Cap.:) The countries of Asia, esp. East Asia.
operand	(Math.) A quantity upon which a mathematical operation is performed.		
operant	Operating; producing effects.	**orientate**	To orient. (A barbarism. Don't use it.)
		oriole	See aureole.
opinion	Belief or judgment; personal view, attitude, or appraisal.	**orotund**	Full in sound, sonorous; pompous.
pinion	1. A small cogwheel that engages with a larger one or with a rack. [Rack and pinion.] 2. The wing of a bird.	**rotund**	Rounded, plump.
		orthoptic	Pert. to or producing normal binocular vision.
piñon	(also **pinyon**) Any of several pines of SW North America, bearing edible nutlike seeds.	**orthotic**	A device or support, esp. for the foot, used to correct an orthopedic problem.
oppose	See appose.	**orthoptics**	A method of exercising the eye and its muscles to improve vision.
opposite	See apposite.		
opposition	See apposition.	**orthotics**	A branch of medicine dealing with the making and fitting of orthotic devices.
or	See oar.		

orthotopic	Of or rel. to the grafting of tissue in a natural position.
orthotropic	(Bot.) Pert. to a mode of growth that is more or less vertical.
oscillate	To swing back and forth, like a pendulum.
osculate	To come into close contact or union; to kiss.
osmatic	Of or pert. to the sense of smell.
osmotic	Pert. to osmosis (a form of diffusion of a fluid through a membrane).
ostomy	An operation (as a colostomy) to create an artificial anus.
-ostomy	(suffix) Creation of an opening into or between.
-otomy	(suffix) Operation of cutting or incising.

otter	*See odder.*
ought	*See aught.*
ours	*See hours.*
overdo	Do (a thing) excessively.
overdue	Past due.
overseas	Beyond or across the sea.
oversees	Surveys; supervises.
overt	*See covert.*
ovoid	*See avoid.*
owe	*See eau.*
owed	*See ode.*
oyer	Hearing in open court re the production of a document.
oyez	Hear ye! A call for silence in court.

P

pa	Short for *papa*.
paw	The foot of an animal; (informal) the human hand.
Pablum	(TM) Baby food.
pabulum	Food, nutriment; intellectual sustenance; an insipid piece of writing.
paced	Covered at a walk; measured by pacing.
paste	Adhesive material; a kind of dough.
pacific	Peaceful.
specific	Particular, clearly distinguished from others.
pacifist	One who opposes war or violence.
passivist	Advocate of passive resistance.
packed	Crammed.
pact	An agreement.
packet	A small package; a small boat.
placket	Opening in a garment.
paddy	A rice field.
patty	A small flat cake of chopped food. (*Also see pâté.*)

paean	Song of joy.
paeon	A metrical foot of four syllables.
peen	Wedge-shaped or spherical head of a hammer. [Ball-peen hammer.]
peon	A member of the landless laboring class.
paid	Gave in return for goods or services. [He paid his bills.]
payed	Coated with a waterproof material; let out. [He payed out the cable.]
pail	A bucket.
pale	(n.) A space or field having bounds. [Beyond the pale.] (adj.) Deficient in color.
pain	Discomfort or distress.
pane	A framed sheet of glass.
pair	Twosome.
pare	To trim; to peel.
pear	A fruit.
pairing	Arranging or designating in pairs or groups of two.
paring	Trimming; peeling.
pal	Buddy; chum.
pall	A cloth spread over a coffin; anything that covers, shrouds, or overspreads, esp. with darkness or gloom.
Paul	Masc. name; Saint Paul; five popes.
pawl	A lever with a catch that engages with the notches of a ratchet wheel.
pol	Politician.

palatal	Of or pert. to the palate.
palatial	Of, pert. to, or resembling a palace.
palate	Roof of the mouth.
palette	A thin board on which a painter mixes pigments.
pallet	A small temporary bed; a portable platform.
pallid	Pale.
pellet	A small rounded or spherical closely packed mass.
palatine	1. Of, near, or in the palate. 2. Having royal privileges; of or pert. to a palace.
Palestine	An ancient country in SW Asia.
pale	*See pail.*
palpate	To examine by touch.
palpitate	To beat rapidly; to throb.
paltry	Inferior; trivial.
peltry	Furs, skins; pelts collectively.
poultry	Domestic fowls.
pan	Cooking utensil. (Etc.)
Pan	1. Ancient Greek god of pastures, flocks, and shepherds. 2. An international distress signal to ships, aircraft, etc.
panne	Lustrous velvet.
pandemic	*See ecdemic.*
pandit	A man in India esteemed for his wisdom and learning.
pundit	A learned person, expert, authority.

pane	*See pain.*
panne	*See pan.*
panoply	*See canape.*
papa	Father.
papaw	(also **pawpaw**) N American tree; its fleshy fruit.
paper	A substance manufactured from wood fiber, rags, etc.; newspaper, etc.
papier-mâché	(also **paper-mâché**) A molded paper pulp, used for making boxes, trays, etc.
papilla	A small nipplelike process or projection.
papule	(also **papula**) A small solid usu. conical elevation of the skin.
papillary	*See capillary.*
par-/para-	Prefix: beside, alongside of; associated in a subsidiary capacity [paralegal]; faulty, abnormal [paresthesia].
per-	Prefix: through, throughout, thoroughly [percolate].
peri-	Prefix: all around [periscope]; enclosing, surrounding [pericardial].
paracardiac	Beside the heart.
pericardiac	Pericardial; pert. to the pericardium, membranous sac that contains the heart.

parados	(Mil.) A protective embankment.
paradox	A statement seemingly contradictory or absurd yet perhaps true.
parallax	An apparant optical displacement of an object.
paragon	A model or pattern of excellence.
perigon	An angle of 360 degrees.
parahepatitis	Inflammation of structures surrounding the liver.
perihepatitis	Inflammation of the peritoneal capsule of the liver and tissues around the liver.
paramastitis	Inflammation of the connective tissue about the mammary gland.
perimastitis	Inflammation of the fibroidipose tissues around the mammary gland.
parameter	(Math.) An arbitrary constant whose value characterizes a member of a system. (Now mostly heard in a sense in which *perimeter* would be more accurate.)
perimeter	Boundary; outer limits.
parametrium	The connective tissue surrounding the uterus.
perimetrium	The serous coat of the uterus.
paraneural	Beside or near a nerve.
perineural	Occurring about or surrounding nervous tissue or nerves.

paraoral	(of medication) Administered by some route other than the mouth.
perioral	Situated or occurring around the mouth.
parasite	An organism that lives and feeds on or in another organism; a person who lives off another and gives no useful return.
parricide	One that murders father, mother, or close relative; the act itself.
parcel	Package; unit (as of land).
partial	Biased; of or rel. to a part, not the whole.
pare	*See pair.*
parental	Pert. to a parent or parents.
parenteral	Taken into the body in a manner other than through the digestive canal.
paring	*See pairing.*
parish	An ecclesiastical unit.
perish	To die.
parity	Equality; equivalence in value, etc.
parody	A comic imitation of a well-known person or literary work; a grotesque imitation, travesty.
Parkay	(TM) Brand of margarine.
parquet	A flooring of patterned inlaid wood.

126

parlay	To increase or otherwise transform into something of much greater value.
parley	To confer; to discuss terms with an enemy.
parody	*See parity.*
parol	Given by word of mouth. [Parol evidence.]
parole	Conditional release of a prisoner.
parotid	*See carotid.*
paroxysmal	Pert. to a sudden violent outburst; a severe attack or sudden increase in severity of a disease.
proximal	Situated toward the point of origin or attachment as of a limb or bone.
parquet	*See Parkay.*
parricide	*See parasite.*
parry	To evade or turn aside something; to ward off a weapon or blow.
perry	Fermented pear juice.
parson	A clergyman.
person	A human being.
partial	*See parcel.*
partition	Division; something that divides, esp. an interior dividing wall.
parturition	The process of bringing forth young.
petition	An earnest request; entreaty.

passable	Capable of being passed through, beyond, or over; capable of being enacted (legislation).
passible	Capable of feeling, esp. suffering; impressionable.
possible	That may or can exist, happen, be done, be used, etc.; that may be true.
passably	Fairly; moderately. [A passably good book.]
possibly	Perhaps; maybe.
passed	Moved, departed; overtook.
past	Rel. to an earlier period.
passible	*See passable.*
paste	*See paced.*
paster	A slip of gummed paper to be pasted on or over something (e.g., on a ballot); one that pastes.
pastor	A minister or priest in charge of a church.
pasture	Grassland, suitable for grazing.
pastiche	A musical or other composition made up of selections from various sources.
postiche	Added inappropriately; artificial, counterfeit, or false.
pastoral	A rural picture or scene; a literary work dealing with shepherds, etc.
pastorale	An opera or other piece of music with a pastoral subject.

pastry	A sweet baked food; a flour dough for covering pies, etc.	**peace**	A state of tranquility or quiet; freedom from war.
pasty	(adj.) Of or like paste; unhealthily pale. [Pasty-faced.] (n., pl.) Small coverings for the nipples of a striptease dancer.	**piece**	A part of a whole.
		peaceable	Not quarrelsome.
		peaceful	Characterized by peace; placid.
patsy	A person who is easily swindled or deceived.	**peak**	Summit; promontory.
		peek	A brief look; glance.
		peke	Short for *Pekinese*.
pasture	*See paster.*	**pic**	Term used in scoring in the game piquet.
pate	Crown of the head.	**pique**	A transient feeling of wounded vanity.
pâté	A meat or fish pie or patty.	**piqué**	(two syl.) A durable ribbed fabric.
patty	A little pie. (*Also see paddy.*)		
		peaked	Came to a peak, point, or maximum.
patent	*See latent.*	**peaked**	(two syl.) Pale and drawn in appearance.
pathos	*See bathos.*	**peeked**	Glanced at.
patience	The ability to bear pains, trials, or delays without complaint.	**piqued**	Aroused anger, irritation, or curiosity.
		peal	To ring (as a bell).
patients	Individuals awaiting or under medical care.	**peel**	To strip off an outer layer.
patrol	A policeman's beat, e.g.	**pear**	*See pair.*
petrel	Seabird. [Stormy petrel.]	**pearl**	A smooth rounded mass found in certain mollusks; something precious or choice.
petrol	(Brit.) Gasoline.		
patsy	*See pastry.*	**purl**	To knit with a particular stitch.
patty	*See paddy and pâté.*		
Paul	*See pal.*	**peasant**	(in some countries) A member of the class of farm laborers and small farmers.
paunch	*See haunch.*		
pause	A temporary stop.	**pheasant**	A long-tailed game bird with bright feathers.
paws	Feet of animals with claws.		
paw	*See pa.*		
pawl	*See pal.*		
payed	*See paid.*		
pea	Vegetable.		
pee	Urine.		

peccadillo	A minor or slight sin or offense; trifling fault.	**pedicel**	A slender basal part of an organism or one of its parts.
Piccadilly (Circus)	A traffic circle and open square in W London; theater district.	**pedicle**	The part of a skin or tissue graft left attached to the original site during the preliminary stages of union.
piccalilli	A relish.		
pecks	Dry measures (four pecks make a bushel); hasty kisses.	**pedocal**	A soil that includes a definite hard layer of accumulated carbonates.
pecs	(informal) Pectoral muscles.		
pectase	An enzyme found in various fruits.	**pediment**	*See impediment.*
pectate	A salt or ester of pectic acid.	**pee**	*See pea.*
		peek	*See peak.*
		peeked	*See peaked.*
pecten	(Zool.) A comblike part or process.	**peel**	*See peal.*
pectin	A gelatinous substance found in ripe fruits, etc., causing jams and jellies to set.	**peen**	*See paean.*
		peeps	Cheeps, as of baby chicks.
peculate	To embezzle.	**Pepys**	(Samuel) His famous Diary was kept in shorthand. (Pronounced peeps.)
speculate	To meditate on or ponder; to assume a business risk in hope of gain.		
pedal	To operate a foot lever; to ride a bicycle.	**peer**	One that is of equal standing with another.
peddle	To sell or offer to sell from place to place.	**pier**	A supporting structure, as for adjacent ends of two bridge spans.
petal	Portion of a flower.		
		peke	*See peak.*
pedant	One who parades his learning.	**pellet**	*See palate.*
		pellucid	*See lucid.*
pendant	(also **pendent**) A hanging ornament.	**peltry**	*See paltry.*
pendent	(adj.) Supported from above; suspended. (*Also see penchant/pennant.*)	**pen**	Instrument for writing; enclosure for animals; (slang) penitentiary.
		pin	Short thin piece of metal used as a fastener. (Etc.)
pediatrist	Specialist in children's diseases.	**penal**	Pert. to punishment.
podiatrist	Specialist in foot problems.	**penile**	(also **penial**) Rel. to or affecting the penis.

penance	An act performed as an expression of penitence.	**peon**	*See paean.*
pennants	Flags or banners.	**Pepys**	*See peeps.*
penchant	A strong inclination, taste, or liking for something.	**per** **purr**	By means of; through. A low vibratory murmur typical of a contented cat.
pennant	A long tapering flag.		
pennate	Winged; feathered.	**perceive**	*See apperceive.*
pinnate	Resembling a feather.	**perception**	*See apperception.*
pencil	A writing instrument.	**peremptory**	Admitting of no contradiction. [Peremptory challenge.]
pensile	Suspended.		
pend	To remain undecided or unsettled; to hang.	**preemptory**	Pert. to prior rights.
penned	Wrote as with a pen; confined in a pen.	**perfect**	Flawless.
		prefect	Chief officer or magistrate.
pinned	Fastened or attached as with pins.	**perform**	To carry out; execute.
pendant	*See pedant.*	**preform**	To form or decide beforehand.
pendent	*See pedant.*		
penicillin	An antibotic.	**perfuse**	To overspread with moisture or color; to suffuse.
penicillium	Any fungus of the genus Penicillium.		
		profuse	Pouring forth liberally; lavish.
penitence	A feeling of remorse for wrongdoing.	**perigon**	*See paragon.*
penitents	Persons who show remorse for wrongdoing.	**perimeter**	*See parameter.*
		perineal	Pert. to the perineum (defined below).
pennant	*See pedant and penchant.*	**perineurial**	Pert. to a perineurium.
pinnate	*See penchant.*	**peritoneal**	Pert. to the peritoneum.
penned	*See pend.*	**peroneal**	Pert. to or situated near the fibula.
pensile	*See pencil.*	**pineal**	A small body (gland) in the brain.
pension	A periodic payment made by the government or former employer to a person who is retired, disabled, or widowed.	**perineum**	The part of the body between the anus and the scrotum or vulva.
pension	(also **pensione**) A boardinghouse in Europe (pronounced pen-SYHON).	**perineurium**	Connective-tissue sheath surrounding a bundle of nerve fibers.
		peritoneum	Abdominal wall membrane.

periodic	*See aperiodic.*
perish	*See parish.*
pernickety	Persnickety.
persnickety	Fussy about small details.
peroration	A lengthy speech—or the last part of one.
proration	A proportional distribution.
perpetrate	To bring about; to commit.
perpetuate	To cause to last indefinitely.
perquisite	Privilege given in addition to wages.
prerequisite	Condition precedent.
perry	*See parry.*
perse	A deep shade of blue or purple.
purrs	Contented-cat sounds.
purse	Handbag; sum of money as a prize or prizes.
persecute	To harass.
prosecute	To institute and carry on legal proceedings.
persecution	Harassment.
prosecution	Legal proceedings brought against a person, etc., for a crime; the person or persons prosecuting another for a crime.
person	*See parson.*
personal	Rel. to a person; private.
personnel	Makeup of an office force, etc.

personality	The complex of characteristics that distinguishes an individual.
personalty	Personal property.
personate	*See impersonate.*
perspective	Outlook, vista, view.
prospective	Likely to happen; expected.
perspicacious	Of acute mental vision or discernment.
perspicuous	Clearly expressed or presented; lucid.
perspicacity	Acute mental vision or discernment.
perspicuity	Clearness or lucidity; clarity.
persuasive	Able or trying to persuade.
pervasive	Diffused through every part of.
persuasion	The act of persuading or seeking to do so; belief. [We are of different persuasions.]
suasion	The act of advising, urging, or attempting to persuade; persuasion.
pertain	*See appertain.*
pertinence	*See appurtenance.*
pertinent	*See appurtenant.*
petal	*See pedal.*
petit	Small—chiefly used in legal compounds (pronounced pet-tit or petty).
petite	Small, dainty.
petty	Insignificant.
petition	*See partition.*
petrel	*See patrol.*

petrol	*See patrol.*
pervade	To become spread throughout all parts of.
purveyed	Provided, furnished, supplied.
pervasive	*See persuasive.*
pervious	*See impervious.*
petty	*See petit.*
phalanges	*See flanges.*
Pharaoh	*See faro.*
pharyngeal	*See laryngeal.*
pharyngitis	*See laryngitis.*
pharynx	*See larynx.*
phase	*See fays.*
pheasant	*See peasant.*
phenol	A caustic compound used in disinfectants, etc.
phenyl	A univalent radical.
phial	*See faille and vial.*
Philip	*See fillip.*
Philippine	*See Filipino.*
philology	Scientific study of languages.
philosophy	Pursuit of wisdom.
philter	*See filter.*
phiz	*See fizz.*
phlegm	A thick mucus in the throat and bronchial passages.
phloem	The soft tissue of plant stems.
phlox	*See flocks.*

phosphate	A salt or ester of a phosphoric acid.
phosphene	A luminous impression due to excitation of the retina.
phosphide	A binary compound of phosphorus usu. with a basic element or group.
phosphine	A colorless poisonous flammable gas.
phosphite	A salt of phosphorous acid.
phosphorous	(adj.) Of or containing phosphorus.
phosphorus	(n.) A chemical element.
photogen	A light oil obtained by the distillation of bituminous shale, etc.
photogene	Retinal afterimage.
photogenic	Forming an attractive subject for photography.
phytogenic	Of plant origin.
photography	The taking of photographs.
phytography	The branch of botany dealing with the description of plants.
phrase	*See frays.*
phyle	*See faille.*
phylon	A group that has genetic relationship, as a race.
phylum	(pl. *phyla*) A division of the animal kingdom; a group of languages somewhat remotely related.
physiatrist	One specializing in physical medicine.
psychiatrist	One specializing in treatment of mental disorders.

physiatry	Physical medicine.		**pickaback**	Piggyback.
psychiatry	Branch of medicine concerned with mental disorders.		**piggyback**	On the back or shoulders or on the top of a larger object.

physic	A medicine, esp. a purgative.
physics	The science that deals with matter, energy, motion, and force.
physique	Bodily makeup.
psychic	Of or rel. to the soul, spirit, or mind.

physical	*See fiscal.*

physical therapy	Physiotherapy.
physiotherapy	Treatment of disease, injury, etc., by massage, exercise, heat, etc.

phytogenic	*See photogenic.*
phytography	*See photography.*

pi	Mathematical ratio; term used in printing.
pie	Type of dessert; a total or whole that can be divided. [Pie chart.]

piazza	An open square or public place in a city or town, esp. in Italy; a large porch on a house, veranda.
pizza	An Italian open pie.
plaza	A public square or open place in a city or town. [Shopping plaza.]

pic	*See peak.*

picaresque	Of or rel. to rogues or rascals.
picturesque	Visually charming or quaint; strikingly graphic.

Piccadilly	*See pecadillo.*
piccalilli	*See pecadillo.*

pics	(also **pix**) Movies (slang).
picks	Choices; heavy tools (pickaxes); pieces of metal, bone or ivory used to pluck the strings of musical instruments.

picture	A portrait, etc.
pitcher	Jug for holding liquids.

Pidgeon	Surname. [Walter Pidgeon.]
pidgin	Simplified speech. [Pidgin English.]
pigeon	A bird; one easily duped.

pie	*See pi.*
piece	*See peace.*
pier	*See peer.*

piety	Reverence for God; the state of being devoutly religious.
pity	Compassion.

pigeon	*See Pidgeon.*
pigment	*See figment.*

pilaster	(Arch.) An ornamental rectangular column.
plaster	A mixture of lime, sand, and water, etc., used for coating walls and ceilings; a medicated or protective dressing. [Plaster of Paris.]

pillar	A vertical structure used as a support or ornament; a person regarded as the chief supporter of something.	**place**	Physical environment. (Etc.)
		plaice	A fish.
		plays	Actions during a game; stage presentations.
pillow	A cushion used (esp. in bed) for supporting the head.	**placeable**	*See placable.*
		placket	*See packet.*
pin	*See pen.*	**plage**	The beach at a seaside resort; a bright region on the sun often associated with a sunspot (pronounced plazh).
pincher	One that pinches.		
pinscher	Breed of dogs (Doberman pinscher, affenpinscher, etc.)		
		plague	An epidemic disease that causes high mortality; any cause of trouble or vexation.
pineal	*See perineal.*		
piñion	*See opinion.*		
pinnate	*See penchant.*		
pinned	*See pend.*	**plain**	An extensive area of level or rolling treeless country.
piñon	*See opinion.*		
pique	*See peak.*		
piqué	*See peak.*	**plane**	A flat or level surface; a tool; an airplane.
piqued	*See peaked.*		
pistil	Ovule-bearing organ of a seed plant.	**plein (air)**	(F., open air) Of or rel. to painting in outdoor daylight.
pistol	A short firearm.		
pitcher	*See picture.*	**plaintiff**	One who commences legal action.
piteous	Evoking or deserving pity.	**plaintive**	Melancholy; mournful.
pitiable	Evoking or deserving pity; lamentable.	**plait**	A braid, spec. a pigtail.
		plat	Chart of a piece of land.
pitiful	Deserving or arousing pity or commiseration.	**plate**	A dish; a smooth flat thin piece of material.
		pleat	A fold in cloth made by doubling material over on itself.
pity	*See piety.*		
pizza	*See piazza.*		
placable	Capable of being placated, pacified, or appeased.	**planar**	Of or pert. to a geometric plane; flat or level.
placeable	Capable of being placed.	**planner**	A person who plans.
		plane	*See plain.*
placate	To appease or pacify.		
plicate	(adj.) Folded, like a fan.		

plantar	Of or pert. to the sole of the foot.	**podium**	*See lectern.*
planter	A person who plants or cultivates; an implement or machine for planting seeds in the ground; plantation owner or manager; a container for ornamental plants.	**poem** **pome**	A composition in verse. A fruit having a fleshy covering around the seed capsule (apple, e.g.)
plastic	A synthetic resinous substance that can be given any permanent shape.	**pogrom** **program**	An organized massacre, esp. of Jews. Plan of intended procedure.
plastique	1. A puttylike substance that contains an explosive charge (used by terrorists and in guerrilla warfare) 2. A ballet technique.	**point** **pointe**	A sharp tapering end. (Etc.) (Ballet, F., pronounced pwant) The tip of the toe; a position on the extreme tips of the toes.
plat **plate** **plaza**	*See plait.* *See plait.* *See piazza.*	**pol** **Polack**	*See pal.* (slang, disparaging and offensive) A Pole or person of Polish descent.
pleas **please**	Entreaties; petitions. To give pleasure.	**pollack**	A food fish, Pollachius pollachius, of the cod family.
pleat **plein (air)**	*See plait.* *See plain.*	**pollock**	A food fish, Pollachius virens, of the cod family.
pleural **plural**	Rel. to the pleura (a membrane that envelops the lungs). More than one.	**polar**	Of or pert. to the North or South Pole, etc.; central, pivotal.
plicate	*See placate.*	**poler**	A person who propels a boat, raft, etc. with a pole.
plum **plumb**	A fruit. (adv.) Straight down or up; perpendicular. [Plumb bob.] (adj., informal) Completely or absolutely. [She was plumb mad.]	**poller** **pole**	One who conducts a poll. A rod; each of the extremities of the axis of the earth.
plume **plural** **podiatrist**	*See flume.* *See pleural.* *See pediatrist.*	**Pole** **poll**	Native of Poland. Casting or recording of votes; a sampling or collection of opinions.

politic	(adj.) Shrewd or prudent in practical matters; diplomatic.	**pomace**	The pulpy residue from apples, etc., from which liquid has been pressed or extracted.
politick	(v.) To engage in political discussion or activity.	**pumice**	A volcanic glass used esp. in powder form for smoothing and polishing. [Pumice stone.]
politics	The science and art of governing a country; maneuvering for power, etc., within a group.		
		pome	*See poem.*
political	*See apolitical.*	**pommel**	The protuberance at the front and top of a saddle.
poll	*See pole.*		
pollack	*See Polack.*	**pummel**	To pound, beat.
poller	*See polar.*		
pollock	*See Polack.*	**pompom**	1. Antiaircraft cannon. 2. Ornamental tuft of wool, feathers, etc. [Pompom girl: female cheerleader.]
polyamide	A polymer in which the monomer units are linked together by the amide group.		
polyamine	A compound containing more than one amino group.	**pompon**	Globe-shaped flower head; ornament on a shako (military cap in form of a cylinder or cone).
polyarteritis	Inflammation of the layers of an artery or of many arteries.	**poof**	(interjec.) Used to express or indicate a sudden disappearance.
polyarthritis	Arthritis occurring in more than one joint.	**pouf**	A high hairdress, with the hair worn in puffs.
polygamy	The state or practice of having more than one spouse, esp. a wife, at the same time.	**poor**	Indigent. (Etc.)
		pore	To study with steady attention or application; to gaze earnestly or steadily.
polygyny	The condition or practice of having more than one wife or female mate at the same time.	**pour**	To cause to flow in a stream. [While poring over the new *JCR*, he absentmindedly poured too much syrup on his waffles.]
polyp	A growth, esp. on mucous membranes.		
pulp	Soft juicy animal or vegetable tissue.	**poplar**	Kind of tree.
		popular	Widely liked.

populace	The common people.	**potassium**	A white crystalline
populist	A supporter or	**bromate**	powder used chiefly as
	adherent of populism.		an oxidizing agent and
	(Cap.:) A member of		as an analytical reagent.
	the People's party.	**potassium**	A white crystalline
populous	Densely populated.	**bromide**	powder used chiefly in
			the manufacturing of
pore	*See poor.*		photographic papers
			and plates, in
portable	Capable of being		engraving, and in
	transported or		medicine as a sedative.
	conveyed.		
potable	Fit or suitable for	**potent**	*See portend.*
	drinking.	**pother**	*See bother.*
		potion	*See portion.*
portend	To indicate in advance;		
	to foreshadow.	**potter**	(chiefly Brit.) To move
portent	An omen.		aimlessly or idly.
potent	Powerful; strong.	**putter**	One putters in the U.S.,
pretend	Assume; display a false		potters in the U.K.
	appearance of.		
		pouf	*See poof.*
portion	A share of something;	**poultry**	*See paltry.*
	part.	**pour**	*See poor.*
potion	A drink; a dose. [Love		
	potion.]	**practicable**	Practical, but with
			emphasis on actual
poser	A person who poses; a		established usefulness.
	puzzling or confusing	**practical**	Of, rel. to, or
	problem.		manifested in practice
poseur	(F.) A person who		or action; not
	poses for effect or		theoretical or ideal.
	behaves affectedly.		
		practice	Habitual or customary
posit	*See deposit.*		performance; operation.
possible	*See passable.*	**praxis**	Practice, as
possibly	*See passably.*		distinguished from
postiche	*See pastiche.*		theory; application or
potable	*See portable.*		use, as of knowledge or
			skills.
		praecipe	(Law) A writ
			commanding a
			defendant to do
			something
			(pronounced pres-i-pe
			or pree-si-pe).
		recipe	A set of instructions for
			making something.

praise	An expression of approval.	**preceding**	Going before in time or place.
prays	Entreats; offers thanks, etc., to God.	**proceeding**	Legal action (often used in plural); transaction.
preys	(usu. with *upon*) Seizes and devours; commits violence.	**precious**	Very valuable or costly; dear, beloved; excessively refined.
praxis	*See practice.*	**precocious**	(of a child) Having developed certain abilities earlier than is usual.
precatory	Of, pert. to, characterized by, or expressing entreaty or supplication.		
predatory	1. (of animals) Preying upon others. 2. Plundering or exploiting others.	**precipitant**	(Chem., n.) Anything that causes precipitation (rainfall, etc.)
		precipitin	(Immun.) An antibody.
precede	To be, go, or come ahead; to surpass in rank or importance.	**precipitate**	Headlong.
		precipitous	Steep.
proceed	To continue; to go in an orderly way; to advance.	**précis**	(F., pronounced pray-SEE) A concise summary.
precedence	The fact of preceding in time; priority. (Sometimes pronounced with a long *e* in the second syl.)	**precise**	Definitely or strictly stated; exact.
		predatory	*See precatory.*
precedents	(Law) Adjudged cases or decisions considered as authority for later or similar cases.	**predominant**	(adj.) Superior; authoritative; in control.
		predominate	To be superior; to be greater in number or intensity.
precedent	(Law) Previous decision taken as an example to be followed.	**predominantly**	Preeminently; preponderantly.
president	Presiding officer.	**predominately**	Numerically superior; predominantly.
precedential	Of the nature of or constituting a precedent.	**preemptory**	*See peremptory.*
		prefect	*See perfect.*
presidential	Of or pert. to a president or presidency.	**preform**	*See perform.*

premier	(n.) The head of the cabinet in France, Italy, etc. (adj.) First in rank, chief; first in time.
premiere	(n.) A first public performance of a play, opera, film, etc.
premise	Something taken for granted.
premises	A tract of land with buildings thereon; a house or other building. [Note: We now sometimes hear the word *premise* as meaning just one apartment, one building in a development, etc.]
promise	A pledge.
premonition	Forewarning; presentiment.
premunition	(Immun.) Relative immunity to severe infection as a result of inducing an active low-grade infection.
preposition	A word used with a noun or pronoun to show place or position, etc.
proposition	Proposal; scheme proposed.
prerequisite	*See perquisite.*
prescribe	To lay down as a guide, direction, or rule of action; to order the use of as a remedy.
proscribe	To condemn or forbid as harmful; prohibit. [Note that these two words have almost exactly opposite meanings.]

prescription	A doctor's written instruction for medicine, etc.
proscription	Something forbidden or rejected.
presence	The fact or condition of being present.
presents	(n.) Gifts; present writings. [Know all men by these presents.]
presentiment	Foreboding; premonition.
presentment	(Law) The written statement of a grand jury of their own knowledge, when no indictment has been laid before them.
president	*See precedent.*
presidential	*See precedential.*
prestigious	Having or bringing prestige.
prodigious	Extraordinary in size, amount, extent, degree, force, etc.
pretest	A preliminary test.
pretext	An excuse; an action that cloaks the real intention or state of affairs.
pretend	*See portend.*
preventative	Preventive (used by people who like extra syllables).
preventive	Serving to prevent or hinder.
preview	Advance showing.
purview	Scope, intention, or range, esp. of a law.
preys	*See praise.*

price	To fix or determine the price of.	**prince**	Male member of a royal family.
pries	Makes a nosy or inquisitive inquiry; moves or pulls apart with a pry or lever.	**prints**	Printed lettering; copies. (Etc.)
prize	To esteem; to press, force, or move with a lever; to pry. [He prized (or pried) off the lid.]	**princes**	A king's sons.
		princess	A king's daughter.
		principal	(n.) A chief or head; chief actor or doer.
prier	One who pries; curious or inquisitive person.	**principle**	A rule or code of conduct.
prior	(n.) An officer in a monastery. (adj.) Preceding in time or order.	**prints**	*See prince.*
		prior	*See prier.*
primate	A top-ranking bishop or archbishop.	**prism**	A transparent body used to deviate or disperse a beam of light.
primate	Any of an advanced order of mammals, incl. man and apes.	**prison**	Jail.
[Note: These words are homonyms; spelled and pronounced the same but of different meanings.]		**prize**	*See price.*
		proactive	Serving to prepare for, intervene in, or control a situation.
primer	(long *i*) A substance used to prepare a surface for painting; a detonator for explosives.	**reactive**	Readily responsive to a stimulus.
		proceed	*See precede.*
		proceeding	*See preceding.*
primer	(short *i*) An elementary schoolbook for children; any book of elementary principles.	**prodigious**	*See prestigious.*
		prodigy	A person with exceptional abilities, esp. a child.
primmer	More prim.	**progeny**	Offspring; descendants.
primogenitor	A first parent or early ancestor.	**profit**	Gain.
primogeniture	The state or fact of being the firstborn of children of the same parents; the system of inheritance by the firstborn.	**prophet**	One who predicts the future.
		profuse	*See perfuse.*
		progeny	*See prodigy.*
		program	*See pogrom.*
		promise	*See premise.*

prone	1. Lying face downward. 2. Likely to do or suffer something.	**protean**	Readily assuming different shapes or roles; variable; diversified.
supine	Lying face upward.	**protein**	A nitrogenous organic compound.
prophecy	A prediction.	**proton**	An atomic particle.
prophesy	To predict; foretell.		

prophet	*See profit.*
propose	To suggest; to set forth.
purpose	To intend; to propose as an aim for oneself. [A good verb not much used now: I purpose going to town.]
proposition	*See preposition.*
pro rata	In proportion; according to a certain rate.
prorate	To allocate or distribute pro rata.
proration	*See peroration.*
pros	Professionals; the affirmative side. [Pros and cons.]
prose	The ordinary language of speaking and writing, esp. as contrasted to poetry.
proscribe	*See prescribe.*
proscription	*See prescription.*
prosecute	*See persecute.*
prosecution	*See persecution.*
prospective	*See perspective.*
prostate	A gland that surrounds the male urethra at the neck of the bladder.
prostrate	Stretched out with face down; prone.

protégé	Someone who is being helped by a person taking an interest in his welfare or career.
protégée	A female protégé.
proud	Having or showing pride.
prowed	(adj.) Pert. to the forepart of a ship or boat.
provenance	A place or source of origin.
providence	Care or preparation in advance. (Cap.:) God.
proximal	*See paroxysmal.*
proximate	*See approximate.*
Psalter	The Book of Psalms.
salter	A person who makes or sells salt.
psi	Letter of the Greek alphabet; parapsychological factors or faculties collectively.
sigh	A long deep breath given out audibly.
psoriasis	A chronic inflammatory skin disease.
psorosis	A disease of citrus trees.
psychic	*See physic.*
psychiatrist	*See physiatrist.*
psychiatry	*See physiatry.*
psychology	*See cytology.*

psychosis	A mental disorder.
sycosis	Inflammation of hair follicles, esp. the beard.
pubes	(pl. *pubes*) The lower part of the abdomen; the hair appearing in the pubic region at puberty.
pubis	(pl. *pubes*) The forward portion of either of the hipbones.
pubic	Of or in the region of the lower part of the abdomen.
public	Of or known to people in general, not private.
pulp	See *polyp.*
pumice	See *pomace.*
pummel	See *pommel.*
pundit	See *pandit.*
punitive	Inflicting or intending to inflict punishment.
putative	Reputed, supposed.
pupal	Pert. to pupa, an insect in the nonfeeding stage.
pupil	1. Student. 2. An opening in the center of the iris of the eye, through which light passes to the retina.
purl	See *pearl.*
purpose	See *propose.*
purr	See *per.*
purrs	See *perse.*
purse	See *perse.*
purser	See *bursa.*
purveyed	See *pervade.*

purview	See *preview.*
pus	A viscous fluid formed in infected tissue. (The adj. form, *pussy*, rhymes with *fussy*.)
puss	Affectionate term for a cat. (Diminutive: *pussy*.)
put	To move a thing to a specified place.
putt	To strike (a golf ball) lightly to make it roll along the ground.
putative	See *punitive.*
putter	See *potter.*
pyel	Trough, basin, pelvis.
pyl	Door, orifice.
pyelometer	Pelvimeter; instrument for measuring capacity and diameters of pelvis.
pylometer	Instrument for measuring obstruction at ureteral opening of bladder.
pyelophlebitis	Inflammation of veins of renal pelvis (kidney).
pylephlebitis	Inflammation of the portal vein.
pyeloscopy	Fluroscopic examination of the pelvis of a kidney.
pyloroscopy	Examination of the pylorus.
pyre	See *fire.*

Q

quad	1. A type-metal space that is one en or more in width. 2. Short for *quadrangle, quadruplet,* etc.
quid	A lump of tobacco for chewing; (Brit., informal) a one-pound note.
quod	(Brit. slang) A prison.
qualify	To modify; to exhibit a required degree of ability to perform in some capacity.
quantify	To determine the quantity of.
qualitative	Of, rel. to, or involving quality or kind.
quantitative	Of, rel. to, or expressible in terms of quantity.
quark	One of three components of elementary particles assumed to exist as the basic units of all matter.
quirk	Peculiarity of action, behavior, or personality.
quarts	Units of measurement.
quartz	A kind of hard mineral occurring in various forms.
quirts	Riding whips.

quash	To put down or suppress; to make void or null.
squash	To crush; to squeeze.
quasi	Resembling; seeming; virtual.
queasy	Inclined to or feeling nausea.
quay	*See cay and key.*
quean	An impudent woman; hussy; prostitute.
queen	A female sovereign or monarch; wife or consort of a king; a woman who is foremost or preeminent in any respect; a male homosexual.
queasy	*See quasi.*
queue	*See clew.*
quid	*See quad.*
quiet	Tranquillity.
quit	To cease.
quite	Wholly; to a considerable extent; rather.
quince	A small tree of the rose family or its fruit.
quints	l. Organ stops. 2. Quintuplets.
quire	*See choir.*
quirk	*See quark.*
quirts	*See quarts.*
quod	*See quad.*
quoin	*See coin.*

R

rabat	1. A vestlike garment worn by a cleric. 2. A piece of unglazed and imperfectly fired pottery.
rabbet	A channel or groove.
rabbit	Small long-eared mammal.
rabid	1. Furious, fanatical. 2. Infected with rabies; mad.
rarebit	Fancy spelling for (Welsh) rabbit, a cheese dish (preferably pronounced rabbit).
rabble	A disorderly crowd; mob.
rubble	Waste or rough fragments of stone, brick, etc.
rabies	An infectious viral disease affecting dogs, etc.
scabies	A contagious skin disease of sheep, cattle, and humans.
race	To move at top speed. (Etc.)
raise	To elevate; to build.
rays	Beams of light, etc.
raze	To destroy to the ground.
racer	One that races.
raiser	One that raises.
razer	One that razes.
razor	Shaving instrument.

rack	(v.) To torture; distress acutely; torment. [To rack one's brains.]
rec	Short for *recreation* [rec room].
wrack	To utterly ruin; wreck.
wreck	To cast ashore; to reduce to a ruinous state.
racket	1. Loud noise or clamor. 2. An organized illegal activity. 3. A light bat used in certain games.
racquet	A game played with rackets and a ball by two or four persons on a four-walled court.
rocket	A firework; a structure that flies by expelling gases produced by combustion.
racketeer	A person who engages in a racket (No. 2 above).
raconteur	A person skilled in telling anecdotes.
radiance	Warm, cheerful brightness.
radiants	Points or objects from which rays proceed.
radical	A person who holds extreme principles; extremist.
radicel	(Bot.) A minute root; rootlet.
radicle	(Bot.) The lower part of the axis of an embryo; the primary root.
radish	A vegetable.
reddish	Somewhat red.

radium	A radioactive metallic element.	**ranch**	An establishment or farm for breeding cattle or other animals.
radon	A gaseous radioactive inert element.	**raunch**	Smuttiness or vulgarity; crudeness, obscenity. (Back formation from *raunchy*.)
rhodium	A hard white metallic element of the platinum group.		
raid	A sudden assault or attack.	**wrench**	A violent or twisting pull; an adjustable tool for gripping and turning nuts and bolts, etc.
rayed	Emitted rays.		
rail	A bar of wood or metal for a support, etc.	**rancor**	Bitter ill will; enmity.
rale	(pronounced rahl) An abnormal sound that accompanies the normal respiratory sounds.	**ranker**	More luxuriant in growth; more offensive or shocking.
		ransom	*See ramson.*
rain	To fall as water; to pour down.	**rap**	A sharp blow or knock.
reign	To rule.	**wrap**	Outer garment or other covering.
rein	To check or stop.		
raise	*See race.*	**rapped**	Tapped or knocked.
raiser	*See racer.*	**rapt**	Enraptured; absorbed.
rale	*See rail.*	**wrapped**	Enveloped.
ramark	A radar beacon serving as a marine navigational aid.	**rappel**	To descend from a steep height by means of a rope.
remark	A casual comment.	**repel**	To drive or force back; to refuse to have to do with.
remarque	(Fine Arts) A mark made in the margin of an engraved plate.		
ramose	Having many branches; branching.	**rapper**	A person or thing that raps or knocks.
ramous	Resembling or pert. to branches.	**wrapper**	A cover of paper, etc., wrapped around something; a loose dressing gown.
ramson	A garlic.		
ransom	The redemption of a prisoner, kidnapped person, et al.; the money paid.		

rapport	(pronounced ra-POHR) A harmonious and understanding relationship between people.	**ray** **re**	A beam of light, etc. (pronounced ray) With regard to. [In re.]
report	A spoken or written account of something, etc.	**rayed** **rays** **raze** **razer** **razor**	*See raid.* *See race.* *See race.* *See racer.* *See racer.*
rapt	*See rapped.*		
raptor **rapture**	Bird of prey. Spiritual or emotional ecstasy.	**reabsorption** **resorption**	Resorption. Absorbing again.
rupture	A breach; a breaking apart.	**reactive**	*See proactive.*
rarebit	*See rabat.*	**read**	To look at so as to take in the meaning of.
raster	(Television) A pattern of scanning lines. (Computers) A set of horizontal lines forming an image on a CRT. (Also consider *arrastre*, a Mexican mining term, often pronounced raster.)	**reed** **read** **red** **redd**	A tall grass. Past tense of verb *to read* (pronounced red). A color. To put in order; tidy. [We must redd the room for company.]
roster	A list showing people's turns of duty, etc.	**readmission** **remission**	A second or later admission, as to a hospital. Reduction of the force or intensity of something. (*Also see emission.*)
rational **rationale**	Having reason or understanding. Underlying reason; basis.	**reagent**	Substance used to produce a chemical reaction.
raucous **ruckus**	Disagreeably harsh, strident. A noisy commotion; fracas.	**reagin**	(Immun.) An antibody found in syphilis and in certain human allergies.
rumpus	A noisy or violent disturbance; uproar.	**regent**	One who rules or reigns.
raunch	*See ranch.*	**real** **reel**	Actual; genuine. A revolving device on which something flexible is wound.
ravage	To wreak havoc on; to devastate.		
ravish	To seize and take away by violence; rape; plunder.		

realign	To align again or regroup.
reline	To line again.
reality	The quality or state of being real.
realty	Real property.
rebate	To return part of a payment.
rebait	To bait again (as a trap or a fishhook.)
rebound	To spring back; to recoil.
redound	To have an effect or consequence; to accrue.
rec	*See rack.*
recant	To withdraw or disavow; retract.
recount	To relate or narrate.
re-count	To count again.
recede	To withdraw or ebb.
reseed	To seed again.
receipt	An acknowledgment.
reseat	To seat again.
recession	The act of receding or withdrawing; a period of economic retraction.
recision	An act of canceling or voiding.
resection	Surgical removal of tissue, etc.
rescission	The act of abrogating, annulling, repealing.
recipe	*See praecipe.*
reck	To reckon. *(Also see rack.)*
wreck	To ruin or damage.

reclaim	To take action so as to recover possession of; to make (flooded or wasteland) usable.
re-claim	To claim or demand the return or restoration of.
réclame	(F., pronounced ray-KLAHM) Publicity; self-advertisement; notoriety.
recognition	*See cognition.*
recognizance	A bond or obligation of record binding a person to do a particular action.
reconnaisance	A preliminary survey to gain information (esp. military).
recognizer	One who recognizes.
recognizor	(Law; accent on last syl.) One obligated under a recognizance (a bond or obligation of record).
recoil	To draw back, start, or shrink back in horror.
re-coil	To coil again.
recollect	To remember.
re-collect	To collect again.
reconnaisance	*See recognizance.*
recount	*See recant.*
re-count	*See recant.*
recover	To regain possession or use or control of.
re-cover	To cover again.
recreate	To refresh by means of relaxation and enjoyment.
re-create	To create anew.

recreation	Refreshment of strength and spirits after work.
re-creation	Creating over again.
recur	To happen again.
reoccur	To recur.
recurrence	Something that has happened again.
reoccurrence	Recurrence.
recuse	*See accuse.*
red/redd	*See read.*
reddish	*See radish.*
redound	*See rebound.*
reed	*See read.*
reef	1. A ridge of rock or coral or sand at or near the surface of the water. 2. (Naut.) A part of a sail rolled and tied down to reduce the area exposed to the wind.
wreath	A band of flowers, etc.
reek	To smell strongly and unpleasantly.
wreak	To inflict. [Wreak havoc.]
reel	*See real.*
reevaluate	To evaluate again; revaluate.
revaluate	To revalue.
reference	The act of referring; something regarded as an authority.
referents	(accent also on first syl.) Objects or events to which a term or symbol refers. [These referents are....]

reflects	Throws back; considers.
reflex	An automatic and often inborn response.
reflux	A flowing back; ebb.
reform	To amend or improve by change.
re-form	To form again.
refraction	*See diffraction.*
refractor	Something that refracts (deflects light, e.g.)
refracture	To fracture again.
refurbish	To brighten or freshen up; renovate.
refurnish	To furnish anew.
refuse	To decline.
refuse	(n., accent on first syl.) Waste material.
regal	Fit for a king.
regale	To feed or entertain well.
regalia	Emblems of royalty; costumes, etc., of an order or person of rank.
regle	A groove or channel for guiding a sliding door.
regardless	*See* [ugh] *irregardless.*
regent	*See reagent.*
regime	Regular pattern; government.
regimen	A systematic plan.
regiment	A military unit; organized group.
register	A written record; roster. [Note: the *register of probate* in Mass. is a person.]
registrar	An official recorder or keeper of records; admitting officer at a hospital, university, etc.

regle	*See regal.*
regretfully **regrettably**	Sorrowfully. Unfortunately.
reign/rein	*See rain.*
relay **re-lay**	To pass along, as a message, by relays. Lay again (as linoleum).
release **re-lease**	To set free. To lease again.
relevance **reverence**	Pertinence. Honor; respect.
relevant **reverent**	Pertinent; germane. Deeply respectful.
relic **relict**	Something that survives from an earlier age. A remnant; survivor, esp. a widow.
relief **relieve** **relive**	Removal or easing of something painful or distressing. To ease or alleviate (pain, distress, anxiety, etc.) To experience over again.
reline	*See realign.*
rem **REM**	A unit of ionizing radiation in human tissue. Rapid eye movement.
remark **remarque**	*See ramark.* *See ramark.*
remission	*See emission and readmission.*

remitter	The relation back of a defective title to an earlier valid title.
remittor	A person or company that makes a remittance.
remittur	A sending back from an appellate or superior to a trial or inferior court of a case and its record for further proceedings.
remuneration	Payment for services rendered.
[renumeration]	No such word!
Renaissance	The revival of art and literature in the 14th-16th centuries; (lowercase) any similar revival.
renascence	Rebirth; renewal.
rend **rent**	To split or tear apart. 1. To lease. 2. Past tense of *rend*.
render	To cause to be or become; to represent; to melt down (e.g., render lard).
renter	One who leases.
renumeration **reoccur** **reoccurrence** **repel**	*See remuneration.* *See recur.* *See recurrence.* *See rappel.*
repertoire **repertory**	Stock of songs, etc., that a person or company is prepared to perform. Theatrical performances for short periods; repertoire.
report	*See rapport.*

reprieve	To delay impending punishment; to relieve temporarily from any evil.
retrieve	To recover or regain.
repulsive	Causing repugnance or aversion.
revulsive	(Med.) Tending to alter the distribution of blood by a diversion technique.
rescission	*See recession.*
reseat	*See receipt.*
resection	*See recession.*
reseed	*See recede.*
reserve	To keep back or save for further use.
re-serve	To serve again.
residence	Domicile; dwelling.
residents	Those who reside in a place.
resign	To give up or surrender.
re-sign	To sign again.
resin	A sticky substance used in making varnish, etc.
rosin	A kind of resin.
resorption	*See reabsorption.*
resort	To have recourse for use, help, or accomplishing something.
re-sort	To sort (papers, etc.) again.
resound	To echo or ring with sound.
re-sound	To sound again.

respectably	Decently.
respectfully	Showing respect or deference.
respectively	In the order given.
respite	*See despite.*
responsibly	Adv. form of *responsible.*
responsively	Adv. form of *responsive.* [He acts responsibly by answering responsively.]
rest	To respose. (Etc.)
wrest	To gain by force or violence.
restive	Stubbornly resisting control; balky.
restless	Uneasy; unquiet.
resume	To get or take or occupy again.
résumé	A summary; statement of one's job qualifications.
retch	To try to vomit.
wretch	A miserable and unhappy person; a vile person.
retinal	Pert. to the retina of the eye.
retinol	(Chem.) A yellowish oil obtained by the distillation of resin, used as a solvent and as an antiseptic.
retrieve	*See reprieve.*
revaluate	*See reevaluate.*

revanche	The policy of a state intent on regaining territory lost to other states as a result of war, etc.
revenge	Retaliation for injuries or wrong; vengeance. (*Also see avenge.*)
reverend	Worthy of reverence. (Cap., after *the*:) a member of the clergy.
reverent	Expressing reverence; worshipful. (*Also see relevant.*)
reveille	A signal to arise.
revel	(often *revels*) Boisterous merrymaking; revelry.
revelry	Boisterous festivity.
reverie	A daydream.
reverence	*See relevance.*
reverent	*See relevant and reverend.*
reversion	Reverting; the legal right to possess something when its present holder relinquishes it.
revision	The act or work of revising.
review	An inspection, esp. military; a survey; a critical examination.
revue	A theatrical production usu. consisting of short skits, dances, etc.
revise	To correct or improve.
revive	To return to consciousness or life.
revision	*See reversion.*
revocation	*See evocation.*
revoke	*See invoke.*
revue	*See review.*
revulsive	*See repulsive.*

rheum	A thin discharge of the mucous membranes.
room	Space; part of a building.
womb	Uterus.
rheumy	Having a watery discharge from the mucous membranes.
roomie	(also **roomy**) Roommate.
roomy	Spacious.
Rhodes	(scholarships) One of a number of scholarships at Oxford University established by Cecil Rhodes.
roads	Highways.
rhodium	*See radium.*
rhombus	A geometric figure.
rhonchus	A wheezing or snoring sound in the chest. (Also consider *bronchus*.)
rhyme	Poetry.
rime	Frost.
rhythmic	*See arrhythmic.*
ribald	(pronounced ribbled) Characterized by coarse indecent humor.
riddled	Permeated; pierced through with holes.
riband	A decorative ribbon.
ribband	A long narrow strip or bar used in shipbuilding.
ribbon	A narrow band of ornamental material used for decoration or tying.

rickrack	Narrow zigzag braid or ribbon used as a trimming on clothing.		**rile**	(Colloq.) To irritate or vex; to roil.
riffraff	The lowest classes; rabble.		**roil**	To make (water, etc.) turbid by stirring; to disturb, irritate, vex.
riprap	Broken stone for use in foundations, etc.		**royal**	Of or pert. to a king, queen, or other sovereign.
riddled	*See ribald.*		**rime**	*See rhyme.*
ridged	Formed into a ridge.			
rigid	Stiff; unyielding. *(Also see frigid.)*		**ring**	To sound (as a bell); to reverberate; to encircle.
			wring	To squeeze or twist, esp. so as to make dry.
rife	Occurring frequently; widespread.			
ripe	Ready to eat; ready, prepared to undergo something.		**ringer**	A person or thing that rings; a racehorse, athlete, etc., fraudulently substituted for another; (slang) a person's double. [Dead ringer.]
riffle	To turn (pages) hastily.			
rifle	1. To ransack and rob. 2. To cut spiral grooves in (a gun barrel).		**wringer**	A device with a pair of rollers for squeezing out water from wet clothes, etc. [They really put him through the wringer.]
riffraff	*See rickrack.*			
rigger	One that rigs; a type of ship.		**ripe**	*See rife.*
rigor	Severity; strictness; austerity.		**riprap**	*See rickrack.*
			rise	An upward slope, small hill; an increase.
right	Entitlement; privilege.		**ryes**	Types of grain; whiskeys.
rite	Ceremony.			
wright	A workman. (Now used mostly in compounds: millwright, playwright.)		**risible**	Causing laughter; laughable. (It rhymes with *visible*.)
write	To form characters on a surface as with a pen.		**visible**	Able to be seen or noticed.
rigid	*See ridged and frigid.*		**risky**	Dangerous.
rigor	*See rigger.*		**risqué**	Off-color.
rigorous	Harsh; severe; very strict.		**rite**	*See right.*
vigorous	Full of physical or mental strength.			

ritz	A pretentious display. (Cap.:) A hotel.	**role**	A character assigned or assumed; socially accepted behavior; part played by an actor. [Role model.]
writs	Legal instruments.		
road	Path; highway.		
rode	Past tense of *ride*.	**roll**	A written document; list of names. (Etc.) [Is your name on the secretary's roll?]
rowed	Propelled a small boat.		
roads	*See Rhodes.*		
roadster	An early open-body automobile.	**rondel**	A short poem.
roaster	A contrivance for roasting something.	**rondelle**	A small glass disk used as an ornament in a stained-glass window; a flat bead used in a necklace as a spacer.
robot	A humanlike machine that performs various functions; a machinelike human.		
		rood	1. Cross or crucifix. 2. A land measure.
rowboat	A small boat designed to be rowed.	**rude**	Unmannerly; crude; vulgar.
roc	A mythical bird.	**rued**	Regretted.
rock	A stone. (Etc.)	**rookery**	*See rockery.*
		room	*See rheum.*
rockery	Rock garden.		
rookery	A breeding place or colony of gregarious birds or animals. 2. A colony of rooks.	**roomer**	One who rents a room.
		rumor	Report; hearsay; gossip.
		roomie	*See rheumy.*
		roomy	*See rheumy.*
rocket	*See racket.*		
rode	*See road.*	**root**	The usu. underground part of a plant; origin; source.
roe	l. Small, agile Old World deer. 2. Fish eggs.	**rout**	A disastrous defeat.
		route	A traveled way; channel. (Prounced rout or root.)
row	To propel a boat with oars.		
row	(pronounced rau) An altercation.	**rosin**	*See resin.*
		roster	*See raster.*
roil	*See rile.*	**rot**	Decay.
		wrought	Worked. [She wrought her magic.]
		rote	A routine; repetition by memory.
		wrote	Past tense of *write*.

rotund	*See orotund.*		**ruff**	*See rough.*
rough	Coarse; harsh; uneven.		**rumble**	To make a deep heavy
ruff	(n.) A fringe or frill, as			continuous sound, like
	of feathers, around the			thunder.
	neck. (v.) To trump a		**rumple**	To wrinkle, tousle,
	trick at bridge.			muss up. (*Also see*
				crumble/crumple.)
rouse	*See arouse.*			
roust	*See arouse.*		**rumor**	*See roomer.*
rout	*See root.*		**rumpus**	*See raucous.*
route	*See root.*			
row	*See roe.*		**rung**	Form of the verb *to ring.*
rowboat	*See robot.*		**wrung**	Form of the verb *to*
rowed	*See road.*			*wring.*
rowel	*See dowel.*			
royal	*See roil.*		**rupture**	*See raptor.*
rubble	*See rabble.*		**ruse**	*See rues.*
ruckus	*See raucous.*		**rutty**	*See ruddy.*
ruddy	Of or having a fresh,		**rye**	A grain; whiskey.
	healthy red color.		**wry**	Bent or twisted. [Wry
rutty	Full of or abounding in			humor.]
	ruts, as a road.			
rude/rued	*See rood.*		**ryes**	*See rise.*
rues	Regrets.			
ruse	A trick, stratagem, or			
	artifice.			

S

saccharin	Sugar substitute.
saccharine	Intensely and unpleasantly sweet.
sachet	A small bag filled with a sweet-smelling substance.
sashay	(informal) To glide, move, or proceed easily or nonchalantly.
sacks	Bags; loose-fitting dresses.
sacs	Baglike parts in an animal or plant.
sax	Saxophone.
saddest	The most unhappy.
sadist	One who delights in cruelty.
sago	A starchy food, used in puddings, obtained from the pith of a palm tree.
sego	A plant of the lily family, with an edible root.
said	Past tense of *say*.
zed	(Brit.) The letter *Z*.
sail	An extent of canvas by which wind propels a ship.
sale	The act of selling.
sailer	A vessel propelled by a sail or sails.
sailor	Mariner; seaman.

sake	Cause, account, interest, or benefit.
sake	Japanese rice wine (pronounced SAH-ke).
salaam	A salutation or ceremonial greeting in the East.
salami	A kind of sausage.
shalom	Used as a Jewish greeting and farewell.
slalom	(Skiing) A downhill race over a zigzag course.
salary	*See celery.*
sale	*See sail.*
sallow	A sickly yellow color.
shallow	Not deep.
salon	An elegant apartment or living room; a stylish shop.
saloon	A tavern.
solon	A wise legislator.
salter	*See Psalter.*
salud	(interjec., Sp.; lit., health) Used as a toast: Salud! [Note to convention reporters: don't confuse with *salute*.]
salute	A gesture of respect, greeting, or polite recognition.
solute	A substance dissolved in another substance.
salvage	Rescue of a wrecked or damaged ship or its cargo; goods or property saved.
savage	Member of a primitive or uncivilized tribe.
selvage	(Also **selvedge**) An edge of cloth so woven that it does not unravel.

155

sanatorium	A hospital for the treatment of chronic diseases.	**Satan**	The devil.
		sateen	A lustrous cotton fabric in satin weave.
sanitarian	A specialist in public sanitation and health.	**satin**	A silky material glossy on one side only.
sanitarium	An institution for the preservation or recovery of health.	**satire**	The use of irony, sarcasm, ridicule, etc., in exposing or deriding folly.
sanatory	Favorable for health; curative.	**satyr**	(Class. Myth.) A woodland deity; a lecherous man.
sanitary	Free from dirt, bacteria, etc.		
sands	Loose granular rock material.	**saucy**	*See sassy.*
sans	(L.) Without.	**savage**	*See salvage.*
sane	Mentally sound.	**saver**	One who saves.
seine	A net for catching fish.	**Savior**	(also **Saviour**) Christ.
Seine	A river in France.	**savor**	The taste or smell of something.
sanitary	*See sanatory.*	**sawed**	Cut or divided with a saw.
sans	*See sands.*	**sod**	Surface of the ground; turf.
sapid	Having taste or flavor.		
vapid	Insipid, uninteresting.	**sawer**	One that saws.
sarcode	A protoplasm.	**sawyer**	A person who saws wood, esp. as an occupation. (Cap.:) Proper name.
sarcoid	A growth resembling a sarcoma (tumor).		
sari	A garment worn by Hindu women.	**sax**	*See sacks.*
sorry	Feeling grief or penitence.	**scabies**	*See rabies.*
sashay	*See sachet.*	**scallop**	1. A bivalve mollusk. 2. Any of a series of curved projections.
sassy	Impudent; saucy.	**scalp**	The skin of the head excluding the face.
saucy	Bold and impudent; flippant.		
sat	Past tense of *sit*.		
SAT	Scholarship Aptitude Test.		

scam	Confidence game or other fraudulent scheme.	**schema**	A diagram, plan, or scheme.
scan	To examine closely. (That's the original meaning; now more often used as its opposite: to glance at or skim through.)	**scheme**	A plan, design, or program of action to be followed; project.
		schematic	In the form of a diagram or chart.
scarf	A long narrow strip of material worn for warmth or ornament around the neck.	**schismatic**	Of or involving schism (a division into opposing groups because of difference in belief, etc.)
scarp	A line of cliffs formed by the faulting or fracturing of the earth's crust; an escarpment.	**schist**	*See cist.*
		schlemazel	(Yid.) An unlucky person.
scarlet	A bright red color.	**schlemiel**	(Yid.) A bungling person. [The schlemiel spills soup—on the schlemazel.]
starlet	A young actress who shows promise of becoming a star.		
starlit	Lighted by the stars.	**schlock**	(slang, from Yid.) Something of cheap or inferior quality; junk.
sterlet	A small sturgeon.	**shock**	A sudden violent blow; a sudden disturbance or commotion. (Etc.)
scat	1. (Jazz) A type of singing. 2. The excrement of animals. 3. Heroin (slang).		
skat	A card game.	**schmear**	(slang, from Yid.) A dab, as of cream cheese to spread on a bagel; a bribe; a number of related things, ideas, etc. [The whole schmear.]
scatological	*See eschatological.*		
scatology	*See eschatology.*		
scene	Subdivision of a play. (Etc.)	**smear**	A smudge or stain; a vilification.
seen	Form of verb *to see.*		
scents	*See cents.*	**schmooze**	(Yid) To chat idly; gossip.
		snooze	Doze; nap.
scepter	Staff carried by a king or queen as a symbol of sovereignty.	**schrank**	(Pa. Dutch furniture) A clothes cabinet.
specter	Ghost; phantom.	**shrank**	Past tense of *shrink.*

scion	A descendant.
sign	A signal. (Etc.)
sine	A trigonometric function of an angle.
syne	(Scotch) Since. ["Auld Lang Syne."]
scirrhous	(Pathol.) Of a hard, fibrous consistency; of or rel. to a scirrhus.
scirrhus	A type of cancer.
scleredema	Edematous hardening of the skin.
scleroderma	A disease in which connective tissue anywhere in the body becomes hardened and rigid.
scleroma	A tumorlike hardening of tissue.
sclerosis	A diseased condition in which soft tissue hardens or thickens.
scoliosis	An abnormal lateral curvature of the spine.
scooter	A child's toy vehicle with a footboard on wheels; a kind of lightweight motorcycle.
scoter	A large diving duck.
scotch	To hinder or thwart.
Scotch	Pertaining to Scotland; a whisky.
Scots	Natives of Scotland.
scow	A flat-bottomed boat.
scowl	A gloomy or threatening look.

scrabble	To scratch or scrape, as with claws or hands. (Cap.:) A word game.
scramble	To move as best one can over rough ground.
scrapple	Cornmeal mush loaf made with pork, etc.
scribble	To write hastily or carelessly.
screw	To fasten or tighten with a screw or screws. (Etc.)
skew	To turn aside or swerve; to give an oblique direction to. (Also see askew.)
scrimp	To be frugal or niggardly.
skimp	To give insufficient or barely sufficient attention or effort to or funds for.
scrip	Paper currency or token issued for temporary use.
script	Something written; manuscript; text of a play, motion picture, etc.
scrum	A Rugby play; confusion, racket, hubbub.
scum	Impurities that rise to the surface of a liquid; the most worthless part of the population.
scrunch	See crunch.
scull	An oar used at the stern of a boat; a racing shell.
skull	The framework of the head.

sculptor	Artist who produces a sculpture.	**secret**	Something hidden or unexplained.
sculpture	A 3-dimensional work of art.	**secrete**	To conceal; to form and release a substance, as a gland.
scum	*See scrum.*		
seal	*See ceil.*	**secretively**	Carried out with secrecy.
sealing	*See ceiling.*	**secretly**	Kept from knowledge or view.
seam	The joining of two pieces.		
seem	To appear (to be.)	**sector**	A geometric figure; a distinctive part (as of the economy).
seamen	Sailors.	**vector**	Something (such as velocity) that has both magnitude and direction; the carrier of a disease or infection. *(Also see vector/vecture.)*
semen	Sperm.		
seamy	Unpleasant, disagreeable; showing seams.		
steamy	Like steam; full of steam.		
		sects	Factions.
sear	*See cere.*	**sex**	Gender; sexual intercourse.
seas	*See cease.*		
season	A period of the year. (Etc.)	**Seder**	*See cedar.*
seizin	(also **seisin**) (Law) Legal possession of land, as a freehold estate.	**seduce**	To persuade by offering temptations.
		traduce	To misrepresent, to slander.
seasonable	Suitable for the season; timely.	**seed**	*See cede.*
seasonal	Of a season or seasons.	**seeded**	*See seated.*
		seeder	*See cedar.*
seated	Placed in a seat.	**seem**	*See seam.*
seeded	Planted with seeds. (Sports) Scheduled so that superior players will not meet in early rounds of a tournament. *(Also note ceded: yielded.)*	**seen**	*See scene.*
		seep	To ooze slowly out or through.
		steep	To soak or be soaked in liquid.
sebum	*See cecum.*	**seer**	*See cere.*
		sees	*See cease.*
		sego	*See sago.*

seigneur	A lord, esp. the feudal lord of a manor.	**seminal**	Pert. to, containing, or consisting of semen; highly individual and influencing the development of future events.
seignior	Seigneur.		
senhor	A Portuguese term of address equiv. to *Mr.* or *sir.*		
senior	A senior person; a student in his last year of high school or college.	**Seminole**	A member of certain Indian tribes. [The *New Yorker* ran as a "newsbreak" an item from a TV program: "...considered to be a Seminole film of the French New Wave"!]
señor	The title of a Spanish-speaking man, equiv. to *Mr.* or *sir.*		
signor	Term of address or title of respect for an Italian man.		
		senate	A legislative council. (Cap.:) Upper house of the legislatures of U.S., Canada, etc.
seine/Seine	*See sane.*		
seize	*See cease.*	**sennet**	1. A small barracuda. 2. A set of notes played on the trumpet to mark the entrance or exits of actors.
seizer	One that seizes. (*Also consider Caesar.*)		
seizure	Taking possession of an item, property, or person legally or by force; a sudden attack, as of disease.	**sennit**	A braided cord or fabric.
		senhor	*See seigneur.*
seizin	*See season.*	**senhora**	A Portuguese term of address equiv. to *Mrs.*
selective	*See elective.*		
sell	*See cel.*	**señora**	The title of a Spanish-speaking woman (*Mrs.* or *madam*).
seller	*See cellar.*		
selvage	*See salvage.*		
		signora	Term of address or title of respect for an Italian married woman.
semantic	Of or rel. to meaning in language.		
sematic	Warning of danger (e.g., labeling a bottle Poison).	**senior**	*See seigneur.*
		sennet	*See senate.*
		sennit	*See senate.*
		señor	*See seigneur.*
semen	*See seamen.*	**señora**	*See senhora.*
		sense	*See cents.*
		senser	*See censer.*
		sensor	*See censer.*
		senses	*See census.*

sensual	Physical, gratifying to the body.	**serge**	A durable twilled fabric.
sensuous	Affecting or appealing to the senses, esp. by beauty or delicacy.	**surge**	A swelling, rolling, or sweeping forward, like ocean waves.
sentence	1. A grammatical unit. 2. Punishment awarded by a law court to a person convicted in a criminal trial.	**serial**	*See cereal.*
		series	Things arranged one after another.
sentience	A feeling or sensation as distinguished from perception and thought.	**serious**	Sober; important; grave.
		serous	Of, rel. to, or resembling serum. *(Also see cereus and cirrous groups.)*
sentry	*See century.*		
separation	State of being set or kept apart.	**serif**	*See seraph.*
		serrate	*See ferrate.*
suppuration	Formation or discharge of pus.	**services**	*See cervices.*
		session	*See cession.*
		setaceous	*See cetaceous.*
septic	Infected with harmful microorganisms that cause pus to form. *(Also see asceptic.)*	**settler**	One that settles somewhere.
		settlor	One that makes a settlement or creates a trust.
skeptic	A person who doubts generally accepted ideas.		
		severally	Separately; singly.
sequence	The following of one thing after another.	**severalty**	(Law; of an estate, esp. land) The condition of being held or owned by separate and individual right.
sequins	Small shiny disks or spangles.		
seraph	A member of the highest order of angels.	**sew**	To unite or fasten by stitches.
serif	(Print.) A small line used to finish off a main stroke of a letter.	**so**	Thus. (Etc.)
		sow	(v.) To plant seed, esp. by scattering. (n.) Fully grown female pig or bear (pronounced sau).
sheriff	A law-enforcement officer.		
sere	*See cere.*	**sewage**	Refuse or waste matter carried by sewers.
serf	A member of a servile feudal class.	**sewerage**	Sewage; disposal of sewage by sewers.
surf	The swell of the sea that breaks on the shore.		

sewer	A conduit for waste matter.	**shatter**	To break at once into pieces.
suer	One that sues.	**shutter**	To provide a window, etc., with shutters; to close a store or business operations for the day or permanently. (*Also see shudder.*)
sewer	One that sews (fastens by stitches).		
sower	One that sows seed, etc. (*Also see soar/sore.*)		
sex	*See sects.*	**sheaf**	Ears of grain, etc., bound together; a collection of papers, etc., held or bound together.
sextain **sextan**	A stanza of six lines. (of a fever) Characterized by paroxysms that recur every sixth day.		
		sheath	An investing cover or case.
sextant	An instrument used in navigating and surveying.	**sheathe**	To put a sword, etc., into a sheath; to cover (a cable, etc.) with a metal sheath for grounding.
sexton	An official who takes care of a church and church property.		
		sheave	(n.) A pulley for hoisting or hauling. (v.) To gather, collect, or bind into a sheaf or sheaves.
sexual	*See asexual.*		
shake	To vibrate.		
sheikh	(also **sheik**) An arab chief. (*Also see chic.*)	**shiv**	(slang) A knife, esp. a switchblade.
shallow	*See sallow.*	**shear**	To cut (as hair or wool).
shalom	*See salaam.*	**sheer**	(v.) To deviate from a course; swerve. (adj.) Transparently thin.
sham	A hoax.		
shame	Disgrace; ignominy.		
shandy	(chiefly Brit.) A mixture of beer and lemonade.	**shepardize**	(Law; now not usually capitalized) Checking a case or statute in Shepard's citator to find all references to it in subsequent cases.
shanty	A shack. (*Also see chantey.*)		
		sherardize	(Metallurgy) To coat steel with a thin cladding of zinc.
shard	*See chard.*		
		sheriff	*See seraph.*
		sherry	*See chary.*

shimmy	An American ragtime dance; excessive wobbling in the front wheels of a motor vehicle.		**shudder**	A convulsive movement of the body, as from cold or fear. [I shudder to think....]
shinny	(n.) A simple variety of hockey. (v.) To play shinny; to climb by holding fast with the hands or arms and legs and drawing oneself up. [He shinnied up a tree.]		**shutter**	A usu. movable cover or screen for a window. *(Also see shatter.)*
			sic	(L.) So; thus. Used after a word or phrase to show it is intentionally written.
shiv	*See sheaf.*		**sic**	(v.; past tense *sicced* or *sicked*) To incite to chase or attack. [Sic 'em!]
shock	*See schlock.*		**sick**	Ill.
shoe	To provide with footwear.		**Sikh**	Member of a Hindu religious sect (pronounced seek).
shoo	To scare or drive away.			
shone	Form of the verb *to shine.*		**sics**	Incites to attack.
shown	Form of the verb *to show.*		**six**	Numeral.
			side	Lateral. (Etc.)
shoot	*See chute.*		**sighed**	Uttered a sigh.
shop	A retail store, esp. a small one.		**sigh**	*See psi.*
shoppe	A shop (used chiefly for quaint effect).		**sighs**	Long deep breaths given out audibly.
			size	Spatial dimensions, bulk, etc., of anything.
shortened	Curtailed.			
shorthand	(Adj.) Abbreviated. [Compare "shorthand version" and "shortened version."]		**sight**	*See cite.*
			sign	*See scion.*
			signet	*See cygnet.*
			signor	*See seigneur.*
shown	*See shone.*		**signora**	*See senhora.*
shows	*See chose.*		**Sikh**	*See sic.*
shrank	*See schrank.*			
			silence	Absence of sound.
shtick	(Yid.) A short comic routine, etc.		**silents**	Movies without spoken dialogue.
stich	A verse or line of poetry; the last trick in certain card games.		**silicon**	A nonmetallic element.
stick	A short piece of wood. (Etc.)		**silicone**	A polymeric silicon compound.

simple	Not compound or complex.	**sin tax**	A tax on cigarettes, liquor, other nonnecessities.
simplistic	Oversimplified. [Many people, trying to be fancy, use this somewhat insulting word when they simply mean *simple*.]	**syntax**	The way in which words are arranged to form phrases and sentences.
		sinuate	*See simulate.*
		sinuous	*See sinews.*
simulate	To copy, represent, or feign. (*Also see assimilate.*)	**Sioux**	American Indian tribes.
		sou	A former French coin.
sinuate	Having the margin wavy with strong indentations. [Sinuate leaves.]	**sough**	To make a sighing or moaning sound (pronounced sou or suff).
stimulate	To excite to activity or growth; arouse.	**sue**	To bring legal proceedings against. (Cap.:) Fem. name.
simulation	Imitation; counterfeit. (Psychiatry:) A conscious attempt to feign some medical or physical disorder to escape punishment.	**site**	*See cite.*
		sits	Is seated.
		sitz (bath)	A bathtub in which one sits immersed to the hips.
stimulation	Exciting to activity or growth.		
		six	*See sics.*
sine	*See scion.*	**size**	*See sighs.*
sinecure	*See cynosure.*	**skat**	*See scat.*
		skeptic	*See septic.*
		skew	*See askew and screw.*
sinews	Tendons.	**skimp**	*See scrimp.*
sinuous	Wavy; serpentine; intricate.		
		skulk	To lie or keep in hiding, as for some evil reason.
sink	To go to the bottom; submerge.	**sulk**	To remain silent or aloof because of resentment or bad temper.
sync	(also **synch**) To synchronize. [Something "out of sync" doesn't quite mesh.]		
		skull	*See scull.*
zinc	A metallic element.	**slack**	To shirk, to leave undone; to make less active [slack off].
		slake	To refresh; to allay thirst.

slalom	*See salaam.*	**slice**	A thin broad piece cut from something.
Slav	A member of any of the peoples of East and Central Europe who speak a Slavic language.	**sluice**	An artificial channel for conducting water in a stream, etc.
slave	A person who is the property of another.	**slick**	*See sleek.*
		slight	*See sleight.*
slay	To kill.	**slingshot**	Y-shaped stick with elastic, for shooting small missiles.
sleigh	A sled.		
sleave	To divide or separate into filaments, as silk.	**slungshot**	Weapon consisting of a strap or chain to which a stone or other weight is attached.
sleeve	The part of a garment that covers the arm.		
sleek	Smooth or glossy.	**slither**	To slide unsteadily.
slick	Smooth and glossy; sly, shrewdly adroit; slippery.	**sliver**	A small often sharp piece of wood or glass; splinter.
sleigh	*See slay.*	**sloe**	Fruit of the blackthorn. [Sloe gin fizz; sloe-eyed beauty.]
sleight	Stratagem; dexterity. [Sleight of hand.]	**slow**	Sluggish; dull.
slight	Slim; frail; meager.		
slew	(v.) Past tense of *slay.* (n.) A large amount. [A whole slew.]	**slog**	To hit hard, as in boxing; to walk or plod heavily.
slough	(pronounced sloo) A bog; swamp.	**slug**	To strike hard, esp. with the fist.
slough	(pronounced sluff) To dispose of or shed (often followed by off), as a snake's skin or dead tissue; to discard at cards.	**slough**	*See slew.*
		slow	*See sloe.*
		sludge	Thick greasy mud.
slue	To turn (a mast) around on its own axis; to swing around.	**smudge**	A dirty or blurred mark.
sluff	To discard at cards; slough.	**slue**	*See slew.*
		slug	*See slog.*
		sluff	*See slew.*
		sluice	*See slice.*
		slungshot	*See slingshot.*
		smear	*See schmear.*

smelled	Past tense of *smell*.	**sol**	1. The fifth note of a scale in music (long *o*). 2. A fluid colloidal solution (short *o*). 3. (Cap.) The sun (short *o*).
smelt	A small food fish.		
smolt	A young silvery salmon or sea trout.		
smirch	*See besmirch.*	**sole**	Undersurface of foot or footwear.
smooth	To make things more agreeable; to palliate.	**soul**	The spirit.
soothe	To calm.	**solecism**	A mistake in the use of language.
smudge	*See sludge.*	**solipsism**	A theory that the self is the only existent thing.
sniff	To draw air audibly through the nose; to show disdain or contempt.	**sophism**	Any false argument; fallacy.
snuff	To inhale noisily; to use or inhale snuff (powdered tobacco).	**soled**	Put soles on shoes.
		sold	Past tense of *sell*.
sniffle	To sniff repeatedly.	**solemn**	Grave, sober, or mirthless.
snivel	To whine.	**solum**	The upper part of the soil profile, which is influenced by plant roots (pronounced with a long *o*).
snooze	*See schmooze.*		
so	*See sew.*		
soar	To fly aloft or about; to rise to heights; to glide.	**solid**	Keeping its shape; firm, not liquid or gas.
sore	Painful. (*Also see sewer/ sower.*)	**stolid**	Not feeling or showing emotion.
soared	Rose in air.	**solipsism**	*See solecism.*
sword	A weapon with a long blade.	**solitaire**	1. A card game for one person; patience. 2. A precious stone, esp. a diamond, set by itself, as in a ring.
social	*See asocial.*		
sodium chlorate	A colorless solid used chiefly in the manufacture of explosives and matches.	**solitary**	Alone; unattended.
		solon	*See salon.*
sodium chloride	Salt.	**solum**	*See solemn.*
		solute	*See salud.*

NOTE: Consult your dictionary for other sodium soundalike compounds, such as sodium nitrate/nitrite and sodium sulfate/sulfide/sulfite.

soma	(Biol.) The body of an organism as contrasted with its germ cells.
stoma	A mouth or small aperture. (Med.) An artificial opening, esp. in the abdominal wall made in surgical procedures.
stroma	(Biol.) The supporting framework or matrix of a cell.
struma	Goiter.
some	An indeterminate quantity.
sum	A total.
someone	Somebody.
some one	A particular one. [Some one of you knows someone who....]
sometime	(adv.) At some indefinite point of time.
some time	An unspecified interval or period of time. [He promised to do it sometime soon, but it will take some time to accomplish.]
sometimes	Now and then.
son	Male child.
sun	Old Sol.
sonde	(Rocketry) A rocket, balloon, etc., used as a probe for observing phenomena in the atmosphere. (It rhymes with *bond*.)
sound	Something heard by the ear. (Etc.)
sonometer	*See centimeter.*

soot	The black powdery substance that rises in the smoke of coal or wood, etc. (Rhymes with *foot* or *boot*.)
suit	A set of clothing, etc. (*Also see grouping under suit.*)
sooth	(old use) Truth, fact. [In sooth.]
soothe	To tranquilize or calm. (*Also see smooth.*)
sophism	*See solecism.*
sordid	*See assorted.*
sore	*See soar.*
sorosis	*See cirrhosis.*
sorption	*See absorption.*
sorry	*See sari.*
sou/sough	*See Sioux.*
soul	*See sol.*
sound	*See sonde.*
sow	*See sew.*
sower	*See sewer.*
spacious	Roomy.
specious	Having a false look of truth or genuineness.
Spackle	(TM) A quick-drying compound for patching plasterwork.
speckle	A small speck, spot, or mark, as on skin.
spade	A garden tool.
spayed	Removed the ovaries of a female animal.
spatial	Pert. to space.
special	Unusual. (Etc.)
spatter	To splash with liquid, mud, etc.
splatter	To spatter; to splash.

spay	To remove the ovaries of a female animal.
splay	To spread out, expand, or extend. [He splayed his feet.]
spray	To scatter in the form of fine particles.
spayed	*See spade.*
spec	(n.) Short for *specification* or *speculation.* [I wrote it up on spec.] v. To provide specifications for. [Note: *The Random House Dictionary* lists past tense as *spec'd, specked,* or *specced* and gives as an illustration, "Their newest truck was spec'd by a computer." *Webster's Ninth New Collegiate* prefers *specced* or *spec'd* as the past.] (Note also *specs,* short for *spectacles.*)
speck	A small spot or particle.
special	*See especial and spatial.*
specially	Specifically; particularly. *(Also see especially.)*
speciality	(chiefly Brit.) Specialty.
specialty	A special subject of study, line of work, etc.
specie	Money in coin. [Note: *Specie,* meaning a single species, a back formation from *species,* is nonstandard. Avoid.]
species	Class; genus; kind.
specific	*See pacific.*
specious	*See spacious.*
speckle	*See Spackle.*

spectrum	Bands of colors as seen in a rainbow; an entire range of related qualities or ideas. (Etc.)
speculum	A mirror or reflector; an instrument inserted into a body passage for inspection or medication.
spiculum	(Zool.) A small, needlelike body, part, process or the like.
specs	*See spec.*
specter	*See scepter.*
speculate	*See peculate.*
spell	1. A word, phrase, or form of words supposed to have magical power. 2. A continuous course or period of work or other activity.
spiel	(informal) A usually high-flown talk or speech, esp. for the purpose of luring people to a sideshow, etc.
sperm	A male reproductive cell.
spurn	To reject with disdain; scorn.
sphenoid	Wedge-shaped; of, rel. to, or being a winged compound bone at the base of the cranium.
splenoid	Pert. to the spleen.

spheroid	A solid geometrical figure similar in shape to a sphere.	**splutter**	To talk rapidly and somewhat incoherently.
spiroid	More or less spiral.	**sputter**	To make explosive popping or sizzling sounds; to talk incoherently.
steroid	Any of a group of organic compounds that includes certain hormones and other bodily secretions.	**stutter**	To stammer.
		spoor	A track or trail, esp. of a wild animal pursued as game.
spiculum	*See spectrum.*	**spore**	One of the tiny reproductive cells of such plants as fungi and ferns.
spiel	*See spell.*		
spinal	Of, pert. to, or belonging to a spine; a spinal anesthetic.	**sprain**	A painful laceration of the ligaments of a joint.
spinel	(also **spinelle**) A hard crystalline mineral.	**strain**	Bodily injury from excessive tension, effort, or use. (Etc.)
spinner	One that spins; a lure (fishing); a play in football.	**spray**	*See spay.*
spinor	(Physics) A type of mathematical vector.	**sprites**	Elves, fairies, or goblins.
		sprits	(Naut.) Spars.
spinose	Full of spines.	**spritz**	To spray briefly and quickly; squirt.
spinous	Covered with or having spines; thorny.		
		spruce	An evergreen coniferous tree.
spiritual	Of or pert. to the spirit or soul.	**sprues**	Openings through which molten metal is poured into a mold.
spirituel	(F.) Showing or having a refined and graceful mind or wit; light and airy in movement.		
		spurge	*See splurge.*
		spurn	*See sperm.*
		sputter	*See splutter.*
spiroid	*See spheroid.*	**squash**	*See quash.*
splatter	*See spatter.*		
splay	*See spay.*	**squashy**	Easily squashed; pulpy.
splenoid	*See sphenoid.*	**squishy**	Soft and wet.
		squshy	Squishy.
splurge	To indulge oneself in some luxury or pleasure.		
spurge	A plant of the genus Euphorbia.	**squire**	*See esquire.*

stabile	An abstract sculpture similar to a mobile but stationary.	**stamina**	Strength of physical constitution. (Also pl. of *stamen*, above.)
stable	A building to house horses.	**staminal**	Pert. to stamina or endurance.
staple	A basic or necessary item. (Etc.)		
		stamp	To strike or beat with a forcible downward thrust of the foot.
stade	(Geol.) A period of time represented by a glacial deposit.	**stomp**	To tread heavily. [He stomped out of the room.]
staid	Sedate; sober.		
stayed	Past tense of *stay*.	**stanch**	To restrain the flow (as of blood).
strayed	Wandered off.	**staunch**	Firm in attitude, opinion, or loyalty. [A staunch Republican, he tried to stanch his opponent's tide of votes.]
staff	A rod; personnel.		
staph	Staphylococcus. [Staph infection.]		
stair	One of a series of steps.		
stare	A fixed look.		
		stannate	A salt of a stannic acid.
stake	A pointed piece of wood. (Etc.)	**stannite**	A gray to black mineral, sometimes called tin pyrites.
steak	A slice of meat.		
stalactite	Hanging calcium deposit (in the roof of a cave).	**staph**	*See staff.*
		staple	*See stabile.*
		stare	*See stair.*
stalagmite	Upright calcium deposit (on the floor of a cave).	**starlet**	*See scarlet.*
		starlit	*See scarlet.*
		static	*See astatic.*
stalk	(n.) The main stem of an herbaceous plant. (v.) To pursue quarry.	**starter**	One that starts.
		stertor	A heavy snoring sound in respiration.
stock	(n.) A supply of goods kept on hand for sale. (Etc.) v. To keep regularly. (Etc.)		
		starve	To perish from lack of food or nourishment.
		stave	To put off, prevent. [This will help you stave off starvation.]
stamen	(pl. *stamens* or *stamina*) The pollen-bearing organ of a flower.		
stamin	A coarse woolen fabric.	**stat**	(informal) Statistic (usu. *stats*: statistics).
		stet	Let it stand. (Used as a direction on a printer's proof, etc.)

stater	An ancient gold or silver coin of the Greek city-states.
stator	A stationary part in a machine in or about which a rotor revolves.
stationary	Immobile; fixed.
stationery	Writing paper, etc.
statue	Sculpture.
stature	Natural height; quality, status.
statute	Law or rule.
staunch	*See stanch.*
stave	*See starve.*
stayed	*See stade.*
steak	*See stake.*
steal	To rob.
steel	To make resolute; to harden.
stele	An upright slab or pillar serving as a monument or marker; the central portion of vascular tissue in a plant stem.
steamy	*See seamy.*
steep	*See seep.*
steer	A male bovine castrated before sexual maturity.
stere	A unit of volume.
step	A ladder rung. (Etc.)
steppe	A vast usu. treeless plain.
stereotape	A stereophonic magnetic tape.
stereotype	Something conforming to a fixed or general pattern.

sterile	Barren; free from living microorganisms.
sterol	Any of a group of complex solid alcohols.
sterlet	*See scarlet.*
sternal	*See asternal.*
steroid	*See spheroid.*
stertor	*See starter.*
stet	*See stat.*
stetor	*See stater.*
stich	*See shtick.*
stick	*See shtick.*
sticker	An adhesive label; one that pierces with a point; a persistent person.
stickler	A person who insists on something; something that baffles or puzzles.
stigmatism	*See astigmatism.*
stile	A series of steps for passing over a fence or wall.
style	1. Fashion. (Etc.) 2. An extension of a flower's pistil.
stimulant	An agent (as a drug) that produces a temporary increase in activity.
stimulus	Something that rouses or incites to activity.
stimulate	*See assimilate and simulate.*
stimulation	*See simulation.*
stipe	A usu. short plant stalk.
stripe	A long narrow band differing in color or texture from adjoining material.

stirp	A line of descendants from a common ancestor.	**straighten**	To make straight.
		straiten	To make narrow; to subject to deprivation. [In straitened circumstances.]
stirrup	A support for the foot of a horseman.		
strip	A long narrow piece of material.	**strain**	*See sprain.*
		strange	*See estrange.*
stock	*See stalk.*	**strap**	A strip of leather or other flexible material for holding things in place.
stodgy	Dull, uninteresting.		
stogie	Cigar.	**strop**	A strip of leather on which a razor is sharpened; an implement or machine serving the same purpose.
stoke	To poke, stir up (a fire).		
stroke	To rub gently. (Etc.)		
stolen	Past part. of *steal*.		
stollen	(Ger. cookery) A sweet bread.	**strass**	1. A flint glass with a high lead content. 2. Silk waste.
stolon	A horizontal above- or below-ground plant branch, a runner. (Also see *solon*, listed under *salon*.)	**stress**	Emphasis; pressure, tension, strain.
		trass	Powdered volcanic rock used in making cement.
stolid	*See solid.*		
stoma	*See soma.*		
stomp	*See stamp.*	**stratagem**	A cunning method of achieving something.
stoop	A posture of the body with shoulders bent forward; a small porch.	**strategy**	A plan for obtaining a specific goal.
stop	A cessation of movement. (Etc.)	**strayed**	*See stade.*
stoup	A stone basin for holy water.	**streptomycin**	An antibiotic.
stupe	1. A hot wet often medicated cloth applied externally to stimulate circulation. 2. (slang) A stupid person.	**streptothricin**	An antibacterial substance produced by a soil fungus.
		strick	A bunch of hackled flax, jute, or hemp.
straight	Direct; uninterrupted.	**strict**	Kept within narrow and specific limits.
strait	(adj.) Narrow, constricted. (n.) An isthmus. [Strait of Gibralter. Straitjacket, straitlaced—but straightedge.]	**stricture**	A narrowing or restriction.
		structure	The action of building; the building itself.

strider	One that strides.	**sucker**	*See succor.*
stridor	A harsh, grating or creaking sound.	**sucrase**	An enzyme (invertase.)
		sucrose	Sugar obtained from plants such as sugar cane or sugar beet.
strip	*See stirp.*		
stripe	*See stipe.*	**sue/Sue**	*See Sioux.*
striped	Having stripes or streaks. (Sometimes pronounced as two syl.)	**suede**	Leather with a napped surface.
stripped	Past tense of *strip.*	**swayed**	Past tense of *sway.*
stroke	*See stoke.*	**suer**	*See sewer.*
stroma	*See soma.*	**suit**	A set of clothing, etc. (*Also see soot.*)
strop	*See strap.*		
structure	*See stricture.*	**suite**	A number of things forming a series or set. (Pronounced like *suit* or *sweet.*)
struma	*See soma.*		
stupe	*See stoop.*		
style	*See stile.*		
suasion	*See persuasion.*	**sweet**	Tasting as if containing sugar. (Etc.)
subliminal	Existing or operating below the threshold of consciousness.		
		sulfate	A salt or ester of sulfuric acid.
sublingual	Situated under the tongue.	**sulfide**	A compound of sulphur with another element or radical.
submerged	Under the surface of water or other enveloping medium.	**sulfite**	A salt or ester of sulfurous acid.
submersed	Submerged. (Bot.) Growing under water.	**sulfurous**	Of, pert. to, or containing sulfur.
subordination	Placement in a lower rank.	**sulphurous**	1. Sulfurous. 2. Pert. to the fires of hell; fiery or heated.
subornation	Inducing someone to commit perjury.		
succor	Relief; help.	**sulk**	*See skulk.*
sucker	One that sucks; cheated person.	**sum**	*See some.*
		summarize	To make a summary of; to state concisely.
succubous	(Bot., of leaves) Overlapping, with the base of each leaf covering part of that under it.	**summerize**	To prepare (a house, etc.) for summer.
succubus	A demon in female form.		

summary	(adj.) Concise; quickly executed. [Summary judgment.]	**surveillance**	A watch kept over a person, group, etc., esp. over a suspect.
summery	Of, resembling, or fit for summer.	**surveillants**	Those under surveillance.
summoned	Convoked; ordered to appear.	**swag**	1. A wreath or spray. 2. Plunder, booty.
summonsed	Summoned by means of a summons.	**swage**	A tool for bending cold metal (pronounced swaj, long *a*).
sun	*See son.*	**sward**	Grassy surface of land; turf.
sundae	A dish of dressed-up ice cream.	**sword**	A weapon with a long blade.
Sunday	First day of the week.		
super-	(prefix) Over and above; higher in quantity, quality, or degree than.	**swatch**	A sample piece (as of fabric).
		swath	The sweep of a scythe; long broad strip or belt.
supra-	(prefix) Above, beyond, earlier (akin to *super*).	**swathe**	(n.) A bandage. (v.) To bind or wrap; bandage.
super	Short for *superfine*.	**swayed**	*See suede.*
supra	Above; earlier in this writing.	**sweet**	*See suit.*
supine	*See prone.*	**swish**	To strike or move or cause to move with a hissing sound.
suppuration	*See separation.*	**switch**	To change positions, etc.
surely	Certainly.	**wish**	To desire.
surly	Churlish; sullen.		
surf	*See serf.*	**swivel**	A device joining two parts so that one or both can pivot freely.
surge	*See serge.*		
surgical	*See cervical.*	**swivet**	A state of extreme agitation.
surplice	Ecclesiastical vestment.	**sword**	*See soared and sward.*
surplus	Excess.	**sycosis**	*See psychosis.*
surveil	(back formation from *surveillance*) To subject to surveillance.	**syllabub**	A drink made by curdling cream with wine or cider.
survey	To look at and take a general view of.	**syllabus**	A summary outline of a discourse, series of lectures, etc.

symbol	*See cymbal.*
symmetrical	*See asymmetrical.*
symmetry	*See asymmetry and cemetery.*
sympathy	*See empathy.*
symphonia	Any of various medieval musical instruments, such as the hurdy-gurdy.
symphony	A long musical composition, usu. in several parts, for a full orchestra.
synchrony	Simultaneous occurrence.

symptomatic	*See asymptomatic.*
synapse	*See asynapsis.*
synapsis	*See asynapsis.*
sync	*See sink.*
synchronism	*See asynchronism.*
synchronous	*See asynchronous.*
syne	*See scion.*
synergy	*See asynergy*
syntax	*See sin tax.*
systematic	Rel. to or consisting of a system.
systemic	Rel. to or common to a system; affecting the body generally.

T

tack	A course or method of action; esp. one widely divergent from previous course.
track	Detectable evidence; a trail; a trace.
tract	1. A large stretch of land. 2. A system of connected parts in an animal body along which something passes (e.g., the digestive tract). 3. A pamphlet containing a short essay, esp. on a religious subject.
trek	A long arduous journey.
tacked	Past tense of *tack*.
tact	Diplomacy.
tracked	Past tense of *track*.
tacks	Attaches with small nails; brings a vessel into the wind.
tax	To assess; to levy a tax on; to charge.
taffy	A chewy candy.
toffee	A candy similar to taffy but more brittle.
tails	Rear appendages.
tales	Stories.
tales	(Law) Persons chosen to serve on a jury when the original panel is insufficiently large (talesmen).
talents	Abilities.
talons	Claws.
talesman	Member of a jury pool.
talisman	A charm or fetish.
talkie	Talking picture.
talky	Talkative; containing too much talk.
talons	*See talents.*
talus	Anklebone.
talus	A slope; a sloping mass of rocky fragments at the bottom of a cliff.
tamper	To meddle with.
temper	To moderate or mitigate; to soften or tone down.
tankard	A large drinking cup.
tanker	A ship, plane, or truck designed for bulk shipment of liquids or gases.
taped	Past tense of *tape*.
tapped	Past tense of *tap*.
taper	A slender candle.
tapir	Animal related to horse and rhinoceros.
tare	A deduction from the gross weight to allow for weight of container.
tear	A rip or laceration.
taro	A tropical plant with a tuberous root, used as food.
tarot	A deck of cards used in fortune-telling (second syl. pronounced oh).
tarry	To delay in coming or going.
terry	A cotton fabric.

tart	A small pie filled with fruit, etc.; prostitute.	**technics**	The study or science of an art or arts in general, esp. the mechanical or industrial arts.
tort	(Law) A wrongful act.		
torte	A rich cake.		
		techniques	Ways in which technical details are treated; methods of accomplishing a desired aim.
taught	Past tense of *teach*.		
taut	Tightly drawn; tense.		
tax	*See tacks.*		
		tee	*See tea.*
taxes	Plural of *tax*.	**teem**	*See team.*
taxus	A genus of plants incl. yews.	**teen**	*See team.*
		tees	*See teas.*
tea	Beverage.		
tee	Mound or peg on which a golf ball is placed. [Note: It's "to a T" and preferably "T-shirt." We also have T-bar (a term in the building trade), T-bill, T-bond, T-bone. (Also T cell and T lymphocyte, no hyphens).]	**teensy-weensy**	(baby talk) Tiny, small.
		teeny-weeny	(baby talk) Tiny, small.
		teether	A device for a baby to bite on during teething.
		tether	A rope or chain by which an animal is fastened during grazing; the utmost length to which one can go. [I've about reached the end of my tether.]
team	To yoke or join in a team.		
teem	To abound; to become filled to overflowing.		
teen	A teenager.	**tegmen**	[Bot.] The delicate inner integument or coat of a seed.
tear	A saline drop emanating from the eye. (*Also see tare/tear.*)	**tegument**	A covering or investment; integument.
tier	A row, rank, or layer of articles.		
		tellurate	A salt of a telluric acid.
teas	Late-afternoon receptions.	**telluride**	A binary compound of tellurium with an electropositive element.
tease	One that teases.		
tees	Mounds for golf balls.	**tellurite**	A salt of tellurous acid.

tellurian	Of or characteristic of the earth or its inhabitants.	**tender**	1. The act of offering something in payment. 2. A person who tends or attends to something.
tellurion	An instrument that shows how the movement of the earth on its axis causes day and night and the seasons.	**tinder**	Highly flammable material.
tellurium	A semimetallic element related to selenium and sulfur.	**tendinitis**	Inflammation of tendons and of tendon-muscle attachments. (Note that there is no *o* in this word.)
temblor	A tremor; earthquake.	**tenonitis**	Inflammation of Tenon's capsule (the fascia of the eyeball).
trembler	A person or thing that trembles.		
tremor	A trembling or shaking; slight earthquake.	**tendon**	A strong band of cord or tissue connecting a muscle to some other part.
temerity	Reckless boldness; rashness.	**tenon**	A projection on the end of a piece of wood. [Mortise and tenon.]
timidity	Lack of courage.		
temper	*See tamper.*	**tends**	Is disposed or inclined in action; attends to.
template	1. A pattern, mold, or the like. 2. (Genetics) A molecule (as of DNA) that serves as a pattern for further generations. 3. (Computers) A small sheet or strip of cardboard, etc., that fits over the keyboard and provides information on software functions.	**tents**	Collapsible canvas shelters.
		tense	Stretched tight; rigid; not relaxed.
		tenere	(L., Law) To have in possession; to retain.
		teneri	(L., Law) A clause in a bond.
templet	A template.	**tenet**	*See tenant.*
tenace	Bridge-whist term.	**tenner**	A ten-dollar bill.
tennis	Popular net game.	**tenor**	The highest natural male singing voice; general sense, purport. [The even tenor of her ways.]
tenant	Lessee; occupant.		
tenet	A principle, belief, or doctrine held to be true.	**tenure**	The holding or possessing of anything.
		tennis	*See tenace.*
		tenon	*See tendon.*

tenonitis	*See tendinitis.*	**terrain**	A geographical area; the physical features of a tract of land.
tense	*See tends.*		
tenser	More tense.	**terrane**	(Geol.) Any rock formation or series of formations or the area in which a particular formation is predominant.
tensor	A muscle that stretches or tightens some part of the body; a term in higher mathematics.		
tensile	Of or pert. to tension; capable of being stretched out.	**terrene**	(n.) A land area. (adj.) Mundane, earthly.
tinsel	A glittering metallic substance used on Christmas trees, etc.	**terrine**	A casserole serving dish.
		train	A locomotive with a series of linked railroad cars. (Etc.)
tenure	*See tenner.*	**tureen**	A deep covered dish from which soup is served at the table.
terete	(adj.) Cylindrical or slightly tapering.		
terret	One of the loops or rings on the saddle of a harness, through which the driving reins pass.	**terret**	*See terete.*
		terrier	A breed of dog.
turret	A small tower.	**terror**	Intense, sharp, overmastering fear.
term	The time for which something lasts. (Etc.)	**terry**	*See tarry.*
therm	(also **therme**) Any of several units of quantity of heat.	**test**	Examination.
		text	The wording of something written or printed.
termer	A person who is serving a term, esp. in prison.	**testee**	A person who is tested.
		testy	Irritably impatient; touchy.
termor	(Law) A person who has an estate for a term of years or life.	**tetchy**	Irritable; touchy.
		touchy	Apt to take offense on slight provocation.
terminable	Able to be terminated.		
terminal	At the end.	**tether**	*See teether.*
termite	Destructive insect.	**tetracaine**	A crystalline solid used chiefly as an anesthetic.
thermite	A metallic mixture that produces intense heat when ignited.		
		tetracene	Naphthacene.
tern	Type of sea gull.	**Tetracyn**	(TM) A brand for a form of tetracycline.
turn	Rotation. (Etc.)		

tetrazene	An isomeric compound; naphthacene.
tetrazzini	(adj.) Served over pasta with a cream sauce.
text	*See test.*
Thai	A native of Thailand.
tie	A bond. (Etc.)
thallous	Containing univalent thallium.
thallus	A plant body without true root, stem, or leaves.
than	Conjunction used to introduce the second element in a comparison.
thane	A man holding land by military service in Anglo-Saxon England.
then	At that time.
the	Definite article.
thee	You.
their	Possessive pronoun.
there	At that place.
they're	Contraction of *they are.*
theirs	Possessive pronoun. (It *never* takes an apostrophe!)
there's	Contraction of *there is.*
then	*See than.*
thence	*See hence.*
theocracy	Government of a state by divine guidance or by officials regarded as divinely guided.
theocrasy	A mixture of religious forms and deities by worshipers.
there	*See their.*

therefor	For or in return for that. [She offered payment therefor.]
therefore	For that reason; consequently.
wherefore	For what reason; for this reason.
therein	In or into that place or thing.
wherein	In what or in which.
there's	*See theirs.*
therm	*See term.*
thermite	*See termite.*
thermophile	An organism that grows best in a warm environment.
thermopile	A device to measure temperature.
they're	*See their.*
thigh	The part of the human leg between hip and knee; corresponding part in animals.
thy	Of or belonging to thee.
thill	A shaft of a vehicle.
thrill	To excite greatly.
trill	To sing or play with a vibrating effect.
thither	*See hither.*
thong	A narrow strip of leather used for binding.
throng	A crowd; multitude of people.

thorough	Painstaking.	**throws**	*See throes.*
threw	Past tense of *throw*.	**thru**	*See thorough.*
through	Extending from one surface to another; finished. [Note: *Thru* is described as an informal, simplified spelling of *through*. Prefer, however, *thruway* to *throughway*.]	**thrum**	To play a stringed instrument by plucking the strings.
		thurm	To carve a piece of wood across the grain. (*Also see therm.*)
thrall	*See enthralled/in thrall.*	**thrust**	An assault; essential meaning.
thrash	To beat soundly with a stick or whip.	**trussed**	Tightly secured; bound.
thresh	To beat out or separate (grain) from husks.	**trust**	Faith; confidence.
		tryst	An appointed meeting, esp. by lovers.
thread	A thin length of any substance.	**thy**	*See thigh.*
tread	Manner or sound of walking; top surface of a stair.	**thyme**	A garden herb.
		time	All the years of the past, present, and future. (Etc.)
threw	*See thorough.*	**tibia**	*See fibula.*
thrice	Three times.	**tic**	Muscular twitching (esp. of the face).
trice	An instant; very short time.	**tick**	A light rhythmic tap or beat; bloodsucking arachnid.
twice	Two times.		
thrill	*See thill.*	**tidal**	Of, pert. to, or subject to tides.
thrips	Minute insects destructive to plants.	**title**	Legal right to ownership of property. (Etc.)
trips	Journeys.	**tittle**	A dot or small mark in writing or printing. [Jot or tittle.]
throes	Pangs; spasms. [Death throes. In the throes of....]		
throws	Tosses.	**tide**	Alternating rising and falling of ocean, etc.
throne	A special chair used by a king, queen, bishop, et al.	**tied**	Past tense of *tie*.
thrown	Form of the verb *to throw*.	**tie**	*See Thai.*
		tier	*See tear.*
throng	*See thong.*		
through	*See thorough.*		

till	(n.) A box, drawer, etc., esp. for money. (v.) To work by plowing, sowing, etc.
till	(conj. and prep.) Until. Note: The *American Heritage Dictionary* says, "'*Til* is a possible variant form of *until*, though most authorities now consider it a needless one. '*Till* is nonstandard."
timbal	(also **tymbal**) 1. A kettledrum. 2. A vibrating membrane in certain insects, as the cicada.
timbale	A pastry shell shaped like a drum.
timber	Growing trees or their wood.
timbre	The quality given to a sound by its overtones.
time	*See thyme.*
timidity	*See temerity.*
tinder	*See tender.*
tinsel	*See tensile.*
tinny	Of, like, or containing tin.
tiny	Very small.
tipple	(n.) A structure where coal is cleaned and loaded into railroad cars or trucks. (v.) To drink (wine or whiskey, etc.)
topple	To fall forward from having too heavy a top; to overthrow, pass from a position of authority.
title	*See tidal.*

titillate	To excite or stimulate pleasantly.
titivate	To make smart or spruce.
titter	To give a high-pitched giggle.
twitter	To make a series of light chirping sounds; to talk rapidly or nervously.
tittle	*See tidal.*
to	Toward. (Etc.)
too	Also. (Etc.)
two	A number.
toad	Tailless amphibian.
toed	Having toes.
towed	Past tense of *tow*.
toady	An obsequious flatterer.
toddy	A sweetened drink of liquor and hot water.
tocsin	A signal, esp. of alarm, sounded on a bell or bells; a bell used to sound an alarm.
toxin	A poisonous substance, esp. one formed in the body by microorganisms.
toed	*See toad.*
toffee	*See taffy.*
togue	A lake trout.
toke	A puff on a marijuana cigarette.
toque	A brimless close-fitting hat for women.
toilet	The process of dressing and grooming oneself.
toilette	Grooming; style of dress.

told	Past tense of *tell*.	**tool**	A thing (usu. hand-held) for working on something.
tolled	Rang a bell.		
tole	A kind of lacquered or enameled metalware, used for trays, etc.	**tule**	A large reed or bullrush (pronounced too-lee).
toll	A tax or duty paid for the use of a public road or harbor, etc.; the loss or damage caused by a disaster, etc.	**tulle**	A kind of fine silky net used for veils and dresses.
troll	(n.) In Scandinavian folklore, a friendly but mischievous dwarf or a giant. (v.) To fish by drawing bait along in the water.	**tooter**	One who causes a horn, etc., to sound.
		tutor	A private teacher.
		topic	Subject of discussion, etc.
tomb	A burial chamber, etc.	**trophic**	Of or pert. to nutrition.
tombé	(F.) A ballet step.	**tropic**	A line of latitude north or south of the equator. [Tropic of Cancer; Tropic of Capricorn.]
tome	A book, esp. a very heavy, scholarly one.		
ton	A measure of weight.	**topical**	Pert. to or dealing with matters of current or local interest; (Med.) pert. to or applied to a particular part of the body.
tun	A large cask for holding liquids.		
tonal	*See atonal.*	**tropical**	Of or found in or like the tropics.
tonality	*See atonality.*		
tong	A Chinese guild, association, or secret society in the U.S.	**topography**	Geographical configuration.
tong	(usu. *tongs*) An instrument with two arms joined at one end, used for grasping and holding things.	**typography**	Style, etc., of typeset material.
		topple	*See tipple.*
		toque	*See togue.*
tongue	The fleshy muscular organ in the mouth.	**tor**	A rocky pinnacle; a peak of a bare or rocky mountain or hill.
tung	A Chinese tree. (It produces tung oil, an ingredient of paint.)		
		tore	Past tense of *tear*.
tonnage	*See dunnage.*	**torr**	A unit of pressure.
too	*See to.*		

Torrens	A system of registration of land titles.	**tracheostomy**	The construction of an artificial opening through the neck into the trachea (windpipe).
torrents	Rushing streams of water or lava; violent outpourings. [Torrents of words.]	**tracheotomy**	The operation of cutting into the trachea.
torso	The trunk of the human body.	**track**	*See tack.*
trousseau	A bride's special wardrobe.	**tracked**	*See tacked.*
		tracker	One that tracks.
tort	*See tart.*	**tractor**	Powerful motor-driven farm vehicle.
torte	*See tart.*		
		tract	*See tact.*
tortious	Implying or involving a tort.	**traduce**	*See seduce.*
tortoise	A turtle.	**tragedian**	An actor esp. noted for performing tragic roles; a writer of tragedy.
tortuous	Winding; circuitous; tricky or crooked.	**tragedienne**	An actress esp. noted for performing tragic roles.
torturous	Causing torture; cruelly painful.		
touchy	*See tetchy.*	**train**	*See terrain.*
tough	(n.) A rough and violent person.	**traipse**	To walk or go aimlessly or idly.
tuff	A volcanic rock.	**traps**	Snares.
tuft	A bunch of threads or grass or feathers or hair, etc., held or growing together at the base.	**tramp**	To walk with heavy steps.
		tromp	(informal) To tramp or trample; defeat.
tousle	To disorganize or dishevel.	**trump**	To play a card of a suit temporarily ranking above others.
tussle	To struggle or fight roughly; scuffle.	**transience**	A transitory state or quality.
towed	*See toad.*	**transients**	Persons or things that stay only a short time.
towel	A piece of absorbent cloth or paper for drying. (*Also see dowel.*)	**translate**	To express in another language or in simpler words.
trowel	A small tool used in gardening or for spreading mortar, etc.	**transliterate**	To represent (letters or words) in the letters of a different alphabet.
toxin	*See tocsin.*		

transverse	Lying or being across.	**trifle**	Something of slight value or importance; a dessert (Brit.)
traverse	To pass or move over, along, or through; to thwart, obstruct.	**truffle**	High-priced fungus—or type of chocolate candy.
traps	*See traipse.*		
trass	*See strass.*		
traumatic	*See dramatic.*	**trill**	*See thill.*
travail	A painful or laborious effort.	**trillion**	A cardinal number, in the U.S. represented by 1 followed by 12 zeros, and in the U.K. by 1 followed by 18 zeros.
travel	A journey.		
traverse	*See transverse.*	**trillium**	A flowering plant.
tray	A flat utensil, usu. with a raised edge, on which small articles are placed for display or carrying.	**triple**	*See treble.*
		trips	*See thrips.*
		triptych	*See diptych.*
trey	The three-spot (cards).	**troche**	Medicated tablet or lozenge.
tread	*See thread.*	**trochee**	A foot in prose consisting of one long followed by one short syllable.
treatise	A written work dealing systematically with one subject.		
treaties	Agreements.	**trochlea**	*See cochlea.*
		troll	*See tole.*
treble	Threefold; having the highest range or part. [Young boys with treble voices.]	**tromp**	*See tramp.*
		troop	A group of soldiers, etc.
		troupe	A group of theatrical performers.
triple	Three times as great or as many.	**trooper**	A soldier in a cavalry or armored unit; police officer.
trek	*See tack.*		
trembler	*See temblor.*	**trouper**	A member of a theatrical troupe.
tremor	*See temblor.*		
trey	*See tray.*		
trice	*See thrice.*	**trophic**	*See topic.*
		tropic	*See topic.*
trickle	To flow or cause to flow in a thin stream.	**tropical**	*See topical.*
truckle	To submit or yield obsequiously or tamely.	**troth**	Faithfulness, loyalty.
		trough	A long narrow receptacle, esp. for holding food or water for animals.
trigon	A triangle.		
trigone	A triangular part or area.		

troupe	See troop.
trouper	See trooper.
trousseau	See torso.
trowel	See dowel and towel.
truckle	See trickle.
truffle	See trifle.
trump	See tramp.

truncheon	The club carried by a police officer; billy.
trunnion	A cylindrical projection on a cannon.

trussed	See thrust.
trust	See thrust.

trustee	One to whom something is entrusted.
trusty	A convict considered trustworthy and allowed special privileges.

tryst	See thrust.
tube	See cube.

tuberculose	Having tubercles (rounded nodules or swellings).
tuberculosis	An infectious disease, esp. of the lungs.
tuberculous	Of or pert. to tuberculosis.

tucks	Folds stitched into cloth.
tux	Tuxedo.

tuff/tuft	See tough.
tule	See tool.
tulip	See julep.
tulle	See tool.
tun	See ton.

tummy	(informal) Stomach.
tunny	Tuna (esp. Brit.)

tun	See ton
tung	See ton.

turban	Headdress.
turbine	A rotary engine.

turbid	Obscure; muddy.
turgid	Swollen; pompous.

turbit	A pigeon.
turbot	A flatfish.

tureen	See terrain.
turgid	See turbid.
turn	See tern.
turret	See terete.

tusche	A greaselike liquid used in lithography.
tush	1. One of the four canine teeth of a horse. 2. (slang) Buttocks.
tusk	A long pointed tooth that projects outside the mouth (in an elephant, walrus, etc.)

tussle	See tousle.
tutor	See tooter.
tux	See tucks.
twice	See thrice.

twirl	To cause to rotate rapidly.
whirl	To swing or spin around.

twitter	See titter.
two	See to.

tympanites	Distension of abdomen with gas.
tympanitis	Otitis media (inflammation of the middle ear.)

typhon	(Naut.) A signal horn operated by compressed air or steam.
typhoon	A tropical cyclone or hurricane.

186

typical   *See atypical.*
typography   *See topography.*

U

ugli   A large sweet variety of tangelo, of Jamaican origin.

ugly   Unattractive; disagreeable.

ultra vires   (L., Law) Beyond the legal power or authority of a corporation, etc.

ultravirus   A filterable virus.

unalike   Not alike.

unlike   Not like.

unapt   *See inapt.*

unbeknown   Unknown; unperceived.

unbeknownst   Unbeknown.

uncal   Pert. to an uncus (hooked anatomical part).

uncle   Brother of one's mother or father.

unceded   Not ceded (i.e., not yielded or surrendered).

unseated   Not seated.

unseeded   Not seeded.

uncooked   Raw.

undercooked   Not thoroughly cooked.

unctuous   *See anxious.*

uncus   *See Incas.*

underdeveloped   Insufficiently developed.

undeveloped   Not developed.

underdone   Not thoroughly done.

undone   Unfastened; not done.

underexposed   Exposed for too short a time.

unexposed   Not exposed (as film).

underlined   Having lines drawn under something; emphasized.

unlined   Without lines; without lining.

underpaid   Not paid enough.

unpaid   Not paid at all.

understated   Stated in restrained form.

unstated   Unsaid.

undertow   Current below the surface of the sea.

under tow   (of a ship) Being towed.

undeveloped   *See underdeveloped.*

undo   Unfasten; nullify.

undue   Exceeding or violating propriety or fitness.

undone   *See underdone.*

unequivocably   (nonstandard) Unequivocally

unequivocally   Leaving no doubt; unambiguous.

unexceptionable   Beyond reproach.

unexceptional   Commonplace.

unexposed   *See underexposed.*

unhuman   *See inhuman.*

unhumane   *See inhumane.*

uninterested   *See disinterested.*

unisex	Of, designed, or suitable for both sexes.
unsex	To deprive of sexual power; to render impotent or frigid.
unlade	To unload.
unlaid	Not laid or placed.
unlike	*See unalike.*
unlined	*See underlined.*
unpaid	*See underpaid.*
unreal	Not real or actual.
unreel	To unwind from a reel.
unrip	To undo by ripping.
unripe	Not ripe.
unsanitary	*See insanitary.*
unseated	*See unceded.*
unseeded	*See unceded.*
unsex	*See unisex.*
unstated	*See understated.*
unwanted	Not wanted.
unwonted	Rare, unusual.
upbraid	*See abrade.*

updraft	The movement upward of air or other gas.
updrift	A slow, upward movement.
uprate	To raise in rate, power, size, etc.; upgrade.
upright	Erect or vertical; righteous, honest, just.
Ur	*See air.*
urban	Of, relating to, or constituting a city.
urbane	Suave; sophisticated.
ureter	Either of the two ducts by which urine passes from the kidneys to the bladder.
urethra	The duct by which urine is discharged from the body.
ureteral	Pert. to or used upon the ureter.
urethral	Pert. to the urethra.
urn	*See earn.*
use	*See ewes.*
utter	*See mutter.*
Uzi	*See oozy.*

V

vacation	*See avocation.*
vain	Conceited.
vane	Device showing wind direction.
vein	Narrow channel; lode; blood vessel. (Etc.)
valance	A short curtain.
valence	The capacity of an atom to combine with another or others.
vale	A valley.
veil	Face covering; something that obscures.
valet	A man's personal attendant who takes care of clothes, etc. (Pronounced VAL-it or va-LAY.)
valley	A long low area between hills.
varlet	A menial low fellow; rascal.
valor	Boldness; courage.
velour	A plushlike fabric.
valuable	Of great price or worth.
voluble	Fluent; glib; talkative.
valuation	*See evaluation.*
valvula	A small valve or valvule.
valvule	A small valve or part resembling a valve.
vane	*See vain.*
vantage	Favorable condition or circumstance. *(Also see advantage.)*
ventage	A small hole or vent, as one of the fingerholes of a flute.
vintage	(n.) The wine from a particular harvest or crop. (adj.) Of high quality.
vapid	*See sapid.*
variance	Dispute; deviation.
variants	Persons or things that vary.
varlet	*See valet.*
vary	To change; to deviate.
very	Exceedingly.
vassal	(in feudal times) A humble servant or subordinate.
vessel	A ship; a hollow receptacle, esp. for liquid.
vault	To leap.
vaunt	To display one's own worth or attainments; to boast.
vector	1. Something (such as velocity) that has both magnitude and direction. 2. The carrier of a disease or infection. *(Also see sector.)*
vecture	A token used to pay transportation fares.
victor	The winner in a battle or combat. (Cap.:) Masc. name.
veil	*See vale.*
vein	*See vain.*
velour	*See valor.*

venal	Mercenary.
venial	Forgivable, as a venial sin.
venerable	Worthy of deep respect because of age, etc.
vulnerable	Able to be hurt, wounded, or injured; unprotected.
venose	Having many or prominent veins.
venous	Of, pert. to, or of the nature of a vein.
Venus	(Roman Myth.) Goddess of love.
ventage	*See vantage.*
venue	*See menu.*
veracious	Truthful.
voracious	Ravenously hungry.
veracity	Truthfulness.
voracity	The state of being voracious.
vermian	Resembling or pert. to worms.
vermin	Small, annoying and often harmful animals or insects; people who are unpleasant or harmful to society.
verses	Poems.
versus	(L.) Against.
vertebra	(pl. *vertebrae* or *vertebras*) One of the bones forming the spinal column.
vertebrae	Often pronounced as to be indistinguishable from the singular.

vertex	The highest point of something.
vortex	A whirling mass of fluid; something resembling a whirlpool.
vertical	Perpendicular to the horizontal; upright.
verticil	A whorl or circle, as of leaves or hairs, arranged around a point or axis.
very	*See vary.*
vesical	Of or pert. to a vesica or bladder, esp. the urinary bladder.
vesicle	A small sac or cyst.
vessel	*See vassal.*
veteran	A person with long experience; one who has served in the armed forces.
veterinarian	A veterinary surgeon or physician.
viable	*See friable.*
vial	(also **phial**) A small vessel for liquids.
vile	Evil; foul.
viol	Stringed musical instrument. [Bass viol.]
vice	A moral fault or failing.
vise	A tool with tight-holding jaws.
vicious	Mean; violent; fierce.
viscose	A viscous solution.
viscous	Thick, sticky, adhesive.
viscus	An internal organ of the body, esp. one (as the heart) located in the great cavity of the trunk proper. (*Also see discus.*)

victor	*See vector.*
victuals	(pronounced vittles) Food supplies; provisions.
vitals	The vital parts of the body.
vigorous	*See rigorous.*
vile	*See vial.*
villain	Cruelly malicious person.
villein	A type of serf.
villainess	A villainous woman.
villanous	Having a cruel, wicked, malicious nature or character.
villose	Villous.
villous	Covered with or of the nature of villi (see below); having long soft hairs.
villus	(pl. *villi*) One of the minute wormlike processes on certain membranes, esp. the mucous membrane of the small intestine.
vineal	Of or pert. to grapes or grapevines.
vinyl	A kind of plastic, esp. vinyl chloride.
vintage	*See vantage.*
viol	*See vial.*
viral	Of, rel. to, or caused by a virus.
virile	Manly; masterful; forceful.

virtu	Excellence or merit in objects of art; taste for or knowledge of such objects.
virtue	Honor; uprightness.
viscose	*See vicious.*
viscous	*See vicious.*
viscus	*See vicious.*
vise	*See vice.*
visible	*See risible.*
visor	The movable front part of a helmet, covering the face; the projecting front part of a cap.
vizier	Formerly a high official in certain Muslim countries.
vitals	*See victuals.*
vocation	*See avocation.*
void	*See avoid.*
vole	*See mole.*
voluble	*See valuable.*
volva	A membranous sac or cup at the base of many gill fungi.
Volvo	Make of automobile.
vulva	The external parts of the female genital organs.
voracious	*See veracious.*
voracity	*See veracity.*
vortex	*See vertex.*
voyager	One who travels, esp. on water.
voyeur	One who seeks sexual gratification by visual means.
vulva	*See volva.*
vulnerable	*See venerable.*

W

waddle	To walk with short steps and a swaying motion.
wattle	1. A structure of interwoven sticks and twigs. 2. A red fleshy fold of skin hanging from the head or throat (as of a turkey).
wobble	To stand or move unsteadily, to rock from side to side.
wade	To step in or through water, etc.
weighed	Past tense of *weigh*.
waif	A person, esp. a child, who has no home or friends.
waive	To relinquish voluntarily.
wave	To motion with the hand.
wail	Mournful cry.
wale	A ridge on woven or knitted fabric; a welt on the skin.
whale	Large marine mammal.
wailer	One who wails.
whaler	A person or ship engaged in whaling.
wails	Mournful cries.
Wales	A country forming the western part of Great Britain.

wain	A farm wagon or cart. (Cap., Astron.:) The Big Dipper.
wane	To decrease in vigor or strength or importance.
Wayne	Masculine name.
waist	The narrowed part of the body between thorax and hips.
waste	Rejected material; garbage, etc.
wait	A delay.
weight	An object's mass; heaviness.
waive	*See waif.*
waiver	Voluntary relinquishment of a right or privilege.
waver	To vacillate.
wale	*See wail.*
walk	A stroll; a sidewalk.
wok	Cooking utensil (for Chinese food).
wander	To ramble; stray.
wonder	To be curious about; to desire to know.
wane	*See wain.*
want	A lack.
wont	Custom, habit, practice.
won't	Contraction of *will not*.
wangle	To scheme; use underhand methods
wrangle	To argue noisily.
wants	*See once.*
war	Combat.
wore	Past tense of *wear*.

ward	(usu. with *off*) To deflect.
warred	Made war on.
ware	Goods.
wear	To bear or have on the person.
where	At, in, or to what place.
warily	Cautiously.
wearily	In an overtired manner.
warm	Moderately hot.
worm	A slender soft-bodied invertebrate; a contemptible person.
warn	To give notice of danger or evil.
worn	Form of verb *to wear*.
warrantee	The person to whom a warranty is made. [Never properly used as a verb.]
warranty	A guarantee. [Note: This is a noun only. The verb is *warrant*.] (*Also see guarantee/guaranty*.)
warred	*See ward*.
wart	A small roundish abnormal growth on the skin.
wort	A plant, herb.
wary	Cautious.
weary	Tired.
wasp	Stinging insect.
WASP	(also **Wasp**) An American of northern European, esp. British, stock and Protestant background. (White Anglo-Saxon Protestant.)
waste	*See waist*.
wat	A Buddhist temple.
watt	A unit of electrical power.
what	Asking for a statement of amount, number, or kind. (Etc.)
wattle	*See waddle*.
wave	*See waif*.
waver	*See waiver*.
wax	(n.) Substance secreted by bees. (Etc.) (v.) To increase in extent, quantity, power, etc. [The moon waxes and wanes.]
whacks	Resounding blows.
way	A thoroughfare. (Etc.)
weigh	To ascertain the heaviness of.
whey	Watery liquid left when milk forms curds.
Wayne	*See wain*.
we	Personal pronoun.
wee	Tiny.
weak	Lacking strength.
week	Seven days.
weal	A sound, healthy, or prosperous state.
we'll	Contraction of *we will*.
wheal	A welt.
wheel	A circular frame designed to turn on an axis.
wear	*See ware*.
wearily	*See warily*.
weary	*See wary*.
weasel	Small fierce animal with long slender body.
weevil	Type of beetle.

weather	State of atmosphere as to heat, cold, etc.
wether	A castrated sheep.
whether	If it be the case that.
weave	To interlace (as threads) into cloth, etc.
we've	Contraction of *we have*.
weaver	One who weaves; a weaverbird.
weever	A small marine fish.
wed	To marry.
we'd	Contraction of *we would* or *we had*.
weed	An undesirable plant.
wee	*See we.*
week	*See weak.*
weepie	(Brit., informal) A tearjerker.
weepy	Tearful; lachrymose.
weever	*See weaver.*
weevil	*See weasel.*
weigh	*See way.*
weighed	*See wade.*
weight	*See wait.*
weir	A small dam; a fence placed in a stream to catch fish.
we're	Contraction of *we are*.
weld	To unite metalalic parts, usu. by heating, hammering, etc.
welled	Past tense of *well* (to rise or spring).
welt	Ridge or wale on the surface of the body.
we'll	*See weal.*

welsh	To cheat by failing to pay a gambling debt, etc.
Welsh	Of or pert. to Wales, its people, its language.
wen	A sebaceous cyst.
when	At what time.
win	To be victorious.
wench	A young woman; a lewd woman.
winch	Machine for hoisting cable.
wrench	A violent twisting; a hand tool.
we're	*See weir.*
were	Form of the verb *to be*.
whir	To move with or to make a continuous buzzing sound.
wet	To douse or dampen.
whet	To sharpen; to stimulate. [This whets my appetite.]
wether	*See weather.*
we've	*See weave.*
whacks	*See wax.*
whale	*See wail.*
whaler	*See wailer.*
what	*See wat.*
wheal	*See weal.*
wheel	*See weal.*
when	*See wen.*
whence	*See hence.*
where	*See ware.*
wherefore	*See therefor.*
wherein	*See therein.*
whet	*See wet.*
whether	*See weather.*
whey	*See way.*
which	What particular one or ones.
witch	Hag.

while	Period of time, usu. short.	**whitish**	Somewhat white.
wile	A trick or strategem.	**widish**	Somewhat wide.
whiled	(usu. followed by *away*) Passed time pleasantly.	**whoa**	(interjec.) Stop (used esp. to horses).
wild	Untamed. (Etc.)	**woe**	Grief.
whine	Prolonged high-pitched cry, usu. of distress or pain.	**whole**	*See hole.*
		wholly	*See holey.*
		whoop	*See hoop.*
wine	Fermented beverage.	**whore**	*See hoar.*
		whored	*See hoard.*
whiny	Whining.	**whorl**	*See whirl.*
whinny	A neigh.		
winy	Of, like, or characteristic of wine.	**who's**	Contraction of *who is* or *who has.*
whir	To move with or to make a continuous buzzing sound. (*Also see were.*)	**whose**	Of or rel. to whom or which, esp. as possessor or possessors.
whirl	A rapid rotating or circling movement. (*Also see twirl.*)	**why**	For what? For what reason, cause, or purpose?
whorl	A circular arrangement of similar parts (as in a fingerprint).	**wye**	A Y-shaped part or object. [In electricity, a three-phase Y-shaped circuit arrangement; in railroads, a track arrangement with three switches and three legs for reversing direction of a train.]
whirled	Past tense of *whirl.*		
world	The universe; Earth and all its people.		
whish	*See swish.*	**widgeon**	A freshwater duck.
		widget	A small mechanical device; gadget.
whiskey	(pl. *whiskeys*) Alcoholic liquor—American or Irish.	**widish**	*See whitish.*
whisky	(pl. *whiskies*) Scotch or Canadian.	**wield**	To hold and use (a weapon, tool) with the hands; to manage.
whit	A particle, bit. [Not a whit better.]	**yield**	To surrender; to produce.
white	The color of snow.		
wit	Intelligence; humor.	**wiggle**	To move repeatedly from side to side.
whither	To which place. (*Also see hither/thither.*)	**wriggle**	To move with short twisting movements.
wither	To dry up.		

wild	See *whiled*.	wolf	A fierce wild animal of the dog family.
wile	See *while*.	woof	1. A filling thread or yarn in weaving. [Warp and woof.] 2. (interjec.) Used to imitate a dog's bark.
win	See *wen*.		
winch	See *wench*.		
wind	(long *i*) To turn completely or repeatedly about an object. (Etc.)		
		womb	See *rheum*.
		won	See *one*.
wined	Served wine.	wonder	See *wander*.
		wont	See *want*.
windlass	A device for pulling or hoisting things.	won't	See *want*.
windless	Without wind.	wood	Lumber.
		would	Form of the verb *will*.
window	An opening in a wall, roof, etc., to admit light and often air.	wore	See *war*.
winnow	To free grain, etc., from impurities.	workaday	Prosaic; ordinary.
		workday	Pert. to a day on which work is performed.
wine	See *whine*.	world	See *whirled*.
wined	See *wind*.	worm	See *warm*.
winy	See *whiny*.	worn	See *warn*.
wish	See *swish*.	wort	See *wart*.
wit	See *whit*.		
witch	See *which*.	worst	Most corrupt, bad, or evil.
		wurst	A sausage.
withe	A slender flexible branch or twig.	worthless	Valueless.
writhe	To twist one's body about, as if in pain; to suffer keenly.	worth less	Of less value.
		wrack	See *rack*.
		wrangle	See *wangle*.
wither	See *whither*.	wrap	See *rap*.
		wrapped	See *rapt*.
woad	A European plant of the mustard family.	wrapper	See *rapper*.
wold	An elevated tract of open country.	wrath	A strong, stern, or fierce anger; vengeance or punishment.
		wroth	(adj.) Angry. [He was wroth to see the damage to his home.]
wobble	See *waddle*.		
woe	See *whoa*.		
wok	See *walk*.	wreak	See *reek*.

wreath	A band of flowers, etc. (*Also see reef.*)	**wringer**	*See ringer.*
wreathe	To encircle or adorn with or as with a wreath; to envelop.	**write**	*See right.*
		writhe	*See withe.*
		writs	*See ritz.*
		wrote	*See rot.*
wreck	*See rack and reck.*	**wroth**	*See wrath.*
wrench	*See ranch and wench.*	**wrought**	*See fought and rot.*
wretch	*See retch.*	**wrung**	*See rung.*
wrest	*See rest.*	**wry**	*See rye.*
wriggle	*See wiggle.*	**wurst**	*See worst.*
wring	*See ring.*	**wye**	*See why.*

X

xanthan	A water-soluble natural gum.
xanthein	The part of the coloring matter in yellow flowers that is soluble in water.
xanthene	A yellow crystalline substance used as a fungicide, etc.
xanthin	The part of the coloring matter in yellow flowers that is insoluble in water.
xenophile	A person who is attracted to foreign peoples, cultures, or customs.
xenophobe	A person who fears or hates foreigners, strange customs, etc.
xero-	A combining form meaning dry (e.g., xeroderma [a disease in which the skin becomes dry and hard]; xerography, etc.)
zero	The arithmetical symbol 0.

Y

Y	*See why/wye.*
yah	(interjec.) An exclamation of impatience or derision.
yea	(n.) An affirmation; an affirmative reply or vote. [Also note use in the South as an adj. in phrases such as ''yea big,'' etc.]
yeah	(informal) Yes.
y'all	You-all.
yawl	A sailboat.
yowl	A long loud mournful wail or howl.
yegg	*See egg.*
yell	A shout or cheer.
yelp	A quick, sharp bark or cry.
yew/you	*See ewe.*
yews	*See use.*
yield	*See wield.*

yippee	(interjec.) Used to express exuberant delight or triumph.
yippie	(also **Yippie**) A member of a group of radical, politically active hippies.
Yuppie	A young, ambitious, and well-educated city dweller who has a professional career and an affluent life style.
yoga	A school of Hindu philosophy.
yogi	A person who practices yoga.
yoke	A wooden frame for joining together draft animals.
yolk	Yellow of an egg.
yore	Time long past.
your	Personal pronoun. (*Also see ewer.*)
you're	Contraction of *you are*. (*Also see ewer.*)
yowl	*See y'all.*
yule	Christmas.
you'll	Contraction of *you will*.
Yuppie	*See yippee.*

Z

zag	To move in one of the two directions followed in a zigzag course.
zig	(Same definition.) [He zigged when he should have zagged.]
zap	(informal) To kill or shoot; to cook in a microwave oven; to skip over or delete TV commercials by switching channels or fast-forwarding (on a VCR).
zip	To fasten or unfasten a zipper.
zappy	(informal) Energetic, lively, or fast-moving; zippy.
zippy	(informal) Lively, peppy.
zealous	*See jealous.*
zed	*See said.*
zero	*See xero-.*
zinc	*See sink.*